ANNE TYLER

Anne Tyler. Photograph by Diana Walker. Used by permission of the photographer.

ANNE TYLER

A Critical Companion

Paul Bail

CRITICAL COMPANIONS TO POPULAR CONTEMPORARY WRITERS
Kathleen Gregory Klein, Series Editor

Greenwood Press
Westport, Connecticut • London

Library of Congress Cataloging-in-Publication Data

Bail, Paul.
    Anne Tyler : a critical companion / Paul Bail.
        p.   cm.—(Critical companions to popular contemporary
    writers, ISSN 1082–4979)
    Includes bibliographical references and index.
    ISBN 0–313–30249–9 (alk. paper)
    1. Tyler, Anne—Criticism and interpretation.   2. Women and
    literature—United States—History—20th century.   I. Title.
    II. Series.
    PS3570.Y45Z56   1998
    813'.54—dc21   98–12152

British Library Cataloguing in Publication Data is available.

Library of Congress Catalog Card Number: 98–12152
ISBN: 0–313–30249–9
ISSN: 1082–4979

First published in 1998

Greenwood Press, 88 Post Road West, Westport, CT 06881
An imprint of Greenwood Publishing Group, Inc.

Printed in the United States of America

The paper used in this book complies with the
Permanent Paper Standard issued by the National
Information Standards Organization (Z39.48–1984).

10 9 8 7 6 5 4 3 2 1

Copyright Acknowledgment

The author and publisher gratefully acknowledge permission for the use of the following
material:

From an interview with Anne Tyler through unpublished personal correspondence March–
December 1997, by Paul Bail. Reprinted with permission of Anne Tyler.

For two grandmothers

Celanire Tessier Rouillard
1883 to 1969
and
Flora Chirinos Bolivar
1926 to 1989

This work is dedicated to Tara.

"We wake, if we ever wake at all, to mystery . . ."

Annie Dillard, *Pilgrim at Tinker Creek*

Contents

x   Contents

Series Foreword

The authors who appear in the series Critical Companions to Popular Contemporary Writers are all best-selling writers. They do not simply have one successful novel, but a string of them. Fans, critics, and specialist readers eagerly anticipate their next book. For some, high cash advances and breakthrough sales figures are automatic; movie deals often follow. Some writers become household names, recognized by almost everyone.

But, their novels are read one by one. Each reader chooses to start and, more importantly, to finish a book because of what she or he finds there. The real test of a novel is in the satisfaction its readers experience. This series acknowledges the extraordinary involvement of readers and writers in creating a best-seller.

The authors included in this series were chosen by an Advisory Board composed of high school English teachers and high school and public librarians. They ranked a list of best-selling writers according to their popularity among different groups of readers. For the first series, writers in the top-ranked group who had received no book-length, academic, literary analysis (or none in at least the past ten years) were chosen. Because of this selection method, Critical Companions to Popular Contemporary Writers meets a need that is being addressed nowhere else. The success of these volumes as reported by reviewers, librarians, and teachers led to an expansion of the series mandate to include some writers with wide critical attention—Toni Morrison, John Irving, and Maya Angelou, for example—to extend the usefulness of the series.

The volumes in the series are written by scholars with particular expertise in analyzing popular fiction. These specialists add an academic focus to the popular success that these writers already enjoy.

The series is designed to appeal to a wide range of readers. The general reading public will find explanations for the appeal of these well-known writers. Fans will find biographical and fictional questions answered. Students will find literary analysis, discussions of fictional genres, carefully organized introductions to new ways of reading the novels, and bibliographies for additional research. Whether browsing through the book for pleasure or using it for an assignment, readers will find that the most recent novels of the authors are included.

Each volume begins with a biographical chapter drawing on published information, autobiographies or memoirs, prior interviews, and, in some cases, interviews given especially for this series. A chapter on literary history and genres describes how the author's work fits into a larger literary context. The following chapters analyze the writer's most important, most popular, and most recent novels in detail. Each chapter focuses on one or more novels. This approach, suggested by the Advisory Board as the most useful to student research, allows for an in-depth analysis of the writer's fiction. Close and careful readings with numerous examples show readers exactly how the novels work. These chapters are organized around three central elements: plot development (how the story line moves forward), character development (what the reader knows of the important figures), and theme (the significant ideas of the novel). Chapters may also include sections on generic conventions (how the novel is similar or different from others in its same category of science fiction, fantasy, thriller, etc.), narrative point of view (who tells the story and how), symbols and literary language, and historical or social context. Each chapter ends with an "alternative reading" of the novel. The volume concludes with a primary and secondary bibliography, including reviews.

The alternative readings are a unique feature of this series. By demonstrating a particular way of reading each novel, they provide a clear example of how a specific perspective can reveal important aspects of the book. In the alternative reading sections, one contemporary literary theory—way of reading, such as feminist criticism, Marxism, new historicism, deconstruction, or Jungian psychological critique—is defined in brief, easily comprehensible language. That definition is then applied to the novel to highlight specific features that might go unnoticed or be understood differently in a more general reading. Each volume defines two or three specific theories, making them part of the reader's understanding of how diverse meanings may be constructed from a single novel.

Taken collectively, the volumes in the Critical Companions to Popular Contemporary Writers series provide a wide-ranging investigation of the complexities of current best-selling fiction. By treating these novels seriously as both literary works and publishing successes, the series demonstrates the potential of popular literature in contemporary culture.

Kathleen Gregory Klein
Southern Connecticut State University

Acknowledgments

A book club discussion on *Dinner at the Homesick Restaurant* organized by Ed Bergman of Leominster Public Library provided the initial inspiration for tackling this project. Many persons assisted in its creation: my editors Barbara Rader and Kathleen Gregory Klein; Anne Tyler, who graciously replied to my written correspondence; Diana Walker, who selected one of her many photographs of Anne Tyler for this book; interlibrary loan specialist Mary Leger at Fitchburg State College; reference librarians Ann Finch, Ed Bergman, and Amy Ricciuti of Leominster and Joanne McGuirk, Kathy French, and Sandy Cravedi of Fitchburg; Dorothy Robinson of Portland, Oregon, who helped with the Internet; Robert Croft, whose excellent bibliography of Anne Tyler was an invaluable reference tool.

In addition, I am thankful for the general support of family and friends, including my children Alexander, Amelie, and Michael, who kept me from narrowly burying myself in this book; my mother Jeanne Bail; my children's mother Patsy Taucer; my stepdaughter Ariana; and others—Wayne Gray, Eda Bennett, and Myrna McPhail, who assisted with child care; and my colleague Chuck Carroll for his good humor. Thanks also for the general emotional support of friends too numerous to mention, including Marit Cranmer, Mark Hart, David Mason, Stu Miller, Lydia Saltzman, Kim and Michael Snow, Gerry Steinberg, Deidre and Lori Taucer, Naomi Zeitz, my cousins Didier, Irene, and Manon

Maurin of Les Taillades, France, and anonymous well-wishers known and unknown. Thanks to Joseph Goldstein and Sharon Salzberg for passing on the aftereffects of their sojourn with T. Urgyen at a time when I was at low ebb.

Special thanks to Gangaji for always being a true friend.

Finally, a source of profound and continuing inspiration has come from the late Karmapa Ranjung Rigpe Dorje and from Professor Chogyal Namkhai Norbu, as well as other mentors whose influence continues to guide me philosophically.

George Orwell once said that completing a book was like struggling with a long illness. I can certainly understand that metaphor. Like Jeremy Pauling of *Celestial Navigation*, I sometimes felt as if my life might be forever strewn out "in bits on the studio floor" as I struggled to give a manageable shape to this mass of material. On the positive side, though, Anne Tyler's compassionate vision has been a worthy companion throughout this process. I have spent the past two years reflecting on her vision. I hope others will benefit from this effort.

The Life of Anne Tyler

Anne Tyler was born in Minneapolis, Minnesota, on October 25, 1941, to Lloyd Parry Tyler, a chemist, and Phyllis Mahon Tyler, a social worker. Both were deeply committed Quakers who expressed their faith through social activism. Anne was their first child, to be followed by three sons. The circumstances of her childhood made Anne Tyler an outsider in relation to the surrounding culture. Her family lived in a succession of communes, or experimental Quaker communities, seeking like Thoreau a "simpler life"—an alternative to the competitive, materialistic lifestyle they saw all around them.

First the family moved to Coldbrook Farm in Phoenixville, Pennsylvania, for two years, then to a community in suburban Chicago, then to Duluth, Minnesota, and then back to Chicago again. The last utopian community they joined was Celo, located in rural North Carolina. Anne was six when they moved there. Initially her parents were content there and persuaded both sets of her grandparents to join them. However, a group of idealists with strong opinions can be difficult to live with at times, and the Tylers eventually tired of the dissension and the authoritarian attitudes of some of the residents.

Anne Tyler and her brothers were primarily home schooled, with excellent results, although Anne's parents did send Anne and her brothers briefly to the local public school so that they could meet some other children and make friends (Evans 1994). The public school nearest to

Celo was a three-room log building, and the teacher would sometimes leave after prayers to go tend his farm, appointing one of the students to lead the class through their spelling words. Anne Tyler was perceived as an outsider there. The pacifists and idealists at Celo were "regarded suspiciously" by the locals (interview by Paul Bail 1997), and she was conscious of being a Northerner transplanted to the South (interview by Bruce Cook 1980).

Anne Tyler believes these years had a formative influence upon her personality and her sensibility as a writer: "I think the fact that I had a fairly isolated childhood influenced me considerably. . . . I learned to be alone and to entertain myself by imagining, and when I left the commune (at the age of eleven) I looked at the regular world from an unusually distant vantage point" (Smith 1989, 141–142).

For milk the family kept goats (bred from stock owned by the wife of poet Carl Sandburg), as Tyler's characters Justine and Duncan Peck do in *Searching for Caleb*. In the evenings the members of the Celo community would engage in handicrafts or gather to listen to recordings of the opera or symphony, and one of the members who worked in the county bookmobile would pick out books that she thought would suit the interests of various residents and would deliver them on her return from work (Evans 1994), just as Miss Vinton does for Jeremy in *Celestial Navigation*.

After five years at Celo, Anne moved with her parents and brothers to Raleigh, North Carolina, leaving behind both sets of grandparents— an event of which artistically transformed traces may perhaps be found in *Searching for Caleb*. In this urban public school, Anne Tyler was again an outsider. She had never used a telephone and was so calloused from roaming the countryside shoeless that she could light a match on the thickened sole of her bare foot. That summer she worked on a tobacco farm outside Raleigh, an experience that is directly represented in one of the chapters of *The Tin Can Tree* and that she drew on in developing such characters as Drum Casey (*A Slipping-Down Life*) and Jake Simms (*Earthly Possessions*) (Sternburg 1980).

In Raleigh, Anne Tyler's parents were active in the Quaker community and in politically liberal social-justice issues, participating in a weekly vigil on the steps of the state capitol in opposition to military weapons production and in support of the overseas relief work of the American Friends Services Committee. Her mother Phyllis, employed as a social worker, lobbied energetically against the death penalty. In the 1960s her parents supported the civil rights movement in Raleigh, which led to threats of violence against them by white militants. After their retirement they travelled abroad to work with political refugees (Croft 1995).

Anne Tyler does not consider herself particularly religious; nevertheless, her Quaker background put her in an outsider status. Her awareness of the Quakers as a minority religion is reflected in a passage from *Morgan's Passing* where Emily attends the only Friends meetinghouse in the county, "small and poor as ever, a gray frame cubicle huddled in the backyard of the Savior Baptist Church" (214). Perhaps in response to this beleagured sense, she occasionally engages in authorial guerilla skirmishes with Baptist ministers and their close cousins, as in the portrayal of a revival meeting in *A Slipping-Down Life*.

Her unique childhood created an atmosphere that supported her penchant for delving deeply into things. She reread favorite books over and over, beginning with *The Little House*, which was read to her as a child and which she read to her children as an adult, as Pearl does with Jenny in *Dinner at the Homesick Restaurant*. During childhood she read *Little Women* twenty-two times, and at fourteen she discovered the short stories of Eudora Welty, beginning with the collection *The Wide Net and Other Stories*.

She read widely as a teenager, "everything from *The Catcher in the Rye* to *The Brothers Karamazov*" (interview by Paul Bail 1997), and as an adult she continued to keep up with new writing and to reread favorite books like Gabriel García Márquez's *One Hundred Years of Solitude*, Christina Stead's *The Man Who Loved Children*, and Eudora Welty's *The Golden Apples* (interview by Bail 1997).

Intelligent and serious, she had a multifaceted interest in the creative arts throughout her growing years. Although she rarely attends the theater now (interview by Bail 1997), at Broughton she was involved in the drama society (Croft 1995) and at Duke she acted the part of Laura in a production of Tennessee Williams's *The Glass Menagerie* (Evans 1994). Throughout her high school years she excelled in the visual arts and dreamed of having a career as an illustrator. Her high school art teacher Alice Erlich thought Anne Tyler had "a gift" for painting but remembers her as being reluctant to display her work publicly (Evans 1994, 7). However, she also excelled at English, which was taught by Phyllis Peacock, a published author and deeply committed teacher, whose earlier prize student Reynolds Price had gone on to become a novelist and English Professor at Duke University. By a twist of fate, Anne Tyler would attend Duke and study under Reynolds Price.

She started college at age sixteen because her early schooling at home

"didn't go strictly by years and so I ended up slightly ahead of myself."
Modestly she adds, "I wasn't a child prodigy or anything like that." She
had "no regrets" about leaving home at such an early age and was "eager" to begin college (interview by Bail 1997). Swathmore was Anne
Tyler's first choice for college. But she was offered a generous scholarship
by Duke, and her parents felt that this was an opportunity to save their
money for the boys' college educations. She later wrote that this was the
only time her being female became a serious issue in her family; and
although her life wasn't ruined, she still doesn't think it was fair or just
(Sternburg 1980, 14).

Duke has had its share of alumni who distinguished themselves in the
field of letters: William Styron, Reynolds Price, James Applewhite, Jo-
sephine Humphreys, Anne Tyler, and Fred Chappell. In Anne Tyler's
freshman year at Duke, she and poet Fred Chappell were students of
Reynolds Price in the the very first creative writing class he taught. Price
remembered her as "frighteningly mature" and a "wide-eyed . . . outsider child, this very watchful child recording, recording, recording the
world" (Willrich 1992, 502).

She also took writing classes with the charismatic William Blackburn,
who had introduced Reynolds Price to Eudora Welty (Cockshutt 1971).
Price had become friends with Welty and had a high opinion of her
talents, referring to her as "the living writer that I admire most. Her
work I have the most natural sympathy for" (Price 1972, 43). On Welty's
recommendation, Price became a client of her literary agent Diarmuid
Russell, and Anne Tyler in turn was represented by him, so that at one
point all three of them had the same literary agent. (Kaufman 1966).

Tyler, Price, and Welty also shared an interest in Russian literature
and the visual arts. Reynolds Price had been a painter before becoming
a writer, and his house was crammed wall-to-wall with photographs,
drawings, and prints, and Eudora Welty worked as a photographer for
the Federal WPA during the Depression years, documenting the exten-
sive poverty she witnessed in rural Mississippi. Although not herself a
photographer, Tyler keeps several bound collections by famous photographers in her study.

Anne Tyler is fascinated by photographs because of their ability to
freeze a moment in time (interview by Bail 1997), and several of her
novels feature characters who are photographers. The experience of time
has been a central preoccupation of Tyler's since she had an epiphany
as a child when her mother read her *The Little House*, by Virginia Burton.
In later years she became enthusiastic about the writing of Gabriel García

Márquez, whose sense of time as a repetitive cycle fit with her own view. Although she continues to admire García Márquez's work, she feels she "overdosed" on magic realism after having read a "whole host" of South American writers (interview by Bail 1997).

Anne Tyler majored in Russian literature at Duke out of a desire to "embark on something new . . . and slightly startling" (Willrich 1992, 501). She became familiar with the giants of Russian literature, such as Chekhov, whom she has cited as influencing her writing (Evans 1994). Long after college for several years she made a practice every summer of reading *War and Peace*, the massive novel by Leo Tolstoy, the excommunicated pacifist Russian nobleman. After graduation she was awarded a fellowship in Slavic Studies at Columbia University in New York, which the hero of her first novel also attends. She took all the required courses for her master's degree but never completed her thesis.

At the end of her year at Columbia, she got a summer job in a seaside town in Maine and fantasized about living in a shack by the sea, a daydream that was worked into the ending of *Celestial Navigation*, when Mary Tell moves into Brian's boathouse. Returning to North Carolina, she began working as the Russian bibliographer in the Duke library. There she met Taghi Modarressi, an Iranian physician, ten years older than she who was completing his residency in child psychiatry at the Duke School of Medicine. He was planning to return to Iran after the completion of his residency. When he proposed to her in 1963 after a seven-month courtship, she said, "Oh, well, why not?" like Evie Decker in *A Slipping-Down Life*.

When Taghi's visa expired, the newlyweds moved to Montreal, Canada, so that he could finish his residency there. Once again Anne Tyler experienced a sense of dislocatedness, the culture of Canada seeming "half foreign, half familiar" (Croft 1995, 30). While looking for a job, she completed the manuscript for her first novel, *If Morning Ever Comes*; and by the time she secured a position at the McGill University Law Library she had received notice that the book had found a publisher. One of her co-workers at McGill was a painfully shy man who became part of the inspiration for the character of Jeremy Pauling in *Celestial Navigation*.

In 1965 their first daughter Tezh was born, and two years later another girl Mitra. Having the children slowed down Anne Tyler's writing for a while, but in the end she felt that motherhood deepened her work and her self (Sternburg 1980). As Croft (1995) has pointed out, Anne Tyler's treatment of women's responses to motherhood has become more complex and nuanced as her children have grown.

In 1967 after her husband, Taghi, had completed his residency in Montreal, he received an offer of employment at the University of Maryland Medical School, which led to the move to Baltimore, where Anne Tyler has remained ever since. After travelling so far from the South, with her marriage to an Iranian and move to Canada, she found herself in what many consider a Southern city (in *Dinner at the Homesick Restaurant* two of the characters have an argument about whether Baltimore is Southern). As in her novels, the movement of life seemed circular. She enrolled her children in private school, as Macon Leary wishes to do for Muriel's son in *The Accidental Tourist*. Finding herself once again in an area with a Quaker presence, she chose a school operated by the Society of Friends, not for religious reasons, but because she appreciates the political and ethical aspect (interview by Bail 1997).

Besides being a doctor, Taghi, who died in April 1997, was also a writer who published an award-winning novel in Persian prior to leaving Iran and another while studying in the United States. He put his writing on hold during the early years of marriage, not publishing his next two novels *The Book of Absent People* and *The Pilgrim's Rules of Etti-quette* until the 1980s. He wrote the manuscripts for these in Persian, and Anne Tyler assisted with the English translation.

Anne Tyler's first literary form was the short story. Though in recent years her writing has been confined to novels, she continues to have an interest in the survival of the short story as an art form and helped edit three anthologies of short stories between 1983 and 1996.

In her introduction to *The Best American Short Stories, 1983*, Anne Tyler defends the short story as a valid art form that is in no way inferior to the novel. She admonishes authors to have a generous spirit and to not hoard their best ideas for the next novel. What she admires most is writing that has a certain vitality—writing that is "stuffed full" of suggestive details until it is "bursting at the seams" (xv), with vivid, spunky characters who are survivors.

By the time she was writing *Dinner at the Homesick Restaurant* Tyler had all but given up writing self-contained short stories. But her novels were now built up out of interconnecting short stories, much as the best cinematographers create movies out of a series of shots, each of which could be individually framed in a gallery. From 1982 onward she published only five short stories, three of which were forthcoming chapters from her novels.

This evolution in her artistic development is paralleled by her character Jeremy in *Celestial Navigation*. He starts with collages and begins layering them so that they become increasingly three dimensional, until finally he is doing huge sculptures. Similarly, Anne Tyler gradually moved from short stories to novels with multiple characters spanning long periods of time.

Anne Tyler's work habits have some parallels to those of fictional Jeremy. Like Jeremy, who would be abstracted for long periods of time before starting a piece, Tyler typically begins her workday by sitting cross-legged and staring blankly for up to thirty minutes until something snags her mind (Croft 1995). And just as Jeremy would soak up the colorful illustrations in art books like a parched man drinking in water, Anne Tyler's study is lined with photography books into which she sometimes sinks "to fill up on when I feel empty" (interview by Michaels 1977, 41). Finally, just as Jeremy embeds pieces of fabric from his children's clothing and other artifacts of his family's daily life into his collages and sculptures, Anne Tyler incorporates much of herself in her writing.

Incidents in Anne Tyler's novels frequently parallel the stage of life that she and her family are going through at the time. In *Breathing Lessons*, the Morans' daughter is getting ready to move to college, which Anne Tyler and her husband had recently experienced with Mitra and Tezh who had both decided to enroll in the Rhode Island School of Design to study visual arts.

With two creative parents as models it was almost inevitable that the Modarressi children would show similar talents. Mitra and Tazh inherited their mother's youthful interest in painting and illustrating, and in recent years she has had an opportunity to collaborate creatively with both of them.

In 1993, Anne Tyler and twenty-six-year-old daughter Mitra created *Tumble Tower*, a children's book about a favorite Tyler theme—clutter, of course! The story humorously illustrates that clutter can have benefits as well as drawbacks. Mitra got credit for illustrating the book, and her mother was listed on the spine as the author, which immediately drew attention in *People* magazine and *Publisher's Weekly*. Since then, Mitra has gone on to write and illustrate three more children's books on her own.

Tazh so far has not tried her hand at writing, but she did the illustration for the cover of *Ladder of Years*, a painting of an empty beach chair, symbolizing Delia's sudden flight from her family while at the beach.

Anne Tyler has some taboos. She does not believe in "researching" her novels because she feels this exercise could inhibit the inner workings of her imagination. In developing the character of Justine Peck, the card reader in *Searching for Caleb*, she did not visit any fortune-tellers, nor in *Saint Maybe* did she base the Church of the Second Chance on any existing congregation. However, she will do meticulous mapping of her "inner" research. For *Celestial Navigation* she constructed a floor plan of the rooming house, a drawing of the front of the house, and a chronology of the characters.

An intensely private person, Tyler studiously avoids publicity, granting interviews only by written correspondence. She made a conscious choice to focus only on writing and family, even though it makes her "narrow," because anything else "fritters" away her energy (Sternburg 1980, 15).

For similar reasons Anne Tyler avoids reading reviews of her own work, whether positive or negative, feeling that they only make her more "self-conscious" as a writer. She began reviewing other writers' books to help pay her daughters' tuitions. From 1972, when she published her fourth novel, *The Clock Winder*, until 1991 when she published her twelfth, *Saint Maybe*, Anne Tyler wrote over two hundred and fifty book reviews. She first started out submitting an occasional review to the *National Observer*; but from 1975 on she was reviewing on average a book a month. With the demise of the *National Observer* in 1977, she began reviewing primarily for the *New York Times Book Review* and *The New Republic*, although eventually her book reviews were appearing in a wide variety of periodicals including, *The Atlantic, Vogue, Washington Post, Chicago Tribune, San Francisco Chronicle*.

Affirming Duke Professor William Blackburn's maxim that one learns to write by reading, Tyler acknowledged that the reviewing process sharpened her analytic skills, forcing her to figure out what makes one piece of fiction work and another not. This mental exercise certainly did not hurt her mature work as she began experimenting with more complex characterizations and narrative structures.

Characteristically, she was a thorough reviewer, reading the book in question through more than once and placing it in context by reading "all of the author's other works I could find" (interview by Bail 1997). Reynolds Price voiced his amazement at her ability to read so voraciously on top of writing. But after almost twenty years of this pace, it becomes tiring. With her daughters' education complete there was no longer the economic pressure to continue. She stopped writing reviews at this point because "I felt I'd used up the vocabulary for it" (interview by Bail 1997).

While generous with those whom she reviewed, she can be a harsh critic of herself. She has disowned her first two novels more than once. Of her short stories she declares rather severely that "there are only four or five that I consider to be any good." Her favorites include "Your Place Is Empty" and "Uncle Ahmad" because they touch upon "the Iranian side" of her life, and "A Knack for Languages" because it is uncharacteristically "strong" (interview by Bail 1997).

One of her reviews provides clues about her thinking on feminist issues. In the 1980s she reviewed books by two prominent feminist authors, Kate Millett and Andrea Dworkin. In both books Tyler admired the factual reporting and the depth of feeling but tried to segregate the ideological interpretation. She felt that much of Dworkin's book was "intelligent, original" and found a strange beauty in the writing style, which she characterized as "a sort of martial poetry." But she felt that neither the style nor the sweeping generalizations worked effectively in the book's genre: political analysis. And she disagreed with its overall sense of life as "an unremitting tooth-and-nail relationship" between the sexes (Tyler 1983, 35). Concerning Millett's book, about the torture-murder of a teenage girl, Tyler wrote that it was "an important study of the problems of cruelty and submission" but disagreed with its superfluous "feminist polemics" (36).

It is not that Anne Tyler is blind to the intersection of gender and power. In a factual piece on corruption in Maryland state government ("Trouble in the Boys Club" 1977) she wrote: "Men's stories always have the same twist: a woman arrives, and the trouble begins. The clubhouse falls to pieces" (16). And on a personal level she was once told by a male instructor that women were not qualified to write fiction about male characters (though apparently he did not hold to the converse). Nevertheless, she wrote her first novel *If Morning Ever Comes*, from the point of view of a young man. Gender was also an issue when she was forced to go to Duke, where she had a scholarship, rather than Swathmore, her first choice, because her parents felt it was more important to save the tuition for the boys' education. Tyler still does not think that was a just decision, although going to Duke turned out to be a stroke of good luck as far as her writing career was concerned (Croft 1995).

These experiences could have created a permanent streak of indignation; but like Justine in *Searching for Caleb*, Tyler is cursed with the "ability to see all sides of every question" (317). An example of this trait is contained in Tyler's essay "Still Just Writing" (1980) in which Tyler describes the many domestic crises, major and minor, that kept interrupting her concentration and threatened to scuttle her efforts to compose *Mor-*

gan's Passing. Her plaint is reminiscent of what Virginia Woolf said of Jane Austen, namely, that she had to write in her family's parlor "where she was subject to periodic interruptions, and would hide her manuscript whenever she heard someone coming in" (Woolf 1929, 52). But Anne Tyler continues: "I could draw some conclusions here about the effect that being a woman/wife/mother has upon my writing, except that I am married to a writer who is also a man/husband/father. His writing fell by the wayside for a long time. . . . Often I wonder what he would be doing now if he didn't have a family to support" (5–6).

Not only does Anne Tyler feel that the feminist perspective is too partial, but her view of literature excludes deliberate promotion of any ideological program. "Much as I would love to think that a novel could make a positive political change, I've never seen it done, and I believe it is always a mistake to aim for anything more than pure storytelling when writing fiction" (interview by Bail 1997). Her personal credo is in line with Eudora Welty's description of Chekhov: "It was his plainest intention that we never should hear him tell us what we should think or feel or believe. He is not trying to teach us, through his characters; he asks us only to understand them" (Welty 1978, 68).

Being such a private person who eschews publicity and does not grant interviews except by written correspondence, Anne Tyler's career would have languished if it depended on self-promotion and book tours. Fortunately, the quality of her fiction has been recognized by some influential fellow writers who drew wider attention to her work. Novelist Gail Godwin's favorable review of *Celestial Navigation* in the *New York Times Book Review* drew critical attention to Tyler's work and was followed by her "discovery" by no less a personage than John Updike, who "put Tyler firmly on the cultural agenda with his review of her next novel, *Searching for Caleb*" (Templin 1994, 181).

When Updike reviewed five of Anne Tyler's novels in succession, "Such attention . . . hinted that Updike was following her career with an eye to ascertaining whether she could be counted among America's foremost novelists" (Templin 1994, 177). The novel he praised most highly was *Dinner at the Homesick Restaurant* because it dealt with some of the darker, grimmer realities of the American family. "Her art needed only the darkening that would give her beautifully shaped sketches solidity," he wrote (Updike 1982, 296) in favorable contrast to his assessment of an earlier novel as giving "the unsettling impression of having been writ in water, or with a cool laser of moonlight" (Updike 1980, 288).

The assessment of her work has depended on the predilections of the critic. Some have been dismissive because of what they judge as an absence of tragedy, moral vision, recognition of the presence of evil. Those who appreciate the comic vision are more receptive to her work. The British in particular seem to easily accept her as a writer in the comedy of manners tradition (Templin 1994).

Anne Tyler has been the recipient of numerous awards. She was Phi Beta Kappa. In 1981 for *Morgan's Passing* she received the prestigious Janet Heidenger Kafka Prize for Fiction by an American woman, and she was nominated for the American Book Award and the National Book Critics Circle Fiction Award. In 1983 *Dinner at the Homesick Restaurant* received the P.E.N./Faulkner Award and was a finalist in the nominations for the Pulitzer Prize (which was won that year by fellow Southerner Alice Walker). In 1985 *The Accidental Tourist* was selected as the National Book Critic Circle's most distinguished work of fiction for the year and was a finalist in the Pulitzer Prize nominations (which was won by Larry MacMurty). Finally, *Breathing Lessons* received the 1989 Pulitzer Prize for fiction. It was also nominated for the National Book Award and was named by *Time* magazine as book of the year and as one of the ten best books of the decade (Croft 1995).

However, awards alone are not enough to guarantee a writer immortality. An enduring readership into the next century requires the blessings of the English Department at the major universities. At present Tyler's reputation among the academic establishment is less than it could be because her work does not easily fit into current intellectual fashions. Charlotte Templin (1994) cites Anne Tyler's "liabilities" as "her realistic forms, her preference for a comic mode, and her hopeful—bittersweet, but more sweet than bitter—outlook" (196). Nevertheless Templin concludes that Tyler's reputation is faring well and that "she stands with a select group of America's most respected writers" (196).

2

Literary Influences on Anne Tyler

"Are not the reviews of current literature a perpetual illustration of the difficulty of judgment? . . . No, delightful as the pastime of measuring may be, it is the most futile of all occupations, and to submit to the decrees of the measurers the most servile of attitudes. So long as you write what you wish to write, that is all that matters; and whether it matters for ages or only for hours, nobody can say."

Virginia Woolf, *A Room of One's Own*

Anne Tyler is not a genre writer and hence cannot be easily classified. Her work is complex and interweaves diverse influences: "Minimalist and feminist as it may seem at times, in other texts Tyler is decorative and anti-feminist. The real sin of pride, in a Tyler lexicon, is that of thinking one has all the answers" (Wagner-Martin 1994, 173). This chapter will examine Anne Tyler's place in literature by looking at her work through three frames of reference: as a Southerner, as a woman, and as a member of a religious minority. First, let us examine the contribution of Anne Tyler's religious background.

RELIGIOUS CONSCIOUSNESS IN LITERATURE

There have been numerous major and minor authors with an explicit interest in religious themes, including Tolstoy, Dostoyevsky, T. S. Eliot, Evelyn Waugh, Somerset Maugham, Aldous Huxley, J. D. Salinger, Graham Greene, Walker Percy, Chaim Potok, Flannery O'Connor, Doris Lessing, and Annie Dillard. They have had varying degrees of success in their attempts since, as Christopher Isherwood (1966) has quipped, "perhaps the truly comprehensive religious novel could only be written by a saint—and saints, unfortunately, are not in the habit of writing novels" (120)

On the other hand, some authors have been so thoroughly steeped in an unconventional religious background that they cannot entirely escape it even when they reject it. Willa Cather said that the writer "may acquire a great many interesting and vivid impressions in his mature years but his thematic material he acquires under fifteen years of age" (quoted by Brown 1953).

If this is so, then an early life as a Quaker must be regarded as an important formative influence on Anne Tyler, who was raised in Quaker communes until just before her teens. Even though Anne Tyler does not consider herself religious, we must presume her background left its imprint, just as Mary McCarthy's Catholicism remained a defining aspect even though she disowned it in her early teens.

The Society of Friends, or Quakers, defines itself as "a religious body which, having never required of its members the acceptance of any formula or belief, holds that the basis of fellowship is an inward experience, and the essentials of unity are the love of God and the love of man conceived and practiced in the spirit of Christ" (Elgin 1968, 74).

An important but controversial figure within nineteenth-century Quakerism was Elias Hicks who preached the primacy of the Inner Light, or the Living Christ within the believer, over the historical Christ of the Bible (Bacon 1986). The American poet Walt Whitman was influenced as a youth by exposure to Hick's powerful preaching. Susan B. Anthony, Lucretia Mott, Jane Addams and several other important social reformers and women's rights advocates were associated with the Hicksite faction in American Quakerism. This emphasis on immanence in spirituality was also one of the essential characteristics of the nineteenth-century Transcendentalist movement as exemplified by Thoreau and Emerson.

Two aspects of the Quaker sensibility that are seen in Anne Tyler's writing are the aesthetic of simplicity and the impulse toward democracy and egalitarianism. The plain style of the Quaker meetinghouse inspired a style of design characterized by clean lines, like Shaker furniture, or Ian Bedloe's woodwork (see Chapter 12). In literature the aesthetic manifested itself as an uncluttered prose style, such as Robert Louis Stevenson admired in William Penn's writing (Bacon 1985). Anne Tyler's prose similarly exhibits clean, spare lines and creates its effects through hand-crafted precision of fit. And her characters share this aesthetic: from Charlotte Emory who disposes of all superfluous household furniture (see Chapter 8) to Ezra Tull who tears down the opulent decorations of Scarlatti's restaurant (see Chapter 9).

The democratic impulse in Quakerism accords well with the modern tendency in literature to abandon the centralized point of view of the omniscient author. As one critic has commented: "Tyler's work is a veritable Quaker meetinghouse in which every voice may be heard as possessing equal opportunity for authority" (Gerstenberger 1994, 139).

During the 1950s and 1960s, beginning with such Beat poets as Allen Ginsberg, there was a rekindling of interest in the worldview of Walt Whitman, Henry David Thoreau, and the sacred literature of the East. And in the 1980s Annie Dillard gained a literary following as a latter-day Thoreau with the publication of *A Pilgrim at Tinker Creek*, which echoed *Walden*'s celebration of nature, simplicity, and solitude.

One of the formative books in Anne Tyler's life was the humble children's story *The Little House*, by Virginia Lee Burton, which her mother used to read to her and which she in turn read to her own children. Tyler felt strongly enough about the book to write an article in the *New York Times Book Review* about its importance in her life and to fictionally commemorate it in a scene in *Dinner at the Homesick Restaurant* in which Jenny Tull observes Pearl Tull reading the book to her grandchild.

The Little House could be seen as the story of an agrarian ideal destroyed by modernism and commercialism and of an attempt to restore that lost way of life. This ideal was, of course, the early quest of Anne Tyler's parents with their noble experiment in communal living, harkening back to an earlier set of American ideals about community and egalitarianism.

The story states that "this Little House shall never be sold for gold or silver and she will live to see our great-great-grandchildren's great-great-grandchildren living in her." Many of Anne Tyler's fictions do involve an ancestral house as the center of the family's identity: *The Clock Winder*, *Earthly Possessions*, *The Accidental Tourist*, *Ladder of Years*. The familial house signifies permanence through continuity and is the nostalgic vestige of what once was a sense of identity formed through a living connection with the land (as in Scarlett O'Hara's drawing strength from the earth of her family estate Tara at the end of the quintessential "Southern" novel *Gone with the Wind*). Thus, the house as the family estate harkens back to an agrarian and premodern ideal that has been somewhat slower to die out in the South.

Anne Tyler's attachment to this children's book, which she admits has become "bleached and ragged . . . with the binding fallen apart," its spine "a strip of naked cardboard," reflects her characters' attachments to their belongings, as with Amanda Pauling, in *Celestial Navigation*, who mourns over her lost suitcase and its little treasures, or Maggie Moran, in *Breathing Lessons*, who imagines being reunited with every favorite item she ever lost.

Physical items encode memory and are a connection to the past, like a relic. In this sense Anne Tyler's sensibility is very *incarnational*, to use a term with which her fellow Southern writer Flannery O'Connor would feel at home. Anne Tyler's old, ragged children's book in itself is just a piece of worthless clutter, but it mediates her memories of her mother's calming voice and of those moments of childhood insight when she could momentarily glimpse a vision of totality that she could not quite grasp and hold. From this perspective the book becomes a ritual object with a sacramental function. It mediates between two ways of "seeing," in Annie Dillard's terms: "At the rim of their conventional meaning" objects momentarily shed their "opacity" and appear to become "translucent" suggesting "a concealed 'eternal' depth, or significance" (Scheick 1985, 62).

SOUTHERN REGIONAL CONSCIOUSNESS IN LITERATURE

It is debatable whether "Southern" is the most apt description for Anne Tyler's body of work. Her first three novels were set in South Carolina and evoke the landscape, the speech patterns, and the mores of the region. However, except for the occasional minor character, like Mr. Stimson in *The Clock Winder*, or the rural Southerner who moves to the big city, like Lucy Bedloe in *Saint Maybe*, most of the characters in Tyler's subsequent novels are not particularly regional, and Tyler's usual setting, the city of Baltimore, is only nominally Southern (in *Dinner at the Home-*

sick Restaurant, Anne Tyler has Pearl and Cody argue over whether Baltimore is a Southern city).

What remains of Anne Tyler's "Southerness" is a certain sensibility:

> The gentle or tactful people ... have been ignored by the Northern novelists. There aren't enough quiet, gentle, basically good people in a novel. Usually whole holocausts happen. But this delicate thing ... between people—that doesn't happen very often in a Northern novel. Most Southern novelists have concentrated on these little threads of connection between people. (interview by Lueloff 1965, 23)

More recently, Tyler has questioned whether regional labels still retain any real meaning. She fancies she notices something "warmer, more ambling" in a Southerner's style of conversation, but "I realize this may be wishful thinking. Americans everywhere, I suspect, cling to the hope that this country still has identifiable regions, in spite of all the changes wrought by modern times" (Tyler and Ravenel 1996, vii).

Book jacket blurbs frequently characterize authors by comparing them to one or more well-known literary landmarks. In Anne Tyler's case the major literary landmarks are the Southern women in the generation immediately preceding hers: Carson McCullers, Flannery O'Connor, and Eudora Welty.

Carson McCullers, born in 1917, was a precocious talent, like Anne Tyler. She was also a prodigious drinker who was disappointed in love and died at fifty after years of chronic illness. Her life is reflected in her fictions, which tend to be melancholy and which focus on the grotesque and seamy sides of the human experience much more than Anne Tyler's works do. Tyler memorializes McCullers in *Ladder of Years* by having the protagonist read McCullers's short story "A Tree, A Rock, A Cloud" about a man who is trying to learn to love by beginning with simple things.

According to Robert Croft (1995), "I Know You Rider," an unpublished Anne Tyler novel written in 1961, "reads like Carson McCullers, complete with a version of the Sad Cafe called Darleen's Grill" (15). In Anne Tyler's published works, however, it is difficult to find a clear example of McCullers's influence, except perhaps in *A Slipping-Down Life*, which has some vague similarities to McCullers's novella *The Ballad of the Sad Cafe* (see Chapter 3).

Eudora Welty was born in 1909. Like Anne Tyler she was an outsider who was not born in the Deep South but whose parents moved there when she was young. Her writing made a deep impression upon the young Anne Tyler, who memorized many of the stories from reading them so many times. *The Golden Apples* (1949) was her favorite collection of stories, a judgment that Welty herself concurs with (Magee 1980, 148–153).

Eudora Welty is foremost a short-story writer, a literary form that Anne Tyler steeped herself in from 1959 to 1977, during which time she produced thirty-six stories. Her production dwindled to seven between 1978 and 1991, since which time she has written none, although she has written introductions to three anthologies of short stories that she helped to select (Tyler and Ravenel 1983, 1985; Tyler, P.E.N. collection 1996). As Doris Betts (1983) has pointed out, Tyler's schooling in the conventions of the short story—the concentration on the implications of small events, the emphasis on rapid disclosure—left its stamp on her technique as a novelist: "Like Eudora Welty, Tyler chose early to make character bear her heaviest load of meaning. Outlining any Tyler plot will illustrate Welty's definition of plot as the 'why' of story, the steady asking of 'why?' and having the question replied to 'at different depths' " (Betts 1983, 27).

The qualities of Eudora Welty's writing that most deeply inspired Anne Tyler are those that Tyler describes in a book review, "The Fine Full World of Welty" (1980). According to Tyler, Welty is "the most faithful of mirrors" because she writes about "what *is*, not what ought to be" (144). Another way to characterize this quality might be "honesty"—the willingness to let the characters tell their own stories.

Paradoxically, this honesty is demonstrated by creating highly believable fictions—or "convincing lies," as Tyler has characterized her own work. Welty's use of incongruities makes her fictions even more convincing: "People are involved in strangely peripheral activities . . . at crucial moments or are caught by irrelevant sights" (Tyler 1980, 146). Tyler has frequently employed this technique, for example, in *Earthly Possessions*, where the protagonist feels happy that her kidnapper has let her have the window seat on the bus.

Anne Tyler also cites Eudora Welty's unerring visual sense—her ability to make the reader *see* through an artful and arresting phrase. The example that Tyler (1980) gives is Welty's description of an old rose bush twining around a post "like the initial letter in a poetry book" (145). Tyler also has this gift for conjuring up an exact visual image through precise and economical language. For example, in *Ladder of Years* Tyler describes an ancient building whose bricks are "worn down like old pencil erasers" (87). This, too, is a kind of honesty, concerning the use of language: the crafting of a telling image or simile to enhance clarity, not just to show off. When we read their metaphors and similes, we have an "aha!" experience because of the goodness of fit between the language and the experience it envelops.

But the most important characteristic of Welty's writing is her kindness. She views her characters with "genuine sympathy and affection" (Tyler 1980, 144). Just as real people instinctively know who to open up to, so do imaginary people. Eudora Welty's characters present themselves to her "hopefully and confidingly, believing that she'll do right by them" (Tyler 1980, 147).

It is this sensibility of Eudora Welty's that most impresses Anne Tyler, who calls her "one of our purest, finest, gentlest voices" (147). In an interview with Welty ("A Visit with Eudora Welty") Tyler (1980) notes that, despite the aging author's frail physical condition, Welty's "eyes are still as luminous as ever, radiating kindness and . . . attention, you would have to call it; but attention of a special quality, with some gentle amusement accompanying it" (149). As Tyler puts it, "it's plain that her *internal* energy is as powerful as ever" (152).

Even though Anne Tyler's primary literary inspiration was Eudora Welty, Tyler shares a penchant for the absurd with Flannery O'Connor. O'Connor is a paradoxical writer. Chronically ill throughout her life, there is a strong religious streak to her writing, beginning with her novel *Wise Blood*. Although a traditional Roman Catholic, O'Connor was also attracted to the modernism and heterodox mysticism of Teilhard de Chardin and Simone Weil (O'Connor 1979).

Despite being born in 1925, O'Connor had a very modern sense of the absurd and used to collect oddities culled from the newspaper and pass them on to friends, much as Anne Tyler has developed some of her more bizarre story ideas from newspaper clippings (such as Evie's self-mutilation in *A Slipping-Down Life*). Anne Tyler (1980) wrote, "I can't shake off a sort of mist of irony that hangs over whatever I see" (12). Similarly, O'Connor (1979) wrote, "The basis of the way I see is comic regardless of what I do with it . . . the Comic and the Terrible . . . may be opposite sides of the same coin" (105).

But what puts Anne Tyler off about O'Connor's humor is O'Connor's willful cruelty toward her characters. This is in decisive contrast to Tyler, who could easily have said, as Eudora Welty does, "I have been told, both in approval and in accusation that I seem to love all my characters"

(Welty 1980, 11). Neither Tyler nor Welty are willing to distort their characters for the purpose of plot or symbolism, nor to torture some kind of moral from the story.

WOMEN AUTHORS AND POPULAR LITERATURE

Prior to the emergence of late-twentieth-century feminist novels, much of the fiction authored by women could be characterized as Gothic, sentimental, or comedy of manners. Anne Tyler's writing falls primarily in the broad tradition of the comedy of manners, as exemplified historically by Jane Austen and as practiced in modern times by Eudora Welty. The comedy of manners is part of the day world of literature: brightly lit, witty, rational. But there is also a strain of the Gothic in Anne Tyler, with her fascination for the twilight, the grotesque, and the mysterious. This Gothic streak is seen in Tyler's fondness for describing her character's dreams, altered states of consciousness, or bizarre, surreal events. It is also seen in her admiration for Gabriel García Márquez and the so-called Magical Realist literature.

As I have discussed elsewhere (Bail 1996), British novelist Anne Radcliffe had transformed the Gothic romance into a highly popular genre by the end of the eighteenth century. With the turn of the century, the novel of manners found its main exemplar in Jane Austen. Meanwhile, the Gothic was revitalized by the Brontë sisters, particularly Emily, whose *Wuthering Heights* is excellent for its depth of characterization and psychological insight. Mary Shelley, the daughter of feminist Mary Wollstonecraft and the wife of the androgynous poet Percy Shelley, had earlier taken the Gothic in another direction with *Frankenstein*, a work of social criticism dressed up as a popular tale, which would later become a cornerstone for the emerging genre of science fiction.

Women novelists were a bit slower to emerge in the former British colonies known as the United States. But in the decades immediately prior to the Civil War, women authors accounted for close to half the literature published (Baym 1988). Some of these women were extremely prolific and immensely popular.

Many of these authors were feminists, in the broad sense of the term. Some, such as Catherine Maria Sedgwick and Lydia Maria Child, were passionately involved in social and political crusades: access to education and voting privileges for women, and the abolition of slavery. This involvement often went hand in hand with participation in the more "open" spiritual climate associated with Unitarian and Quaker ideals.

Until recently, these authors were forgotten, dismissed as "sentimental" or "popular," their works unread until they were reclaimed by feminist scholars. There is a certain ambivalence in the critical and academic community toward Anne Tyler's writing, some considering her to be a unique and independent voice in American fiction, others feeling she is too popular and saccharine and not political enough. Many of the criticisms of Tyler's works have traditionally been used to devalue women's writing, namely, that it is domestic and regional and utilizes a small canvas and that it is quiet and uplifting. It remains to be seen whether the critical establishment will preserve Anne Tyler's writing in the coming century or will dismiss it, as has happened in the past to so many well-loved women authors.

SELECTION CRITERIA

Anne Tyler has published thirteen novels. The first three are set in North Carolina and involve individuals in their late teens or early adulthood who are in the process of establishing a love relationship. With the fourth novel, *The Clock Winder*, there begins a series of stories about young women, including Elizabeth Abbott (*The Clock Winder*), Mary Tell (*Celestial Navigation*), Emily Meredith (*Morgan's Passing*), and Lucy Bedloe (*Saint Maybe*), who migrate from North Carolina or Virginia to Baltimore. At some point, each of these characters marries and has children. *Searching for Caleb, Dinner at the Homesick Restaurant, Breathing Lessons*, and *Ladder of Years* focus more on a later stage of family life, often including several generations, with a mature heroine dealing with grown-up children and contemplating the meaning of her life. *Earthly Possessions* also deals with some of these themes but on a smaller scale. The progression of the novels to a large extent mirrors the changes in Anne Tyler's life experience as it has moved from the first blush of marriage, through the experience of being a mother and a writer, to becoming a widow with adult daughters.

Owing to limitations of space, I have focused on twelve of the fourteen novels so that I can explore them in some depth. Her most recent novel, *A Patchwork Planet*, was released as this book was going to press, and a brief analysis of it has been included. I have chosen not to analyze her earliest works, *If Morning Ever Comes* and *The Tin Can Tree*, feeling that there is more to be gained from studying her later work. Anne Tyler (1981) herself has disowned these first two novels, declaring to Wendy Lamb that they should be "burned" (58). However, Tyler is her harshest critic. The earliest novels are not without merit, and readers who have digested all of her later novels may be curious to explore the earlier manifestations of her talent.

In addition to writing novels, Anne Tyler has produced a number of short stories and book reviews and has written a few essays and book introductions. I have occasionally drawn on these where it has shed further light upon the novels being analyzed.

A Slipping-Down Life
(1970)

"I'm always hurt when a reader says that I choose only bizarre or eccentric people to write about. . . . Even the most ordinary person, in real life, will turn out to have something unusual at his center."
Anne Tyler, "Because I Want More Than One Life"

A Slipping-Down Life is the last of Anne Tyler's three North Carolina novels. Unlike the first two, it was written after she moved to Baltimore. All of her subsequent eleven novels are set in Maryland, generally in Baltimore. The first two North Carolina novels, *If Morning Ever Comes* and *The Tin Can Tree*, have been disowned by Anne Tyler, who has wished she could buy up every copy and burn them (Tyler, 1980). Although they lack the full power of her later work, they are nevertheless of interest in tracing the evolution of her style and her thematic concerns.

If Morning Ever Comes deals with a young law student who returns to visit his family home, which is inhabited by three generations of women, including six sisters. Alice Hall Petry hailed *If Morning Ever Comes* as a feminist novel because it portrays a family of strong women who bond together without seeming to need a family patriarch. But that is only one dimension of it. Anne Tyler herself avoids the label "feminist" and has a distaste for fiction that is self-consciously political or ideological.

One sees already in Anne Tyler's first novel her occasional touch of surrealism: On the night when Ben Joe's father dies, the reader is suddenly jarred out of the flow of the narrative by the out-of-place appearance of a drunken soldier who is marching around the family's lawn and playing a single piercing note over and over on a broken bagpipe. This bizarre character appears as if he wandered in off the pages of another book, like an actor in costume getting lost and walking onto the wrong movie set.

The plot of *The Tin Can Tree* is set in the immediate aftermath of a young girl's death. In this respect it anticipates some of the themes of *The Accidental Tourist*. The mother of the dead girl becomes so self-absorbed in a stupor of grief that she fails to attend to her surviving child's needs. She only awakens from her cocoon after her son runs away from home. This novel, like its predecessor, is self-consciously Southern and draws heavily on regional speech patterns, particularly in the scenes with the tobacco workers.

Anne Tyler will continue to demonstrate an interest in the language and culture of poor Southern whites in her subsequent novels, including *A Slipping-Down Life, Earthly Possessions, Celestial Navigation, Breathing Lessons*, and *Saint Maybe*.

With the birth of her second child in 1967, life had become too hectic for Anne Tyler to write anything longer than a short story. For similar reasons, *A Slipping-Down Life*, which was completed before her daughters had reached ages three and five, is her slenderest novel. Nevertheless, it retains a special place in Anne Tyler's heart and is the only one of her North Carolina novels that she does not wish she had destroyed. An abridged form of the novel appeared in the January 1970 issue of *Redbook* magazine. At one point, the film rights were optioned by Paul Newman, but it was never made into a movie.

The idea for the plot began with a newspaper article that Tyler read about a girl in Texas who cut Elvis Presley's name into her forehead in a bid for his attention (Croft 1995). The character of Drum Casey is one whom Tyler feels a special affection for. He is the "direct inheritance" of the summer days she spent working on the tobacco farm, absorbing the speech patterns of the laborers (interview by Ridley 1972, 23).

Anne Tyler was fascinated with the language of the poor Southerner, both black and white. She once told Jorie Lueloff (1965), "A Southern conversation is pure metaphor and the lower you get in the class structure, the more it's true. Up North they speak in prose, and the conversation doesn't have as much color" (23).

PLOT

This novel has a very simple, straightforward plot and no subplots. With the exception of the last page of the novel, the entire narrative is told from the point of view of a single character, Evie Decker. There are no flashbacks or other complicated narrative structures. There are only a handful of other characters, and of these the only significant one is Drumstrings Casey, whose story is almost entirely subordinate to Evie's. The action of the novel takes place within a tightly circumscribed rural geography over a period of a few months.

Evie Decker is a seventeen-year-old high school student living with her father, a schoolteacher. Shy and overweight, Evie is ignored by her peers. Her only friend Violet Hayes is heavier but more self-confident. Evie develops a crush on Drumstrings (Drum) Casey, a rock musician whom she hears interviewed on the radio. Evie learns from a schoolmate, Fay-Jean, that Drum performs at the Unicorn, a roadhouse tavern on a "lonesome highway" (17). Evie and her friend Violet soon become regulars at the Unicorn, but Evie has competition for Drum's attention from a gaggle of prettier fans. She feels that if she wants to get Drum's attention she will have to do something on impulse. Evie goes into the restroom and carves "Casey" into her forehead by using fingernail scissors. The letters are cut backward as if she had been looking into a mirror when she did it.

Discharged from the hospital, Evie skips school, looking for ways to keep Drum's attention. The publicity from her act of self-mutilation leads to a big career break for Drum. He is offered a gig at the Parisian nightclub in Tar City. When Evie asks permission to watch him perform at the Parisian, Drum angrily refuses. Hurt, Evie tells Drum that his music is boring and that carving his name in her forehead was a waste. She hopes he will be a failure.

After Drum is fired, he turns to Evie. He now believes that she is his good luck charm and that her "curse" on him was the cause of his failure. She brings him luck, he says, but he wishes she would smile more and not "weigh on" his head so much. When Evie begins questioning Drum about the future of their relationship, he runs off again. Drum returns to Evie's a week later. He surprises Evie by proposing marriage.

They lie about their age and elope, then move into a primitive tar paper shack on the outskirts of town where the tenant farmers live. Drum's career and his mood keep going downhill. He seems to have become a shell of his old self, not even writing songs anymore, sitting around singing sad ballads, feeling his life has already hit its high point and it's all downhill from now on—just nineteen years old and already leading "a slipping-down life" (148).

Evie tries to think up more publicity schemes, hoping to revive Drum's career and his spirits. She learns that Brother Hope is preaching to a revival meeting that a girl in town had "ruined her face" at an orgy over a rock idol (149). Evie decides fate has thrown a photo opportunity into their laps. Brother Hope, the traveling revivalist, represents Anne Tyler's most savage takeoff on fundamentalist preachers. The clergymen in her other novels—*Earthly Possessions, Searching for Caleb, The Clock Winder, Saint Maybe,* and *Ladder of Years*—are sympathetically drawn by comparison.

Evie confronts the preacher in front of his congregation and gets herself in the newspaper again. The notoriety leads to fans' calling the Unicorn and asking for Drum, so the manager rehires him. Evie decides to manufacture more publicity by staging a fake "kidnapping" of Drum by his "fans" without his consent. Shortly after Violet and Fay-Jean overpower Drum, the high-school principal drives up and tells Evie that her father has just had a heart attack. Evie's father is already dead by the time Evie gets to the hospital.

Evie spends the night at her father's house and is driven out to her shack the next day only to discover Drum in bed with Fay-Jean. However, Evie is less upset about this than about the general aimless quality of her life and Drum's. She reveals to Drum that she is three months pregnant, and she tells Drum that she wants him to move with her into her father's house, which she is going to inherit. But Drum refuses. He tries to convince Evie to stay with him, reminding her that she once cut his name into her forehead. In response, Evie tells Drum a revised version of the event: It wasn't she who carved those letters in her skin but some other female fans who were angry at her. Drum is no longer sure what to believe.

Despite her ambivalence about leaving Drum, for the baby's sake Evie steels herself and drives off. The tale ends with Drum, back in the Unicorn, wondering which is the true version of how Evie got her face scarred.

CHARACTERS

The principal character is Evie Decker, an only child whose mother died shortly after childbirth. Evie feels alone in her house; her father is always absorbed in some type of project, and the housekeeper Clotelia has a bantering, teasing style of relating that discourages Evie from confiding in her. Evie does well academically at school, but socially she is an outsider. She is bored and starved for both affection and excitement.

When Evie cuts "Casey" on her forehead, she is glad she has done something "out of character" for once. This desperate act is also a daring leap that serves the positive function of irrevocably proclaiming her deeply buried desires to be noticed. Evie gradually transforms herself from a passive, unpopular teenager, watching life pass her by, to someone who speaks her mind and asserts herself. She starts becoming more direct with Drum.

As she becomes more assertive, her sense of middle-class propriety comes more to the fore. Even though she is desperate to marry Drum, she surprises herself by refusing to run off to South Carolina because that's where the "trash" go when they "have to" get married (116).

More and more, Evie becomes the decision maker, and Drum reluctantly goes along after mounting only a token protest. It finally comes to the point where Evie stops informing Drum of her decisions. When she decides to stage a kidnapping, Evie just invites her girlfriends over and the women dominate Drum by use of brute force.

Evie begins asserting herself with others as well. When Fay-Jean, acting nonchalant about Evie's catching her in bed with Drum, has the gall to ask for a ride home, Evie curtly informs her that she's too busy and tells her to walk down the dirt road to the highway in her high heels and flag down the bus. This is quite a different Evie from the shy, deferential girl we met in the opening pages. At the end of the novel as Evie is about to drive away from the tar paper shack for good, Drum asks her if she might not change her mind later on. "I never back down on things," Evie replies (186).

Drum Casey, also known as Betram "Drumstrings" Casey, is a dark-haired, dark-eyed, brooding, aloof nineteen year old. If there were a movie version of this novel, Nicholas Cage could be cast as Drum. In many ways Drum is a rural version of Jesse Moran, the would-be rock star whose wife leaves him in *Breathing Lessons*. Drum, like Jesse, has a mother who encourages his dreams and a father who tries to puncture them, calling him lazy and irresponsible. Drum also is hypersensitive and becomes defensive at any hint of criticism, like Jake, the bank robber, in *Earthly Possessions*.

Drum is a high school dropout who comes from a social class lower than Evie's. His family lives in Farinia, a town in which there is only one paved street. Drum's favorite meal seems to be breakfast: biscuits with ham and syrup. His primary expectation of marriage is to have a wife who will be able to fix him such a breakfast. His idea of a luxury item is to be able to taste artichoke hearts just once before he dies.

Rock stardom seems his only chance to rise above his family's lot. He appears boastful and full of himself. But this conceit is covering a deep streak of insecurity. He is dependent upon outside adulation to reassure himself of his worth. On the way home at the end of a performance, away from the female fans who surrounded him, he seems vulnerable and uncertain.

When Drum's mother denigrates him for getting fired from the Parisian he protests against her loss of faith in him after "one little setback." But in the next breath, Drum reveals that he has taken his mother's assessment to heart. "I will never get anywhere in this life" (105). After Drum and Evie get married, Drum is reluctant to have Evie stray too far away from him. If she is in a different room of the shack, he asks her to come in and keep him company. On the nights when he is playing at the Unicorn, he insists that she put aside her homework and come with him.

Drum gradually becomes more passive in his dealings with Evie, letting down his protective wall, talking about his feelings and fears, making only a token protest against her getting a job. When Evie wants to go to the revival at the Tabernacle of God for publicity, Drum adamantly refuses; but when she and David decide to go without him, he protests against being left behind and reluctantly accompanies them rather than sit at home alone. When Evie finally decides to leave Drum and move to her father's house, Drum asks Evie whether she can't just stay with him until his "luck" changes (183). Drum cannot move with Evie into her deceased father's house for the same reason that Evie could not run off to South Carolina to be married: It's a matter of pride and ingrained social class codes.

Mrs. Casey, Drum's mother, is a frustrated woman who is living out her ambitions through her son: "He's carrying all my hopes," she says (84). Drum's success reflects on his mother. It proves that she was right about his being special and shows that he has inherited musical ability from her side of the family. It means that she was justified in defending her son. But Drum's failures also rebound upon her. If Drum's career fails, his father will say to her "I told you so." Evie comes to replace Drum's mother as Drum's source of support, and this transference is subtly signaled by the use of equivalent phrases in describing both Drum's mother and Evie. Early in the novel, Mrs. Casey is described as spinning a "web of words" whereby she puffs up Drum's self-confidence (84). But after Drum and his mother have their falling out it is Evie who is now described as winding a "net of words" around Drum (104). These kinds of verbal parallelisms are a device that Anne Tyler frequently uses to signal correspondences between certain characters.

Sam Decker, Evie's father, is a small-town school teacher, like Charlotte Emory's mother (*Earthly Possessions*) and Mary Tell's mother and father (*Celestial Navigation*). Lanky, bony, awkward and mild-mannered, his students ignore him and pass notes around the classroom in his presence. He is equally ineffective in dealing with his daughter. He is a ghost of a man, more of an absence than a presence, always off in the yard or some other part of the house, doing a fix-it project or solving a crossword puzzle or listening to his shortwave. Clearly, he doesn't understand teenage girls, particularly his own daughter, and feels uncomfortable around them.

As one critic (Nesanovich 1994) has pointed out, the contrast in physiques between father and daughter is in itself a sign of the gulf between them (as is true of Charlotte Emory and her parents in *Earthly Possessions*). Nesanovich underscores Mr. Decker's inability to speak forthrightly to Evie, even about the most obvious problem—her weight. Stumbling over his words, he retreats into euphemism. He tells her that the boys will be going crazy over her "when you lose a—when you're older" (37).

LITERARY DEVICES

This is Anne Tyler's most "gothic" novel—a term overused in describing Southern literature (see Chapter 2). The two main characters are an unlikely pair of misfits, starkly outlined, motivated by emotional compulsions that they take for granted. The author's tone is cool and somewhat ironic. It's all somewhat mythic—a mood that is reinforced by the author's frequent references to movie and newspaper formulas and popular songs, whose themes the characters fit their lives into. The overall effect is reminiscent of the tone of Carson McCullers's novella *The Ballad of the Sad Cafe*.

Anne Tyler invests bits of herself in the main characters. Evie accepts Drum's proposal of marriage with the same words that the author used in real life, "Why not?" And Anne Tyler spent a number of years working in a library, just as Evie does. Drum is an artist, of sorts. His spontaneous "speaking out" in disconnected sentences in the middle of a song, reflecting the images that pop into his mind, is similar to a certain tendency of Anne Tyler's, whereby she inserts odd little cryptic or surrealistic bits into the plot that are somewhat disconnected from the main narrative.

As with Drum, Anne Tyler thinks in images (and almost became a visual artist instead of a writer). While Anne Tyler is able to integrate within herself both the visual and verbal languages of representation, Evie and Drum speak opposing "languages," which reflect in part their different social classes. Drum's people are closer to the soil, and his is an aural culture of musical rhythms and visual images, while Evie's middle-class town style is a literate one, focusing on the written word.

When Evie begins working in the town library, she begins to be drawn away from Drum. Miss Simmons the librarian becomes a kind of mother substitute. Evie begins to internalize the organized atmosphere of the library. It makes her see that she and Drum have to get their life "organized" (183). When she decides to leave Drum, she feels a deep tugging at her heart; but then, drawing strength from her days of working in the great middle-class temple of books, she "squared her corners," as though she were a stack of library cards, and drove off (183).

While Evie's verbal-literary style draws her increasingly into a linear, ordered world, Drum's aural-imagistic style could leave him more open to the dimension of *mystery* in life. The most peculiar aspect of Drum's music is his "speaking out," whereby he breaks into unplanned speech in the middle of a song—perhaps distantly related to the old-fashioned Pentecostals' being moved to speak a message. The lines come to Drum spontaneously as he articulates images that come to his mind. They are disconnected and dreamlike, like the lyrics of some early Bob Dylan songs. At times, they are almost mystical.

THEMES

On the surface, *A Slipping-Down Life* could be considered a coming-of-age novel, as Evie faces poverty, pregnancy, infidelity, and the death of her father and develops from a passive teenager who is seeking an identity to an increasingly assertive woman. As Evie becomes increasingly active, Drum reveals more of his own passivity. This role reversal is an extreme example of what commonly happens to couples in Anne Tyler novels—they begin absorbing parts of each others' personalities.

But at a deeper level, the story is a postmodern parable about the role of narrative images in shaping our lives and the manipulation of images by commercial interests.

For example, Evie receives a piece of mail containing a newspaper clipping of her in the hospital after she mutilated her forehead, with a note from Sonny Martin, "Pulqua County's Biggest Real Estate Agent," congratulating her on her "recent achievement" (60). This commercial message is characterized by a sense of missed connection or dislocation. The message doesn't match the reality because of the carelessness of the person with commercial interests. Evie's cutting her face and being photographed with Drum Casey is not an "achievement" in the usual sense. Nor is it a "sacrifice to false gods" (155), as the publicity-seeking revivalist Brother Hope calls it, twisting Evie's private suffering to serve his own evangelistic ends.

Even in the very beginning, the novel starts off with an example of commercialized misconnection. Appearing on a new radio interview show, Drum gets annoyed when it is obvious that the host has never heard his music. Why did he invite him onto the program then? Drum asks. Because the higher-ups instructed him to, the interviewer exasperatedly replies. "Heavens, boy . . . Let's get this over with" (4).

When the news cameraman Mr. Ogle tries to get a caption for Evie's photograph, she is speechless, so he begins putting words in her mouth, making up a quotation for her: "That sound about right?" he asks off-handedly (42). Likewise, the newspaper photograph of her protest at Brother Hope's revival comes out distorted and strange looking.

Distortion and the failure to connect is also shown, more subtly, in the formulaic newspaper reviews of Drum's music. When Evie gets angry at Drum, she borrows negative phrases from a review and throws them in his face. Although Drum believes in his music and has some inner spark, as revealed by his "speaking out," his creativity is mixed in with excessive commercial ambitions. The more the characters begin emphasizing the importance of publicity, the more Drum begins to lose faith in his music, until in the end he concludes that the songs he has written are just the same as everyone else's, maybe even worse, so why should he want to write more?

Anne Tyler often demonstrates the interplay between fictional texts and the characters' narrative constructions of their lives as revealed in their self-images. This process of narrative filtering and shaping of one's "story" of oneself is an everyday occurrence that largely goes unnoticed. In *Celestial Navigation*, Jeremy derives his notions of courtship from antiquated novels and contemporary television programs, and Olivia imagines herself living in a movie about the life of Jeremy Pauling, artist. In *Ladder of Years*, Delia, who is addicted to romance novels, invents an alternate identity for herself—Miss Grinstead—and imagines herself in a movie. Charlotte Emory in *Earthly Possessions* sees herself over and over on television where the nightly news shows video footage of her and Jake Simms taken during the bank robbery.

In *A Slipping-Down Life*, movies, television soap operas, and women's magazines provide prescriptions for the characters on how to behave. There is a thin line in the novel between real life and fictional images, real achievement and publicity. The characters demonstrate their confusion about image and reality when watching soap operas. Clotelia speaks familiarly about the characters as though they were her relatives, and Drum talks back to the television characters on the screen.

Evie walks a narrow line between fantasy and reality, consciously adopting a new, romanticized image by putting on a black dress and sitting at Drum's feet while he performs. She makes it clear that she will not do anything that, in her mind, is "play acting" (74). But when she accepts Drum's proposal of marriage, one of the arguments he uses to persuade her is that they will get their picture in the newspaper as a human interest story.

On Evie's wedding day, she feels like "a star in an old movie" (120). The movie motif appears again a few months after Evie and Drum's marriage, when it becomes clear that Drum will not move into Evie's father's house with her. Evie begins packing her bags; she has seen this scene "rehearsed for her" so many times on television and in the movies that every move seems "prescribed" (183–184).

In the movies, the Drum character would end up changing his mind and coming with Evie, but Evie doesn't expect this to happen because Drum is ignorant of "things like that" (185).

As Evie is leaving Drum, she tells him that she didn't cut her forehead but that "someone else did" (185). She tells him that two girls at the Unicorn held her down in the bathroom and did it. Some critics have taken this retraction quite literally (Voelker 1989). On the other hand, one could interpret Evie's statement symbolically; she could be saying, "The 'I' that did that (or needed to do that) no longer exists. It feels like 'someone else.' " This would be consistent with Anne Tyler's view of the self in a state of flux, as presented in *Ladder of Years*. But in the context of the plot of this novel, Evie's denial that she inscribed herself with Casey's name seems to be just a way of getting back at him. And her denial produces the same sense of uncertainty in Drum as her denunciation of his musical ability during their fight when he got hired at the Parisian months earlier. "Life is getting too cluttered," he declares, confused by what Evie is telling him (185).

"Clutter" is a multimeaning motif that appears frequently in Anne Tyler's novels. Here it refers to the surplus of meanings, the indeterminacy that ruins the clean, aesthetic lines of Drum's naive sense of certainty about life. In the final paragraphs of the novel, he "speaks out" during his song at the Unicorn, calling, *"But the letters was cut backwards. Would you explain?"* (186).

Drum wonders aloud about the letters' being cut backwards because this would be consistent with Evie's cutting them herself while looking in a mirror, rather than someone else's doing it to her. This type of uncertainty, and multiple versions of past events, is a motif that Anne Tyler explores in other novels, notably *Earthly Possessions*, where Charlotte remembers her mother's saying that there had been a mix-up of babies at her birth, though later her mother denies it, and *Saint Maybe*, where the meaning of Danny's and Lucy's deaths changes and remains uncertain.

The reference to "circular stairs" is more puzzling. Circular stairs, of course, form a spiral. Without getting overly symbolic, the spiral does represent Anne Tyler's view of time, and she has used stairs as a metaphor for the passage of time, both in *Ladder of Years*, where it figures in the title, and in *Celestial Navigation*, where Olivia and Jeremy come to view the stairs as a symbol of the futile repetitiveness of life. In *A Slipping-Down Life*, the circular pattern is also present. At the end, Drum is back at the Unicorn and Evie is back at her father's house, alone, reenacting with her unborn baby the role of a single parent that her father carried through with her. It is almost a cliché that her father's death so closely coincides with her pregnancy, dramatizing the cycle of the generations as life is renewed through death and birth.

The beginning and end of the circular movement are framed by mirrors. Early in the novel, when Evie looks into the mirror at the Unicorn and cuts Casey's name into her forehead, she steps "through the looking glass" into a different life. At the end of the novel, just before leaving Drum, she looks at her face in the mirror and undoes the cutting by saying, "I didn't do it," then steps back through the looking glass to her middle-class home, like Alice awakening from her dream of Wonderland. In this verbal undoing of her action, Evie is in effect agreeing with her father, who also wanted to undo the damage, but through plastic surgery.

A MULTICULTURAL READING OF *A SLIPPING-DOWN LIFE*

A multicultural reading involves examining the text from the perspective of ethnic groups that are peripheral to the social, economic, and political "mainstream" of the dominant culture. This approach reveals the overt and covert ways in which those who are culturally "other" are ignored, misperceived, thwarted, or oppressed.

Anne Tyler's fictional treatment of most political and social issues has been indirect and muted. Schooled in the democractic atmosphere of the Quaker meetinghouse, Tyler is sensitive to social injustice and prejudice. Tyler has wiped away her daughters' tears after they experienced anti-Iranian hatred at school during the 1970s. Yet her political orientation is always communicated with unintrusive subtlety: Pearl Tull in *The Accidental Tourist* throws away junk mail from the Republican Committee and the National Rifle Association without even bothering to open it; Maggie Moran in *Breathing Lessons* tries to talk Serena out of an abortion, but also fights with the anti-abortion picketers; Mrs. Emerson in *The Clock Winder* is oblivious to the frightening reality of the Vietnam War.

One of Tyler's few overt references to civil rights issues was a very subtle one. The opening pages of *If Morning Ever Comes* describes the divided waiting room at the train station: "Since times had changed the wooden letters saying 'White' and 'Colored' had been removed, but the letters had left cleaner places on the wall that spelled out the same words still" (39). This image reveals the limits of what can be accomplished through political and legislative change and aptly symbolizes how the promise of equality remains unfulfilled despite desegregation.

In a multicultural analysis, minor characters, who are marginal to the text, may suddenly assume a magnified importance because they embody ethnocultural "difference." This is the case with Clotelia, the housekeeper in Evie's home. She is one of the few African American characters who is developed to any degree in Anne Tyler novels, the others being Missouri, the tobacco worker in *The Tin Can Tree*; Alvareen, the Emerson's cook in *The Clock Winder*; Rick Rackley, an ex–pro-football star who is scorned by his white father-in-law in *Ladder of Years*; the elderly Mr. Otis in *Breathing Lessons*; and White-Eye, the blind street musician to whom Caleb attaches himself but never speaks with in *Searching for Caleb*.

Other black characters are only glimpsed momentarily in Tyler's novels: Sulie Lafleur, the maid in *Searching for Caleb*, the man playing the harmonica in the final chapter of *Celestial Navigation*, the little boy mimicking the marching band from the sidelines in *Earthly Possessions*, the black diners who never talk to Morgan at the No Jive Cafe in *Morgan's Passing*, and some unemployed men standing on the sidewalk, glimpsed by Macon Leary in *The Accidental Tourist*.

Clotelia is the closest thing that Evie has to a maternal presence in the house. Clotelia potentially could play a significant role in Evie's life since she is perceptive and much more aware of Evie's situation than the father is. For example, Clotelia recognizes that Evie is pregnant without being told. But aside from her constant nagging, Clotelia is not the motherly type. She never gives Evie a hug or a pat or a sympathetic word. She seems more involved in the lives of her favorite soap opera characters than in the life of the young girl who sits before her in flesh and blood.

Nevertheless, when Evie needs housewifely lore passed on to her— the kind that is not written down in books—she turns to Clotelia. It is she who instructs Evie on how to make the kind of biscuits that Drum Casey and "his kind" crave. The secret ingredient is bacon drippings (127).

Clotelia also comes to keep Evie company the night her father dies. But Clotelia admits that she didn't inherit her mother's talent for consoling people and keeps on with her nagging tone so that Evie is forced to make do with cupping her mug of hot chocolate for warmth. But Clotelia also hints, in her usual ironic style, at her willingness to help Evie with child care.

One critic (Nesanovich 1994, 29) criticizes Clotelia's "blunt selfishness," arguing that though Clotelia's presence is a relief from the gloomy silence of the household, her banal chatter fails to hold out any "possibility of intimacy" to the maternally deprived Evie.

But while it may be fair to say that Clotelia is neither efficient nor especially industrious as a housekeeper, it seems presumptuous to expect her to play the role of an understanding mother to a moody, sullen teenager who feels free to order her about, instructing her imperiously to "go fix some lemonade" for a guest whom her father has forbidden her to entertain. In any case, Clotelia doesn't have the temperament for administering hugs and kisses, as she herself confesses on the night of Evie's father's death (176).

Clotelia stubbornly insists on maintaining her Otherness and refuses to "turn into a member of the family" by Evie's definition, which would apparently mean making herself totally available to meet Evie's every expectation—like the elderly maid in *The Clock Winder* who is expected to clean the baseboards with a Q-tip. Clotelia carries her purse with her from room to room as she works, as if she feels mistrustful of leaving it untended. Nevertheless, Evie feels uninhibited about dipping into the purse and consuming a packet of snack crackers that she finds in there, or perusing the magazines that Clotelia hides under the furniture.

There is a complexity to Clotelia's relationship with Evie that reflects the ambivalence and hypocrisy of the social structure, with its rigid hierarchy, whose "on-stage" roles are too confining to be consistently maintained "off-stage." Clotelia wonders if a character in her favorite soap opera acts so stuck-up because it is "*his* way" or if he just acts that way "for the play" (106). In front of guests, Clotelia allows Evie to order her to fetch things; but in private, Clotelia is apt to tell Evie to get it herself.

Although of a younger generation, Clotelia bears some resemblance to the black housekeeper Maroon in Anne Tyler's short story "The Geologist's Maid" (1975). There is something not easily assimilable about the presence of Clotelia and Maroon that constitutes some kind of "affront" to their employers' sensibilities—an inborn resistance to becoming unobstrusive and invisible. And yet both have an intense awareness of social class and of what is "proper" behavior.

Clotelia believes that Evie should remain within the prescribed boundaries of her social class. Like a sheepdog guarding the fold, Clotelia makes it her duty to nag Evie into living up to these standards. As Evie gets more involved with Drum Casey and neglects her studies, Clotelia protests that her years of being "nursemaid" to Evie have been a waste—"all for nothing" (107).

But there is an ambiguity to Clotelia's internalization of social pre-scriptions, since these same standards repressively prescribe for her an inferior status based on skin color and occupation. When Clotelia catches Evie reading her *Revealing Romances* and her black magazine *Jet*, she de-mands to know why Evie is reading "that trash" that will "snarl" her mind. Evie replies that she wants to see where Clotelia gets her "outlook on life" (47).

This ambiguity about prescribed social caste is particularly apparent in the way in which Clotelia treats Drum Casey. On the one hand, she derides Drum as white trash; and yet when he shows up at the house, she has prepared just the kind of down-home breakfast she knows "his kind" would like. In fact, she prepares much more mouth-watering fare for Drum than what she serves the members of Evie's family, who get frankfurters, instant mashed potatoes, and jello for supper.

There is a hidden kinship between Clotelia and Drum. Evie complains that Clotelia never does what she is supposed to do. Drum is also re-calcitrant, and never does what Evie expects him to do either. Both Clo-telia and Drum are peripheral to the hierarchical mainstream. Neither of them quite measures up to middle-class expectations of how they should behave.

Clotelia also embodies the awkward transition from the legally seg-regated to the legally desegregated South, an indigestible remnant of still-unresolved historic grievances, like the still-divided train station in *If Morning Ever Comes*. She comes to work wearing ski pants, an African cape, and cream-colored high-heeled suede boots and wears her hair in an "Afro," which at the time was a political statement of black pride. To Evie it seems that Clotelia is always angry and scornful. When Clotelia leaves Evie's house at the end of the day it feels as though Clotelia leaves behind an "angry" silence. Seen through Evie's eyes, Clotelia's earrings seem "as big as slave bands" and they flash "knives of light" (48). Clo-telia herself admits that she goes home from Evie's house in an "evil" mood of irritation (49).

Like Sulie the maid in *Searching for Caleb*, Clotelia is the keeper of the family secrets whom Evie's father never thinks to consult. Clotelia un-derstands all the things that Evie's father doesn't. She knows that Drum Casey has been coming around before Evie tells her. She knows when Evie has stopped attending school. She knows when Evie is pregnant. She doesn't reveal any of this to Evie's father. It is not clear whether Clotelia is being protective of his feelings or protective of Evie's secrets or whether she feels that it is not her role to get involved. But she does inform Evie that her behavior is breaking her father's heart. When Evie replies that Clotelia has never seemed to care a thing about his feelings before Clotelia replies in her typical oblique style that she still doesn't care but it hurts her to see someone's heart broken.

Anne Tyler succeeds here both in creating a complex and believable character and in demonstrating the misunderstandings that arise from the persisting legacy of institutionalized inequality.

The Clock Winder
(1972)

The Clock Winder marks the transition from the North Carolina novels to the Baltimore novels. Like Anne Tyler in her youth, the protagonist Elizabeth Abbott comes from rural North Carolina. The novel marks the point in Anne Tyler's development when she was beginning to reveal herself more openly through her characters—a kind of risk taking that intensifies in her next novel *Celestial Navigation*.

In the youthful character of Elizabeth Abbott there appears to be a bit of the teenage Anne Tyler: "There was a period in my life, starting at 17 or 18, when I seemed determined to do whatever seemed the most contrary thing," she once told Clifford Ridley (1972). "When I decided to get married, for instance, I remember thinking 'Oh, well, why not?'" (24). There is this same quality to Elizabeth's footloose impulsivity.

The novel ends with the ambiguity that is Anne Tyler's signature. In her estimation, it "condemns what it praises and vice versa" (interview by Ridley 1972, 27).

PLOT

The main narrative centers on the relationship that develops between Elizabeth Abbott, an aimless college dropout from a small town, and the upscale Emerson family of big city Baltimore, particularly the family's aging patrician matriarch Mrs. Emerson whose huge house lies empty with her children grown and her husband recently dead. She fires her handyman in a fit of pique and hires Elizabeth to replace him. Although Elizabeth, like Ezra Tull (*Dinner at the Homesick Restaurant*), is by nature "butter-fingered" (62), clumsy and accident prone, from the instant she enters the Emerson household she manifests "miraculous repairing powers" (70).

On Thanksgiving Elizabeth has her fateful first encounter with Timothy, one of Mrs. Emerson's four sons who is attending medical school. Mrs. Emerson sends Elizabeth with an ax to slaughter the Thanksgiving turkey, but the fowl slips away from her and she only halfheartedly gives chase, being reluctant to actually kill it. Timothy drives up as Elizabeth is trying to herd the turkey back into the yard. Timothy suggests that Elizabeth and he sneak off to the grocery store and buy a turkey carcass at the meat counter, which Elizabeth agrees to. But when Mrs. Emerson discovers the deception, she raises such a fuss about her orders not having been followed that Timothy, in irritation, catches the escaped turkey and slaughters it himself over his mother's last minute cries of "Timothy? Wait" (43).

The scenes of chasing the turkey mostly serve a comic function, but the grim climax demonstrates the power that Mrs. Emerson's disapproval has over her son. His mechanical follow-through in killing the turkey, despite his mother's last minute change of mind, reveals a streak of grim determination that foreshadows his capability of committing suicide later in the story.

Once Timothy begins something, he has to follow through to the end. He develops a romantic interest in Elizabeth, and they spend many weekends doing things together. But she, exercising her right to be footloose and free, begins also spending time with Timothy's brother Matthew. When Elizabeth decides to visit her parents and to take Matthew with her, Timothy becomes jealous. Compounding his upset, he has just been accused of cheating and expects to be expelled from medical school. He is afraid that the disappointment will devastate his mother. After Elizabeth refuses to break a date so that they can go away together, Timothy puts a gun to his head. When Elizabeth struggles to get the gun away from him, it goes off, and Timothy dies with a surprised expression on his face. This is the first turning point in the plot.

Traumatized by this incident, Elizabeth leaves town. In the bus station, at the last minute, Matthew proposes marriage, but she refuses. He writes letters to her at her parents' home, but she doesn't reply. Yet the

Emersons appear in her dreams, and memories of them haunt her days. She finally rouses herself out of her depression by agreeing to act as a companion for old Mr. Cunningham, whose is gradually becoming senile. Caring for him comforts her, but she takes his death as a personal failure.

Next, Elizabeth begins working in a handicrafts shop making wood-carvings. Still traumatized by Timothy's death, she contemplates a "safe" marriage to the bland and baby-faced Dommie Whitehill. Margaret Emerson confides to Elizabeth that her own marriage is haunted by her unresolved feelings for her first love, Jimmy Joe. This revelation triggers a realization in Elizabeth that she does not actually want to marry Dommie. At the last minute, she calls off the wedding. This is the second turning point in the plot.

Elizabeth blames herself for ruining yet another life—Dommie's. Although Margaret applauds Elizabeth's action as courageous, Elizabeth castigates herself: "Flashes of courage are easy," she says (202). She regrets her inability to choose a course of action and endure in it. Eventually, she regains confidence in herself and resumes a caretaker role, this time teaching crafts to wayward girls at a reform school in Virginia—a significant breakthrough since in the past Elizabeth was afraid to be responsible for children. Elizabeth is settling into her new life when Mrs. Emerson suffers a stroke and asks for Elizabeth. Margaret pleads with Elizabeth to take a six-week leave of absence to help Mrs. Emerson during her convalescence. In the course of her stay at the Emersons's house, Elizabeth becomes reinvolved with Matthew. Andrew, Timothy's mentally disturbed twin brother tries to shoot Elizabeth, but the bullet only grazes her. The final chapter, which acts as an epilogue, shows that Elizabeth and Matthew have married and are expecting their second child.

In addition to the main plot, which centers on Elizabeth, a minor plot involves Mrs. Emerson's daughter Margaret who had allowed her mother to bully her into choosing a respectable "good" marriage, but who now is plagued by regrets about the loss of her first love Jimmy Joe. Like Charlotte Emory in *Earthly Possessions*, Margaret finally makes peace with her past by realizing that she was not a passive victim but rather that her life has been a product of her own decisions.

CHARACTERS

Mrs. Emerson is a former Roland Park debutante and a bit of an aristocrat. Although well past her middle years, she still wears the "frail and spiky" shoes of her youth, refusing to make any concessions to aging (206). She is used to being catered to, having been spoiled by her husband, a successful businessman with humble origins. When we first meet Mrs. Emerson, her husband has been dead three months, and she misses the quiet competence with which he cushioned her life. At the start of the novel, she has already fired her maid Emmeline for letting the portable radio's batteries run down; and in the opening scene, she fires Richard, her handyman of twenty-five years. It is as if she is trying to take control and not be a victim of her husband's death, transforming it with her stubborn will by actively running off all those who, like her late husband, had been her daily support for many years. People in general are constantly failing her, she thinks. But she is really referring to her husband, who failed her by being mortal.

Mrs. Emerson is proud of her independence, although she is in fact no more independent than other humans. When she trips on the stairs and falls, she struggles to her feet, feeling ridiculous, and curtly refuses Elizabeth's solicitude as though it were beneath her. She is the matriarch of a clan of seven grown-up children, three of whom are females whose names all start with "M." She dictates letters to her children for future transcription. Although it is she herself who eventually transcribes them, nevertheless the act of her dictating into a recorder reinforces her image of herself as some kind of executive—an imperial figure issuing commands to the far-flung provinces.

Mrs. Emerson is used to giving orders as well as being pampered. In her world there is a clear distinction between employers and employed. When she first meets Elizabeth, she asks her for help in moving the lawn furniture inside. In the beginning, they carry the furniture together. But in the course of conversation, Mrs. Emerson agrees to hire Elizabeth, and from that moment Mrs. Emerson stops helping, feeling, "that was her privilege, now that she was paying" (18).

Although Mrs. Emerson in actuality cultivates a personal relationship with her employees, and benefits emotionally from their presence, she will not admit to it. When her maid Alvareen, a black woman, quits after her request for sick pay is refused, Mrs. Emerson reflects upon why she is reluctant to let her maid take sick time. Mrs. Emerson is paying Alvareen not just for her labor but for her presence. However, Mrs. Emerson will not admit that to Alvareen because Alvareen might "puff up" and ask for a raise. Although Mrs. Emerson knows she will be unable to find a satisfactory replacement for Alvareen, in her stubbornly prideful and imperious fashion Mrs. Emerson thinks, "good riddance," she'll just do without (207).

Mrs. Emerson's deceased husband fell into an ambiguous category. Although he was not an employee, his role had certain similarities. He buffered Mrs. Emerson and the children from the nuts-and-bolts aspect of life. It was he who oiled the machinery that sustained Mrs. Emerson's grand illusions.

Elizabeth Priscilla Abbott comes to play an analogous role to that of the deceased Mr. Emerson. This is symbolized by the fact that she and he were the only ones who could figure out how to wind the house's many pendulum clocks so that they would all strike the hour at exactly the same moment.

Like the protagonist with a Quaker background from *Morgan's Passing*, Elizabeth is comfortable with long silences. She doesn't like to plan ahead because she wants to be free to respond to the promptings of the moment. She has an odd, whimsical slant on life. For example, she tells Mrs. Emerson that she looks forward to old age because early-morning insomnia will give her more time to do things. Like Ian Bedloe of *Saint Maybe*, Elizabeth is a caretaker who enjoys doing things with her hands, especially working with wood. Like Ian, she is burdened with feeling responsible for someone's suicide.

Unlike her Baptist preacher father, a man with a sense of mission, Elizabeth is one of those Anne Tyler characters who feels she has no right to meddle in other people's lives and who worries about influencing someone to choose a course in life that turns out to be disastrous. She violates this principle when she lunges for the gun that Timothy has pointed at his head. From the look of surprise on his face when the gun goes off, it appears possible that his death might have been avoided if she had not tried to wrest the gun away.

Elizabeth is someone who never cared to be around children because, "I don't like people you can have so much effect on" (11). She used to comfort herself against the fear of making unalterable mistakes by believing in reincarnation. But when Timothy dies, she can no longer sustain the belief that there are extra chances or extra lives "stashed away somewhere." She now feels that "things are so permanent. There's damage you can't repair" (202). At that point she withdraws back to her rural home town to hide from the world.

The pivotal point in Elizabeth's coming-of-age is a revelation that for every grown-up person she sees there was someone who must have "had the patience to lug them around, and feed them, and walk them nights. . . . People you wouldn't trust your purse with for five minutes, maybe, but still they put in years and years of time tending their children along and they don't even make a fuss about it"(247).

Elizabeth realizes that for all these years she has been afraid to move on to something new for fear of causing some kind of harm, as though she were a "special case" of some kind (247). Suddenly she sees she is not any different from these people she now imagines, who somehow carried on and succeeded in raising another human being. At this point she takes a job working with children for the first time.

But at the end of the novel, Elizabeth has given up her own identity to become an appendage to the Emerson family, married to Matthew and still caring for his mother. This abandonment of her identity is symbolized by the fact that everyone now refers to her as "Gillespie," a distortion of her name that came about accidentally during the days immediately following Mrs. Emerson's stroke when she could not pronounce the name "Elizabeth" correctly.

Apart from Elizabeth and Mrs. Emerson, all the other characters are minor and derive more importance from their role in the plot than from their personalities. The twin brothers Timothy and Andrew are of interest as mirror images of each other. Timothy deeply wounds Elizabeth by shooting himself; Andrew frees her by shooting her and grazing her flesh. Although superficially Timothy is the successful brother and Andrew is the psychiatrically disturbed one, underneath they share the same morbid streak. They perhaps can be seen, from one perspective, as a burlesque upon the cult of nostalgia for the Southern past with its "romantic" mythos of honor and pistol duels.

THEMES

One of the consistent themes of this novel is people's opposing styles of relating to the world and how these contraries fit together. Relationship in the fictional world of Anne Tyler is frequently between opposites. It is "two *differentnesses*" coming together, as Julian says in *The Accidental Tourist* (197). Anne Tyler reveals the unstable nature of the emotions inspired by the beloved. The very traits of differentness that initially seem exotic and fascinating can at other times seem strange and irritating. Attraction can instantaneously shift to dislike, or back again—the two emotions being inextricably linked like the sides of a revolving door. As Matthew declares to Elizabeth, "Sometimes the things I like most about you make me dislike you" (172), a Tylerian insight that is also expressed by Adrian Bly-Brice in *Ladder of Years*.

Mrs. Emerson and Elizabeth embody opposite approaches to life, much like Cody and Ezra Tull. Mrs. Emerson keeps her posture erect and her stomach sucked in. She applies makeup and wears sheer nylon stockings even to eat breakfast. She believes in formality of dress and manner, in "character" and self-discipline, in having "fixed destinations" in life and not getting "sidetracked" (8). Whereas Mrs. Emerson is all sharp edges, Elizabeth is fluid like Ezra Tull. She drifts through life serendipitously, priding herself on never turning down an invitation from anyone, not having to worry about being diverted from any particular goal or obligation. The shapelessness of her well broken-in moccasins symbolizes the unformed quality of her life.

Where Mrs. Emerson comforts herself with wealth, social status, and the role of matriarch, Elizabeth cushions herself from the shocks of life through her belief in her reincarnation, an outlook that enables her to escape a sense of finality. She uses this outlook as a protective mechanism, just as Jenny Tull uses humor (*Dinner at the Homesick Restaurant*), to evade the wrought-up intensity that comes from things always having to be perfect. In the Emerson house, which represents a kind of respite from her life as a preacher's daughter in Ellington, North Carolina, Elizabeth experiences a sense of competence. Here, as with many of Anne Tyler's characters, she can escape "other people's notions about" her (62).

Elizabeth's belief in reincarnation is her way of dealing with the brute fact of mortality—the various forms of loss that life deals out. As with Morgan Gower of *Morgan's Passing*, and Maggie Moran of *Breathing Lessons*, Elizabeth experiences life as a dress rehearsal. Elizabeth consoles herself with the thought that there is no finality. Mrs. Emerson never consoles herself; like an ascetic, she deals with loss by voluntarily inflicting more loss upon herself. Elizabeth dislikes dealing with children because she is afraid she might affect them too much. In contrast, Mrs. Emerson's dealings with her children are for the purpose of having the maximum effect possible upon them.

Mrs. Emerson in fact is depending upon Elizabeth to help her hold her life together, and Elizabeth benefits by finally having someone who depends upon her. In their differentness, Elizabeth and Mr. Emerson fit together "like puzzle pieces" (69).

While Elizabeth is able to support Mrs. Emerson after the death of her husband, Elizabeth is unable to be of help after the death of Mrs. Emerson's son Timothy. Elizabeth herself has been too deeply touched by this death. The young woman who couldn't bear to put an ax to the turkey's neck was only inches away from Timothy's face when the bullet went through his head. Having been confronted with death so directly, she can no longer deny its finality. "Death is never going to be easy," Matthew's Aunt Dorothy replies when told that a closed casket is easier to deal with (113).

Mrs. Emerson remarks (reflecting, one suspects, Anne Tyler's sentiments) that she never had the "knack" for feeling religious (115). This is a trait that she and Elizabeth share. Elizabeth's father is a rural Baptist preacher, and his mother fits the role of a minister's wife more neatly than Charlotte does in *Earthly Possessions*. But Elizabeth does not fit the expectations of a preacher's daughter. She cannot relate to the experience of her teenage friend who keeps getting "saved" each year at the annual revival and who vows to change her life, only to lapse into her habitual ways. But Elizabeth marvels at these glimpses of Sue Ellen in an "altered state," looking "flushed and intense" (133).

Elizabeth's parents' religiosity is sincere but formulaic, their charity self-conscious like that of the heroine's family in Anne Tyler's short story "The Saints in Caesar's Household" (1961). Like the casseroles for bereaved parishioners that she prepares far ahead and stores in the freezer till the next death, Elizabeth's mother would have happily "deep frozen her sympathy ahead of time too" if it were possible (130). Her parents overlook Elizabeth's form of charity because it does not fit their preconceptions. When Elizabeth agrees to act as a companion to the senile Mr. Cunnigham, her father tries to discourage her, suggesting that such assistance would be a "waste" of her talents (141).

It could be said that *The Clock Winder* is in some ways a feminist novel, in the same sense that Alice Hall Petry so classified *If Morning Ever Comes*. With the exception of Mrs. Emerson's deceased husband, whom we never meet, all of the strong characters in the novel are women, and the men orbit around them. Mrs. Emerson's remark after Timothy's funeral illustrates the difference between the "acceptable" sentiments sanctioned by the official culture and the "alien" views that women might only voice privately: "The trouble with ministers . . . is that they're not women. There he was talking about young life being carried off in its prime. What do I care about the prime? I'm thinking about the morning sickness, labor pains, colic, mumps—all for nothing" (115).

AN EXISTENTIAL READING OF *THE CLOCK WINDER*

Twentieth-century writers and thinkers described as "existential" have covered quite a broad spectrum. At one pole, Jean-Paul Sartre and Simone de Beauvoir represent an atheistic strain of existentialism that they hoped would be compatible with organized Marxism. At the other pole, Gabriel Marcel developed a Christian existentialism (whose antecedents are in Kierkegaard), and the German philosopher Martin Buber developed an existential humanism that was a reinterpretation of Jewish mysticism. Stephen Batchelor (1983) has sketched out a Buddhist existentialism that draws on the philosophical vocabulary of Heidegger. Buber, Marcel, Kierkegaard and Batchelor have all emphasized the living kernel of religious experience as a bare encounter with the ground of (one's) being, and have deemphasized the conventional religious trappings and dogmas that can obscure this kernel of direct experience.

A movement so broad and multifaceted must be difficult to define. There is not one existentialism; there are as many existentialisms as there are existential authors. But all have as their starting point a concern with the human experience as it is lived in its concreteness and immediacy. An existential approach begins, therefore, with the fundamental categories of human existence, one of which is the shadow that death casts over all activities. The unreflective human tendency is to gloss over the fragility of life and the certainty that every individual life will end. Habitual daily activity is used as a distraction from this all-pervading truth, and the ultimate utility or value of these activities is not questioned. But when the ultimate fact of death is nakedly acknowledged and deeply absorbed in all of its reverberations, there is a momentary shattering of the superficial approach to life. Death is the most dramatic illustration of the general truth of impermanence: all meetings end in parting, all building ends in destruction.

Existential concerns were very prominent among the nineteenth-century Russian novelists whom Anne Tyler studied, particularly Dostoyevsky. The existential strain in Anne Tyler's work is primarily seen in the way in which she deals with death. She shows death's double-edged capacity to either imprison individuals in a cocoon of grief or awaken them to the call to live purposefully. These themes are elaborated in *The Tin Can Tree*, *The Accidental Tourist*, and *Saint Maybe*, in Pearl Tull's deathbed musings in *Dinner at the Homesick Restaurant*, and in the novel under consideration here, *The Clock Winder*.

In *The Clock Winder*, Anne Tyler uses a particularly forceful image as a metaphor for death. When Mrs. Emerson suffers a stroke, she collapses onto the carpet and is lying on her back looking up at the underside of her hall table, thinking: "The undersurface of the table was rough and unfinished, a cheat. From above, it had always been so beautifully polished" (212).

The table's polished finish represents the surface of life with its illusory veneer of permanence. The raw quality of the underside reveals what lies beneath the surface of the illusion. Both sides are inseparable in the actual table, just as life and death are inseparable. Every moment of life is a moment of change—therefore, a moment of death for what went before, a moment of birth for what comes next. Life and death are inseparable, simply two sides of the same thing.

In *The Clock Winder*, the sudden revelation of the table's hidden underside is connected with Mrs. Emerson's sudden sense of estrangement from her own body, which has been revealed as a mortal object. One of her arms has become unresponsive. It feels "dead and cold," like a piece of furniture (211). Even her mind reveals its uncontrollable, thinglike nature to her, "floating away" from her like a balloon whose string she keeps grasping at (212). Loosed from its usual moorings, her subjectivity begins to drift disconcertingly.

As powerful as this scene is for the reader, the near brush with death does not appear to exert any transformative effect on Mrs. Emerson. At the end of the novel, we find her still as petulant and controlling as at the beginning. For Elizabeth, on the other hand, the encounter with death has more far-reaching effects. We first see her struggling with death when she is ordered to kill the Thanksgiving turkey. While she does not mind eating meat, she flinches away from the actual process of transforming a living creature into food. Her attraction to the belief in reincarnation comes from the fact that it softens the sense of finality about death.

When Elizabeth is forced to watch Timothy's violent death, it provokes a realization of the potentially unalterable consequences that flow from her casual decisions and actions. Frightened by this new sense of responsibility, she retreats to the safety of her small town and the security of a conventional life style. She begins to admire the "responsible" citizens who wait patiently in the ballot line to cast their "single votes that hardly matter" and return to their repetitive jobs and interminable chores. "Just plodding along . . . till they die" (202). She confines herself to a boring existence "for fear of some harm" she might otherwise cause (247).

Later, when Andrew shoots her with a pistol and grazes her flesh, the experience for her is a release. She thinks, "Now I know that nothing I can do will change a bullet in its course" (254). No longer something external for her to flee, death is now something she has literally taken into herself, and she has allowed it to make its mark upon her. She has seen how the two faces of life and death are inseparably joined. At the end of the novel, we find her among the Emersons, batting away the cicadas that terrify her mother-in-law, the only one present who can live fearlessly.

Celestial Navigation
(1974)

"It is possible, in deep space, to sail on solar wind. Light, be it particle or wave, has force: you rig a giant sail and go. The secret of seeing is to sail on solar wind. Hone and spread your spirit till you yourself are a sail, whetted, translucent, broadside to the merest puff."

Annie Dillard, *Pilgrim at Tinker Creek*

Anne Tyler is an artist whose earlier works are in no way inferior to the popularly acclaimed novels of her later career. *Celestial Navigation*, first published in 1974, is an example of one of these early gems that effortlessly withstands the test of time. More than any of her other novels, it gives the reader a peek into Anne Tyler's creative process; therefore, it was the most difficult novel for her to write. She told Wendy Lamb (1981), "It took two years and it made me sick all the way through" (58).

STRUCTURE AND POINT OF VIEW

In this novel, Anne Tyler experiments with constructing a story from chapters that are narrated from different points of view—a technique that she perfects in *Dinner at the Homesick Restaurant*. A unique feature is that each character's chapter is narrated in the first person, except for Jeremy's.

The opening chapter is related in the first person by Amanda Pauling, Jeremy's sister. The next chapter is Jeremy's but is narrated by an authorial third person. The succeeding chapter reverts to first person, but this time the narrator is Mary Tell. The chapters are self-contained. Each could stand on its own, like a short story. They continue to alternate in this rhythm, interspersing segments focusing on Jeremy with personal reminiscences by different female characters who live in Jeremy's boardinghouse, including Olivia and Miss Vinton.

The contrast between the women's first-person narratives and Jeremy's limited third-person one is a significant feature of the novel. The sections dealing with Jeremy are always in the authorial voice and suggest Jeremy's limited sense of self-awareness. In a sense, Jeremy is the construction of the women around him, and this phenomenon is reinforced by the very fabric of the narrative. Jeremy is the cipher to whom the women respond with anger, love, or need.

The fragmentary structure of the novel mimics Jeremy's characteristic mode of consciousness by which he apprehends things piecemeal, in momentary snapshots and fragmentary details: "He had tried looking at the whole of things, but it never worked out" (39).

There are large temporal gaps between the chapters that jump abruptly from 1961 to 1968 and then again to 1971. And some significant events, like the death of Jeremy's sister Laura, occur offstage and receive only the barest mention in passing, as though there were no centralized author who was trying to shape the narratives into a seamless story.

PLOT

Set in Baltimore, the story begins with the death of Jeremy Pauling's mother. Jeremy has lived all his adult life with his mother in her boardinghouse. He is so anxiety ridden that he refuses to leave the house to accompany his sisters to the funeral. The reader begins to realize what a fragile person Jeremy is when informed that he has been sitting motionlessly on an interior stairway in the dark since his mother's death.

Several months after Mrs. Pauling's death, Mary Tell and her five-year-old daughter Darcy move in to the boardinghouse. Mary has run away from her husband Guy in Virginia at the urging of her married lover John, who is from Baltimore. But when it becomes apparent that John is not going to divorce his wife after all, Mary stops accepting money from him. She begins looking for work that she could do in her room, like stuffing envelopes, since she has no one to watch Darcy during the day. But finding work without job skills is more difficult than she expected, as a newly widowed Lucy also discovers in *Saint Maybe*. Mary nervously tells Jeremy that she will be late with her rent.

Jeremy brushes aside Mary's concerns about the rent; he has fallen in love with Mary, although he hardly knows her, and his mind is preoccupied with his elaborate fantasies of courting as in the old-fashioned novels his mother used to read. But when he starts coming around her room with flowers, Mary thinks he is trying to take advantage of her financial straits to coerce her into becoming his mistress—an idea she would realize was totally ludicrous if she had any idea of how timid and sheltered Jeremy really is.

Penniless, frustrated, and bored, Mary becomes increasingly irritable and on one occasion is horrified, like Jenny Tull in *Dinner at the Homesick Restaurant*, to find herself slapping her daughter. She fears Darcy will carry the memory of this for the rest of her life. As Mary's financial situation becomes more grim, Jeremy dreams of rescuing her. He proposes marriage, but at first Mary doesn't really take him seriously. Then she informs him she is still legally married to Guy. Jeremy suggests that they could *pretend* to get married—get all dressed up, go out, come back, and tell the other boarders they've been to City Hall and exchanged wedding vows.

Mary accepts Jeremy's proposal and soon begins to actually love him. Over the next seven years, she gives birth to five additional children. One day Mary gets an impulse to write to her mother-in-law, of whom she was always fond, and learns that Guy has divorced her for desertion. She tells Jeremy that they can get married for real now, if he wants to. (Ironically they will have to sneak off to get married, since everyone who knows them assumes they already are husband and wife.) But Jeremy in his insecurity focuses on the fact that Mary wrote to her mother-in-law and was therefore thinking about her past life. He begins to imagine that all this time she preferred her husband Guy to him. To avoid these painful feelings, he plunges himself into working on a new artistic piece, becoming feverish, working on it even in his dreams, unable to stop because "he might drop dead by nightfall, leaving his figure unfinished and his life in bits on the studio floor" (165). He becomes abstracted, ignoring Mary's knocks at the locked studio door, ignoring the tray of food that is left outside the door. Food is irrelevant at this stage; the thought of it makes him feel sick. The day of their proposed marriage comes and goes, and he has only the vaguest sense that perhaps he has forgotten something. When his lunch fails to be delivered to his door and the house seems too quiet, he stumbles downstairs to find Mary gone.

Humiliated and hurt by Jeremy's failure to materialize for the wedding, Mary has taken the children, abandoning home suddenly, on impulse. She moves into a dilapidated shed on a lake, where Jeremy's art dealer Brian docks his boat. Like Charlotte of *Earthly Possessions*, Mary had hoped something would stop her at the last minute from carrying through her plan to leave. And like Delia of *Ladder of Years*, after Mary has succeeded in running away; she keeps hoping that Jeremy will come to fetch her back home. But he never does; instead he sinks into a paralysis in the rooming house, abandoning his artwork. When Mary and the children were with him, with all their noise and disorder, he had imagined that without them around he could concentrate on his art more seriously. But now that they have gone, they have taken all the life with them, and he finds himself sterile, unable to produce.

In Mary's absence, Olivia, a troubled teenager, begins tending to Jeremy. She aspires to become his confidante in a spirit of feminine rivalry with Mary, her substitute mother figure, whom she resents for having left her behind. Olivia becomes closer to Jeremy only in the sense that she begins to participate in his withdrawn, autistic depression. Finally, Miss Vinton intercedes and metaphorically dashes cold water on Olivia who, waking up, packs her measly belongings and hits the road again, hitchhiking to another city.

With Olivia's departure, Jeremy too wakes up from his lotus world, realizes he misses Mary, and takes what for him is an unprecedentedly bold action. He braves the outside world to take the long bus ride to where Mary is holed up. When he finally arrives at the boathouse, the reconciliation, which one would expect in a more sentimental novel, fails to materialize because of the crossed signals in Jeremy and Mary's communication. (Anne Tyler has stated that she wanted to effect a reconciliation between Jeremy and Mary but her creative process simply would not let her honestly write such a scene.)

The reader's final view of Jeremy in this next-to-last chapter is of his sitting forlornly in Brian's sailboat as it circles in wider and wider arcs around its moorings—a symbolic representation of the kind of circularity of people's lives that is addressed in *Earthly Possessions* and *Breathing Lessons*. The final chapter, which is only a page and a half long, is more of an epilogue, which fleshes out the symbolic circularity. Its first sentence is: "This house is back at its beginnings now" (247). Miss Vinton has become Jeremy's caretaker. Jeremy's art is thriving, and he has progressed to making "great towering beautiful sculptures" (247), but he remains an isolated and reclusive figure.

CHARACTERS

The sibling dynamic between the three Pauling children resembles that of the Tull family (*Dinner at the Homesick Restaurant*). Amanda is the angry eldest; Jeremy is the dreamy, artistic youngest; and Laura, the middle child, is the peacemaker between her temperamentally opposite siblings. Of the three, the one central to the novel is Jeremy, a thirty-eight-year-old bachelor at the beginning of the narrative. He has the perpetual anxiety of an Ingmar Bergman character. His interest to the reader is twofold. First, one wonders how such a shy and retiring person, so far from the mainstream of life, will possibly win the hand of Mary Tell, and one winces for him when each of his tentative, delicate advances bounces off the oblivious Mary, who doesn't even perceive that she is rebuffing him. Second, one marvels at the richness of his interior life and revels in being allowed to glimpse the mysteries of his creative process. As Miss Vinton, one of his boarders, puts it, Jeremy lives his life at a distance, creating his art in the way that people make maps, namely, "setting down the few fixed points that he knows, hoping they will guide him as he goes floating through this unfamiliar planet" (129).

Jeremy feels so self-conscious around Mary that he leaves his orange juice untouched at breakfast. He can't relax enough to swallow with her watching him. After marriage, Jeremy feels as though he lives in Mary's shadow. He feels a conflict between their actual relationship, which is more like mother-son, and the stereotypes of what the man of the house should be. Jeremy had once fantasized about Mary's coming to him for support with tears in her eyes, but after their marriage she seemed so much stronger than he. Even his art studio is not a safe sanctuary; when she enters he feels as though she takes over the room, trailing in "a long tail of noise and energy . . . pluming out behind her" (159). And with the children, Jeremy feels that Mary's strong genes have eclipsed his; his offspring seem more self-confident and fearless than he ever was.

Mary Tell is a straight arrow, raised by small town, Baptist parents. As a teenager she chafed at the narrowness of her well-ordered existence. Later, like Morgan Gower (*Morgan's Passing*), she wants to enter into the world of every person whom she sees on the street. She feels a great expansive need, as though *"full* of life, with not enough people to pour it into" and laments how narrow her world has become (73–74).

Just as Jeremy's mode of being is watery, Mary's elemental affinity is to earth. She describes herself as "landbound" (191). While Jeremy spends his days and nights charting the depths propelled by the winds of imagination, Mary is like a lighthouse keeping him mindful of the shore, preventing him from getting lost at sea. At the beginning of the novel, Mary reminisces about her girlhood, and the key image is of her staidly planted on dry land while she watches her future husband Guy Tell frolicking gaily in the water. Near the end of the novel, she finds herself and the children living near the water's edge, caretaking the sailboat, and disdaining the queasy feeling that floating gives her.

When Jeremy is courting Mary, he imagines her as an ethereal goddess, picturing her garbed in the light-blue shade associated with her namesake, the Virgin Mary, a heavenly figure. But she sees herself more as mythic Earth Mother, nurturing the hordes out of her bounteous vitality. Mary is a nurturer—one of those women who enjoys having babies. During the years when she is with Jeremy, not more than a few months passes between the time when the most recently born infant stops nursing at the breast and the new pregnancy begins. It is the process of creating and the early stage of nurturing that is most important to Mary. Once her creations are "completed," in the sense of being able to stand on their own, it is time to start incubating a new one. In this sense, she resembles Jeremy, except that her creations are biological and his are artistic compositions into which he attempts to breathe life.

When she states that she and Jeremy are "more alike than anyone knew" (199), she is referring to the fact that in order to pursue their respective vocations both of them must depend upon others to sustain them during their periods of absorption in creation. She depends upon a string of men to cope with the material side of life, starting with her husband Guy and continuing possibly through Brian the art dealer. Jeremy must depend upon a sucession of women, beginning with his mother and continuing through Miss Vinton, to keep him anchored to the earth, to prevent him from becoming "too removed" (220).

Olivia is an eighteen-year-old hippie runaway, confused, searching for her identity, and badly in need of a mother. She is obviously intelligent and has some familiarity with art, knowing who Toulouse-Lautrec is, for instance. She makes art almost into a type of religion, believing that artists hold some kind of essential key. There is a certain passivity about her; she is looking for someone else to define her. After Mary leaves,

Olivia turns to Jeremy, the artistic genius, hoping he will define her. She has many illusions, wondering why Jeremy doesn't hang out at a cafe and get drunk with wild bohemian friends as she has always imagined artists do. She imagines participating in Jeremy's reflected glory. Like Delia in *Ladder of Years*, Olivia imagines herself living in a movie—a romanticized movie about her life with Jeremy in which she is a minor character, but nevertheless a powerful influence: "the last scene would show me holding his head as he died. Some major transformation in his art would be dated from the time he met me" (206).

She begins preparing meals for Jeremy and buying his art supplies for him, but then realizes that she is in danger of becoming another Mary—his link to the outside world—when what she wants to do is enter his inner world and share it with him. Soon she begins spouting her own somewhat paranoid-sounding theories to Jeremy, who barely pays attention to them. Much of her theorizing has to do with time, one of Anne Tyler's favorite subjects.

Olivia believes Jeremy is not from our time but got caught here in a "time loop" (214). She thinks he is progressing from two-dimensional, to three-dimensional, to four-dimensional art and that his current piece is a time machine. She thinks ghosts are really ancestors visiting from the past in a time machine and that what we call Martians are our descendants who are visiting from the future. She wonders whether Jeremy is an ancestor or a descendant. She thinks Jeremy is interested in these theories, but he is only interested in having her cook breakfast. Since Mary left him, Jeremy has been ravenously hungry, pillaging Miss Vinton's groceries, eating a whole jar of mayonnaise. The more Jeremy tries to fill his inner void with food, the more Olivia becomes anorexic—watching him eat fills her up.

Olivia and Jeremy are unable to help each other because they are too much alike, in their neediness, to fill each other. As Jeremy says, Olivia is cold whereas Mary was warm. Grieving their abandonment, together they descend into a clinical depression like Macon Leary's at the beginning of *The Accidental Tourist*, but more extreme. Olivia experiences herself as communicating telepathically with Jeremy: "Look at stairs, we thought, silently, together: what a perfect example of pointlessness. They go up and down, both. If you go up you must come down. You undo everything and start over" (217).

Mary Tell's husband Guy and his mother Gloria are minor characters in the novel. Guy's widowed mother—chewing-gum snapping, Southern Comfort drinking, with peroxide hair, shorts, and a halter top—has the vulgar vitality of Serena's mother in *Breathing Lessons*. Self-reliant, spunky, and maternal, Guy's mother brings Mary out of postpartum depression with a nonstop round of shopping, experimenting with hair styles, watching soap operas, and reading true confession magazines, all the while keeping up an incessant stream of chatter in a "fake-tough" tone (63).

Drawn from her teenage summers when she worked alongside such characters in the tobacco barns, Anne Tyler depicts those characters as heroic, despite society's tendency to negatively stereotype them. Like Tyler's patrician old ladies who expend tremendous amounts of effort to keep up appearances, they are *survivors*, a trait that Anne Tyler greatly admires.

AUTHORIAL SELF-REFERENCE

In *Celestial Navigation* it seems particularly clear that Jeremy and Mary stand for two complementary sides of the author's personality that are in creative tension: her identity as writer and her identity as mother. Jeremy shares Anne Tyler's need for privacy and creative absorption in an inner world. But without the Mary side of her personality the artist could become too single-minded, self-absorbed, and ultimately half-mad, like the nameless foreign woman in *Earthly Possessions*. Whereas in the novel the author is ultimately unable to reconcile the two characters' differences, in real life Tyler has been able to harmonize these two sides of herself in an uneasy but mutually enriching balance.

Anne Tyler likes to strew parts of herself in all of the characters, like the fragments of real objects that Jeremy embeds in his collages. Besides Jeremy and Mary, there are parts of the author in Daphne, a wise child like the precocious Tyler, and in Jeremy's mother Wilma, who likes to clip unusual stories from the newspaper, a penchant of Tyler's that has provided the initial ideas for some of her novels. And Olivia, with her ability to enter so completely into Jeremy's inner world, may represent Tyler's ability to imaginatively "live more than one life" through her characters.

THEMES

The primary theme of the novel is the nature of the creative process. Jeremy is a visual artist, as Anne Tyler once wished to be. Just as Tyler gradually moved from short stories to complex novels, so too Jeremy's collage pieces become increasingly layered and textured until they become sculptures. Recognizable pieces of ordinary objects are included— bus tickets, Dixie cups, snippets of material from his children's clothing. Like Tyler ("Still Just Writing"), Jeremy has fantasies of escaping to the desert and finding a "small, bare, whitewashed cubicle" where he can work in privacy (153). Like her, too, he drinks in the illustrated art books that Miss Vinton lends him, like a parched and starving survivor, the way that Tyler refreshes herself with the images from the photography books that line her study.

Jeremy's is a child's world of ambient sounds, familiar comforting smells, captivating visual details, and colors whose slight variations in tint each evoke a different mood. He even has the capacity to translate the experiences of one sensory modality into another—visuals can become sound, colors and textures can "make him hungry" (227). He is defenseless against the intensity of the most seemingly trivial sensations. Sometimes colors burn him. It is as if his internal wiring is crossed. This kind of synesthesia has been explored in Peter Greenaway's disturbing film *The Pillow Book* (1997).

When Jeremy is working, he experiences Mary's domestic conversation as a kind of background music that he filters out. If he detects some note of urgency in her voice, he has to struggle up "from under layers and layers of thought" (137). Even then, he has trouble getting her into focus, for the exact shade of color he has been searching for to complete his latest piece may suddenly swim into awareness, sending him into a frenzy of rummaging about through drawers searching to find the exact match, while Mary calls, "Jeremy? . . . Jeremy?" (138).

The difference between Mary's practical way of seeing the world and Jeremy's is illustrated by their opposite perceptions of what Mary conventionally designates as "chicory and poison ivy" (192). Jeremy sees it very innocently as a beautiful pattern of green wild flowers and glossy blue leaves that he associates with "Mary-blue . . . the blue from a madonna's robe" (82).

The novel tries to show that being an artist is both a blessing and a curse. Jeremy's theory is that the artist's activity is a way of trying to compensate for being handicapped at normal living. He quips that the Stone Age rock paintings of animals were probably created by a lame cave man as a way of consoling himself for being unable to participate in the hunt. Olivia counters this with a different theory: the artist begins as a normal human, but the artistic endeavor is itself so all-consuming that it leaves the artist a human wreckage, only marginally able to relate to other people. Whichever of these theories one holds to, it is clear that artists create because they are compelled to and that their lives are often dwarfed by their art.

Although thematically the novel is primarily about a certain type of creative personality, as represented by Jeremy, the narrative architecture simultaneously brings to the foreground the styles of the four women—Amanda Pauling, Mary Tell, Miss Vinton, and Olivia—as alternate ways of relating to love, art, and their own mothers.

Mary had a good relationship with her mother, despite some teenage rebellion. Mary's strategy is to become totally submerged in the role of mother. She feels happiest when she is pregnant or nursing. As she adopts this role, she is drawn into "a world made up of women"—her mother, her mother-in-law, and the neighboring women—who encircle her in a protective embrace that she sinks into as comfortably as a lukewarm bath (62). This blurry, boundaryless existence is a bit like the unfocused space of Jeremy's creative reveries—but it is intensely social, whereas his is solitary.

Jeremy's oldest sister Amanda has a horror of such symbiotic intimacy. Hers is a world of definite boundaries. Feeling deprived by her mother, who seemed to discount girls, she resolves her ambivalence toward her mother by pushing it out of mind and becoming self-sufficient. Her relationship to her mother is marked by fulfillment of the role of daughter as propriety demands, but without intimacy or genuine feeling.

Olivia is the most damaged character. Like Amanda, she has an intense ambivalence about her mother but does not have Amanda's strength of will. Nor has she been able to repress the side of herself that longs for dependency. We are given no details about her relationship to her own mother, but the text implies that her mother was too "earthbound," unable to understand or tolerate her unconventional interests (201). Nevertheless, Olivia craves nurturance and was drawing close to Mary, until Mary proved to be an unreliable mother-figure by running away without warning.

Miss Vinton, one of Jeremy's boarders, is the most resilient of the characters, except perhaps for Mary. But while Mary exceeds Miss Vinton in sheer vitality, Miss Vinton has a certain elasticity that enables her to bridge Jeremy's imaginative world and the ordinary earthbound world in a way that Mary cannot quite manage. For Miss Vinton is a kind of paradoxical character. She is capable of Mary Tell's symbiotic, self-forgetting intimacy, as she demonstrated in caring for her deceased mother, her constant companion from whom nothing was hidden. And yet she relishes solitude and privacy and is quite capable of operating just as independently as old Amanda Pauling. And from within her solitude she can understand Jeremy's needs and the meaning of his art.

These characters illustrate the fundamental ambivalence in relationships and the difficulty of finding the right balance between distance and closeness—a balance that is symbolized in the image of the rooming house itself where everyone can have a "single room with a door that locks, and then a larger room downstairs where people can mingle or not as they please" (125).

A FREUDIAN INTERPRETATION OF *CELESTIAL NAVIGATION*

Sigmund Freud was a Viennese physician and neurologist whose career spanned the late nineteenth and early twentieth centuries. His psychological theories greatly influenced twentieth-century thought. Freud investigated the role of the irrational in human life, particularly unconscious emotional tendencies shaped by early childhood experiences. Freud used hypnosis to uncover unconscious mental processes. Later, he abandoned hypnosis and founded a method called psychoanalysis that attempts to track down and uncover hidden, or unconscious, wishes and motives through a sort of psychological detective work. He made a detailed examination of what caused someone to use the wrong word in a "slip of the tongue" and decoded the language of nighttime dreams. He studied the hidden connections between a person's thoughts through a method called "free association," in which the person says everything that comes into his or her mind without censorship.

Freud at times applied his method to the analysis of myths and works of literature and art, and for a while a school of literary analysis flourished that was based on Freudian ideas. Freud's central concept was the Oedipus complex, which he named after the Greek tragedy of Oedipus, who unwittingly kills his father and marries his widowed mother. Freud theorized that at a certain point in early development children have fantasies of becoming the love partners of the opposite-sexed parent and in conjunction with these fantasies feel a rivalry toward the same-sexed parent. These feelings and desires are abandoned in most children by the time they reach school age, and all traces are erased from their memory.

One criticism of Freud's theory was that it seemed very male oriented, stressing specifically sexual wishes and the role of "castration anxiety" in boys and "penis envy" in girls. A second wave of Freudian theorists, some of them with feminist sensibilities, began using the psychoanalytic method to look at the stages of child development that precede the appearance of the Oedipus complex—the "pre-Oedipal" period.

According to these Freudians, both male and female children begin their lives with a powerful attachment to their mothers. The male child's main psychological task is to break away from the mother in order to establish a separate male identity, which involves creating some psychological boundary for himself that defines woman as "Other." Perhaps the best symbol of this paradigm of male identity is the medieval knight errant whose armor is an emblem of his heroic individualism. According to this theory, intimacy is a double-edged proposition for the male. While he needs interludes of intimacy to escape the narrowness of constructed selfhood, if he swims too long in the waters of intimacy it can have a corrosive effect on his armor, bringing up fears of dissolution as he becomes nostalgic for a return to undifferentiated life in the amniotic pool. This fear is reflected in the mythology of mermaids and water nymphs—feminine archetypes whose embrace entangles males in the watery depths in which they will drown.

For Freudians there occurs a violent discontinuity in the male's psychological development at the point where he as a male individuates from his mother, who represents all females. It is theorized that a girl's psychological development is a more continuous, evolutionary process. She need not subject herself to this fundamental rupture in her primal relationship. She can continue to enjoy a relatively fluid relationship with her mother—and by extension with all women.

The symbiosis of prolonged intimacy is certainly not threatening to Mary Tell; in fact, she may be too comfortable with it: "All events, except childbirth, can be reduced to a heap of trivia in the end," she declares (200). Through her repeated pregnancies, she continually reestablishes that primal relationship of mother-infant unity, herself now representing the maternal pole of the equation. Here is the image of her that we are finally left with: she is buoyed up by her childen, their warm bodies "smelling of milk" pressed against her on all sides (200).

In contrast, Jeremy's sister Amanda is an example of a disturbance in the symbiotic mother-daughter bond. Consequently, Amanda cannot stand to be touched. Like Amanda, Olivia the hippie boarder tends to suppress her longing for maternal holding, but the need in her is too strong to be denied. When Olivia criticizes Mary's "domesticity," the reader can see that it is really "sour grapes"—a concealment of her rage and disappointment over Mary's abandonment of her. In her forlorness, she seizes upon Jeremy and, imagining herself to be Mary's rival, begins an incestuously flavored relationship with him that is symbiotic, or pre-Oedipal, in its aims: she desires not to have sex with him but to merge her mind with his.

As for Jeremy, it is quite clear that Mary functions as his mother substitute. When he imagines asking her to marry him, he pictures himself kneeling at her feet to propose, as in the old-fashioned romances. He projects himself into the scene so vividly that he is able to visualize how she would appear to him from that angle: the proximity of her sandal and the hem of her skirt, and at a distance the underside of her bosom and jaw. Later, when he accompanies her on a walk two blocks away from his house and faints on the sidewalk, he looks up and, seeing her as in a deja vu from that same peculiar angle, the well-rehearsed proposal of marriage spontaneously pops out of his mouth.

It is no accident that Jeremy's view of Mary at that moment is from the visual perspective of a child. This is how Jeremy would have seen his mother as a toddler, as he crawled about on the floor and looked up. This image conveys, in deliciously understated form, the psychological equivalence of Jeremy's attraction to Mary Tell and his childhood romance with his mother. The strength of this image demonstrates why Anne Tyler values photographs so much. Although she paints her snapshots in words, the visual image that is verbally conveyed encodes information that it would take several paragraphs of text to unpack.

6

Searching For Caleb
(1976)

"I can't shake off a sort of mist of irony that hangs over whatever I see."

Anne Tyler, "Still Just Writing"

Searching for Caleb was Anne Tyler's sixth novel and was more ambitious in scope than earlier ones, covering almost a century in the life of the Peck dynasty. She told Wendy Lamb (1981) it was "fun" writing about a "huge" family (58). The novel was a significant one for her career because of its review in the *New Yorker* by the respected novelist John Updike (1983) which closes with the signature phrase, "This writer is not merely good, she is *wickedly good*" (278).

STRUCTURE AND PLOT

The first three chapters introduce Justine Peck, her grandfather Daniel, and her husband Duncan, beginning the current time narrative. The fourth chapter traces the history of the family from the 1870s when Justine's great-grandfather and namesake Justin Montague Peck began a successful importing business in Baltimore and founded his dynasty. The next three chapters trace Justine and Duncan's childhood courtship and early years of marriage, after which the narrative returns to present time.

The novel is basically a series of character studies held together by a loose plot. The framework for the plot is the history of the Peck family. The rich and successful Justin Peck has two sons, Daniel and Caleb, by two different wives. They are expected to carry on the family business, but Caleb is more interested in music. The only person in the family whom Caleb feels is a kindred soul is Daniel's wife Margaret Rose. Stifled by the controlling ways of her patriarchal husband, Margaret Rose becomes one of Anne Tyler's runaway wives. Caleb pleads with Daniel to go after her, saying, "Life is not the same here when Maggie Rose is gone" (62). But Daniel refuses, and Caleb finally runs away too and becomes a street musician in Louisiana.

Daniel has six children, and his descendants continue to occupy the family estate in Baltimore, the men switching from the importing business to the practice of law. The one maverick is Daniel's grandson Duncan Peck who runs away from the family compound, much like Caleb did. Shortly thereafter, Duncan's first cousin Justine, also Daniel's granddaughter, defies her parents to join Duncan and live the life of a vagabond. However, they never travel far away but always stay within Maryland and Virginia, circling the Peck family compound in Baltimore. Daniel eventually comes to live with Justine and Duncan and participates, disapprovingly, in their eccentric lifestyle.

The suspenseful element of plot involves Justine and her grandfather Daniel who take bus trips together to various parts of the country, trailing down possible leads as to the whereabouts of Daniel Peck's missing half-brother Caleb who vanished some sixty years ago.

Periodically, Justine and her grandfather journey to some distant city to track down clues as to where Caleb might have gone, but they only find dead ends. Finally, near the end of the novel, Daniel's sons hire a private detective, Eli Everjohn, to track down Caleb. Eli, who makes a return appearance as a detective in *Saint Maybe*, succeeds in finding Caleb, but Daniel Peck is displeased by the news that Caleb is living in a public institution for the aged indigent, since this seems a disgrace to the Peck family.

Every anticipated climax in this novel turns into an anticlimax. Daniel Peck dies of a heart attack shortly after receiving the news of Caleb's whereabouts and is never reunited with the long-lost brother for whom he has been searching all these years. Instead, Justine is the one who meets Caleb and helps him to escape from the institution where he is living. She brings him home to live with her and Duncan, but he runs away after a while. Justine is disappointed and disturbed by him. She goes into a kind of emotional crisis that, it appears, might resolve itself by her returning home to the Peck family estate in Baltimore. But even this homecoming becomes an anticlimax since Justine decides instead that she and Duncan will join the carnival. Like Caleb, she has been gone too long and cannot really return home again.

There are two main subplots: the story of Caleb's life, told retrospectively, and the marriage of Justine's daughter Meg. Both of these subplots develop anticlimactically and end unresolved.

CHARACTERS

In contrast to the staid and proper Pecks of Baltimore, Justine and Duncan lead lives that are scandalous. Although presented sympathetically by Anne Tyler, the average social worker would have to label Duncan and Justine's household "dysfunctional." Neither Justine nor Duncan likes to cook or do housework. They wait until the family members are wearing the last of their clean clothes before making a trip to the laundromat.

Although of upper middle class origins, Justine and Duncan have practically no furniture or appliances (they have to toast their bread in the oven), yet they are pack rats who haul around cartons filled with secondhand books and spare machine parts. Periodically, grandfather Daniel will try to make the house look cared for, but he is handicapped by the lack of cleaning supplies. For example, he has to scour the pots with a piece of dried gourd that Duncan eccentrically insists has excellent scouring properties.

Gypsy-like, Justine and Duncan never stay in one place for long and are on the move again before they have even gotten around to completely unpacking from the last move. As a result, their daughter Meg frequently retreats to her room in tears while Duncan plays solitaire in a withdrawn silence.

Duncan Peck, Justine's husband, is also her first cousin, and had a reputation for being shiftless ever since he was a youngster. Duncan is a magnet for useless information—the more esoteric the better. His secondhand book collection ranges from quantum mechanics, to obscure anthropology, to the mystical writings of the Chinese sage Lao-tzu. He is addicted to a constant acquisition of new ideas as a way to escape the fear that he is just another Peck "treading an endless round of days just as his pinched, unimaginative family had done" (35).

Temperamentally, Duncan resembles Morgan Gower, the manic protagonist of *Morgan's Passing*, who leaps from one enthusiasm to another, never able to stay with any one thing for long. When Duncan is working on a project, he plunges into it with intensity. Upon achieving success, however, he loses interest. Like Sherlock Holmes between cases, Duncan grows restless and melancholy, seeking solace in a bottle of bourbon rather than in Holmes's seven-percent solution: "That was the pattern of Duncan's life—ventures begun light-heartedly, with enthusiasm but only half his attention, the other half devoted to plans for a perpetual motion machine . . . or a method of breeding stingless honeybees" (34).

In his vagabond ways, Duncan resembles Caleb, the wastrel, and is the object of reserved disapproval from his grandfather, Daniel Peck, a retired judge, who still gives the impression of judging everything that comes his way; when Daniel is offered a Cheez Doodle, he frowns at it. "What *is* this?" he asks, as if uttering a verdict rather than asking a question (3).

Like most Pecks, Daniel is a settled and prosaic person. Daniel voices disapproval of an acquaintance who left his hometown and blames such behavior on a lack of endurance: "He wanted something new, something different, he couldn't quite name it" (4). But without realizing it, Daniel is disapprovingly describing himself in his quest after Caleb. Even as a younger man he used to sometimes, late at night, "drive aimlessly over moonlit roads" (65) looking for something he was never able to name until shortly before his death: "I was trained to hold things in, you see. But I . . . assumed that someday, somewhere, I would again be given the opportunity to spend all that saved-up feeling. When will that be?" (264).

Daniel Peck is waiting for a specific time. He thinks in a very linear fashion, like Cody Tull of *Dinner at the Homesick Restaurant*. He pursues his quest for Caleb as though he were seeking some external object, but he is really seeking to be reunited with a lost and undeveloped part of himself, though he doesn't realize it. When he does finally learn Caleb's whereabouts, he still doesn't know how to express his saved-up feeling and writes to his long-lost brother a cramped, formal letter filled with petulant accusations and empty conventions, with no real sense of intimacy. Caleb never responds to the letter, and Daniel dies without ever getting to spend his saved-up feeling. His last words: "I had certainly hoped for more than *this* out of life" (267).

Daniel's granddaughter Justine Peck, who always wears a Breton hat, has three primary attributes—her devotion to her grandfather, her adaptability (some might say passivity), and her intuition. Justine has an inborn aptitude to foretell the future because she can sense a change before it occurs. Her mentor Madame Olita tells her this ability comes from having led a very still life.

Justine's dominant trait is her placid adaptability, her lack of finality: "Her curse was her ability to see all sides of every question" (317). This is what allows her to put up with Duncan's restlessness and his need to uproot the family at least once a year. Meeting Caleb, who seems "spineless" and eternally marked by the "musty cabbage smell of a public institution," forces her to an unpleasant confrontation with the ultimate consequences of being too adaptable (307). It throws her into a kind of emotional crisis so palpable that her husband is finally ready to agree to return to the Peck family estate if that will ease her mind. However, it doesn't come to this because Justine hits upon the compromise of attaching themselves to Alonzo Divich's travelling carnival, so that they can have both stability and unconventionality in their lives.

Although Justine the fortuneteller has adapted to Duncan's gypsyish lifestyle, it wreaks havoc with their daughter Meg's sensibilities. Meg, age seventeen, is an important minor character. The offspring of two nonconformists, she is a throwback, manifesting all the orderly, commonsense instincts of a true Peck. In the midst of her parents' scatteredness, she essentially rears herself. She is conscientious and does well scholastically, in spite of having to change schools once a year. A creature of routine, she tidies up regularly, leading Duncan to complain, "Do you have to put everything away all the time?" (177).

Even as a young child, Meg was serious, putting away her toys and asking for an alarm clock at age six. Like her mother, Meg chooses a husband that her parents don't approve of. But while Justine's choice of a mate was a rebellion against Peck conservatism, Meg's rebellion is a reversion to it. She begins dating Arthur Milsom, a Protestant minister, expecting to lead a more normal family life. However, in one of life's anticlimactic ironies, Arthur's domineering mother turns out to be as odd in her own way as Justine and Duncan. "I thought when I got married we would be so—regular," Meg tells Justine. But instead of a "normal happy life," she finds herself living "among crazy people."

It seems clear that this novel in some way pays tribute to Anne Tyler's family. The cover illustration of Caleb fiddling was based upon an old photograph of Tyler's great-grandfather, Charles Tyler. The character of Daniel Peck is modelled after the author's grandfather. The Peck family compound in Baltimore perhaps has some echoes of the Cello community where three generations of Tylers lived on the same grounds. Justine and Duncan's goat raising is reminiscent of that period, when Anne Tyler's father kept a herd of goats for milking.

LITERARY DEVICES

Anne Tyler is an author who avoids doing factual research, feeling it constrains her creative process. This novel is exceptional for the degree to which it dazzles the reader with obscure historical detail such as the brand of rouge worn in the 1900s or the accoutrements of the 1908 Ford.

As usual, Anne Tyler evinces a bemused interest in the fads and trends of popular culture, such as Justine's using raw spaghetti stalks as a substitute for divining sticks in casting the Chinese oracle, the *I Ching*. In this novel Tyler also turns the clock back to give an historical view of turn-of-the-century American health fads. Justine's ailing great-grandfather orders all his window panes replaced with amethyst glass, which was believed to promote healing. And he dines only on squirrel meat, "easiest on the digestive tract" (56).

Once again in this novel Anne Tyler uses physical differences to signal estrangement within the family. Thus, all the Pecks have clear blue eyes except Caleb, the misfit, who was born with brown ones, said to have "snuck in" from his mother's side of the family.

THEMES

Anne Tyler illustrates the self-defeating effects of disdaining and disempowering others, reflected in the Peck's attitude toward their African American servants. Sulie Lafleur, the maid, was in a quandary about what to tell the family if they asked where Caleb Peck had run off to. Sulie didn't want to give away Caleb's secret, but she also didn't want to lie. Her husband told her not to worry, the family would never ask her: "Them folks . . . don't reckon just old us would know *nothing*" (247). And they never do. Daniel searches for years for his missing brother, when all he had to do was ask the maid.

Anne Tyler demonstrates that these self-defeating attitudes are difficult to overcome. Being enamored of African American music, Caleb attached himself to a black street musician nicknamed White-Eye (because he is blind) when Caleb ran away to New Orleans. Without any discussion, he simply began dogging the footsteps of the blind musician, accompanying White-Eye's guitar with his fiddle. They spoke very little, and never about anything personal. When White-Eye first heard Caleb's voice, he expressed surprise, and perhaps dismay, that the fiddler was a white man. But Caleb was determined to hang on his side, and the guitarist seemed to recognize this as unavoidable. Each night they went their separate ways without ever exchanging a personal word, although sometimes they hesitated, "as if wishing for something more to say" before heading off, each in his separate direction. And during the day "their two stringed instruments spoke together continuously like old relations" (284).

Caleb's music seemed to get into old White-Eye in such a way that White-Eye couldn't keep himself from dancing, sometimes wandering off if the music was too fast and lively, so he tied a string from his belt to Caleb's to keep them together, and Caleb came to be called "the Stringtail man" (253). But for all that, Caleb never so much as laid eyes upon his musical partner's family until the old man died and his widow sought him out to invite him to the funeral.

The image of these two linked together by an umbilical-like string illustrates the often invisible links of mutual dependence and interconnection between individuals who on the surface seem entirely separate, even opposed. This ties in to a universal theme that some of Anne Tyler's most successful novels have explored: the tension between radically different ways of being in the world. *Celestial Navigation*, with its contrast between the earthbound Mary Tell and the free-floating Jeremy Pauling, is one example. *Dinner at the Homesick Restaurant*, with its rivalry between Ezra the dreamer and Cody the achiever, is another. *Searching for Caleb* turns upon a similar opposition between Caleb the brown-eyed vagabond musician and Daniel the blue-eyed sedentary judge.

Yet, as Lynn Ross-Bryant has pointed out, these oppositions are not absolute polarities. Each contains within it an element of the other, as in the Chinese yin-yang symbol. Thus, "Caleb maintains some of the habits of the Pecks and [the sedentary] Daniel takes up traveling in search of Caleb"(196). This kind of unity within polarity may also be symbolized by the waitresses Red Emma Borden and Black Emma Borden, whose names are like two facets of the same person, red and black being opposing colors on the checkerboard. At the end of the novel, Justine realizes that she and Duncan must continue vagabonding. The Pecks in some sense depend upon them as a counterweight to their own overly settled ways. Justine and Duncan are living out a way of being that the Pecks cannot otherwise integrate; so that in the very process of acting in opposition to their family, Justine and Caleb are paradoxically being loyal to their fundamental Peckishness.

A JUNGIAN READING OF *SEARCHING FOR CALEB*

Carl Gustav Jung (1875–1961) was a contemporary of Sigmund Freud who developed his own school of psychology. Like Freud, he was interested in the deep undercurrents of the mind more than surface thoughts and behaviors. Whereas Freud confined his investigation to the personal unconscious, which includes one's repressed memories from childhood, Jung was interested in the collective unconscious. The collective unconscious is that deeper layer of mind that is universal and represents the common inheritance of all human beings. It is due to the collective unconscious that experience tends to structure itself universally along certain lines. For example, Jung would say the sense of religious awe, or "the sacred," is a category of experience that is built into the collective unconscious. For Jung, an ancient Egyptian worshipping Ra, the sun god, and a modern Hindu paying homage to Devi, the divine mother, are both tapping into the same primordial human experience, though through different avenues. The collective unconscious may also contain powerful collective evolutionary memories. For example, human beings seem to be predisposed to developing a fear of snakes, perhaps because of a long history of human encounters with poisonous snakes.

Because of its transpersonal nature, the collective unconscious can be difficult to access. Universal symbols, or archetypes, found in myth and religion throughout the world, act as a bridge to the collective unconscious. These archetypes are personifications of unconscious forces; they are not purely subjective and individual; they have a certain independent reality though they are ultimately not distinct from the mind in its broadest sense. This statement may have been grasped more easily in the days when Platonic philosophy of mind was part of the curriculum. Notwithstanding, an example may help. One could say, from Jung's point of view, that if Mary Smith experiences for a moment the feeling that her innermost being has been graced by the divine mother, this cannot be dismissed as just a figment of Mary Smith's imagination. To Jung, the archetype of the divine mother is "outside" of Mary Smith's "small," individual, mortal consciousness, but resides "within" the broad continuum of human consciousness stretching back for thousands of millenia. This point may be a little difficult to grasp at first, but further reflection may clarify it.

For Jung, wholeness is the ultimate goal that human life is aiming toward. The achievement of wholeness requires the integration of fragmented aspects of personality and experience. Therefore, Jungians emphasize the importance of understanding and integrating the so-called shadow, which consists of the aspects of oneself that are disowned and denied. Jungians also stress integrating those parts of one's self that are usually suppressed by virtue of one's assigned gender identity. For males this means integrating the *anima*, or "feminine" archetypal principle. For females it means integrating the *animus*, or "masculine" energy within themselves.

Jung regarded this process of integration as important not only for restoring balance to the individual but also for society as a whole. Therefore, he applauded the resurgence of female representations of the sacred, such as the development of the popular cult of Mary, as representing a necessary correction to a one-sided male emphasis within Christianity. No doubt, he would have also welcomed the current rediscovery of the many mythological faces of the goddess, seeing it as a continuation of this process.

The archetypes are often experienced as having a "numinous" or awe-inspiring quality, that Rudolf Otto called the experience of "the holy." Jung regarded contact with the numinous dimension of experience as pointing the way to wholeness. A necessary part of this process of evolving wholeness in oneself is to open up a channel of communication to the collective unconscious. Jungians place a great deal of emphasis on art, dreams, and visions as ways of contacting the unconscious. Jung also developed a rationale for fortune-telling through his concept of synchronicity, or meaningful coincidence. Anne Tyler seems to also be interested in these dimensions of human experience.

Although she is not religious in any formal sense, Anne Tyler seems to have a certain fascination with popular manifestations of the spiritual, whether it takes the form of Baptist fundamentalism or New Age metaphysical beliefs. *A Slipping-Down Life*, *The Clock Winder*, *Earthly Possessions*, and *Saint Maybe* feature evangelical preachers. *Ladder of Years* includes a character who believes in reincarnation and dispels negative vibrations by burning herbs. Fortune-telling through reading cards and casting the *I Ching* is central to *Searching for Caleb*.

Altered states are also frequently explored in Anne Tyler's novels—

the madness of the foreign woman and the vision that Saul Emory interprets as a call to preach in *Earthly Possessions*, the eerie mind-merging between Olivia and Jeremy near the conclusion of *Celestial Navigation*, or the disembodied reveries of Delia in her cubicle at Belle Flint's rooming house in *Ladder of Years*. Dreams, which are also a type of altered state, are frequently included in Tyler's narratives and are particularly central to *Saint Maybe* where Ian receives communications from the dead—or from a part of his unconscious—in his dreams.

Although these phenomena are subordinate aspects in most of Anne Tyler's novels, there is a short story of Tyler's in which they are central, "Half Truths and Semi-Miracles" (1974), written shortly before the publication of *Searching for Caleb*. The heroine, Susanna Meagan, discovers that she can channel healing power through her hands. Sick people begin flocking to her, and she reluctantly becomes drawn into the role of a spiritual healer. Her family begins treating her strangely, and her friends drift away. When her child has an accident, she tries to heal him but is unable to save his life and begins to lose faith in God. Finally, she travels to see another healer who, through the simple human gesture of a hug, communicates to her that the healing power comes from within the sick people themselves: "While they performed their magic, you held tight to their hands. . . . When they said you were responsible, you accepted the burden. . . . Believe my half-truths, they are all we have" (302).

This short story anticipates themes that are further developed in *Searching for Caleb* and *Saint Maybe*. The incident of the healer who is unable to cure her own child is repeated in a different form in *Searching for Caleb* in the episode with Mrs. Milsom, Meg's mother-in-law. Although she is a healer who practices the laying on of hands, she is unable to cure her son Arthur of his headaches. Likewise, her father, from whom she inherited "the gift," cured a blind man but was unable to heal his own deafness (237).

The nonfundamentalist attitude that Susanna Meagan has toward healing in "Half Truths and Semi-Miracles" is very akin to Justine's attitude toward fortune-telling. The future is changeable, and the cards themselves have no inherent power except as a catalyst for releasing one's own intuitions. Madame Oliva tells Justine: "You must thinks of these cards as tags . . . with strings attached. . . . The strings lead into your mind. These cards will pull out what you already know but have failed to admit or recognize" (137).

Another aspect of the novel that is relevant to the Jungian viewpoint is the lack of integration between the two sides of the Peck family. Daniel clearly represents the *animus* principle with its one-sided linear rationality. Caleb, the intuitive one, is more in tune with feeling states and therefore more closely allied with the *anima*. This difference is reflected in the way the two brothers relate to Margaret Rose. Daniel merely posseses her as a wifely object and child breeder and does not enter into communion with her. When Margaret disappoints the family's expectations, she is cast aside without much conscious regret. Caleb, however, is attuned to her on a soulful level.

The search for Caleb is the search for something missing—some vital ingredient necessary to find wholeness, as in the Grail myth. But the end of the novel brings only partial integration. Daniel dies without ever reconciling in any meaningful way with Caleb. And it becomes clear that Caleb would never be able to fit into the Peck family, so he runs away again. Likewise, Meg is left in a limbo state, not fitting into her parents' lifestyle but also feeling out of place in her mother-in-law's household. Duncan and Justine too have no place to go. In the end, they join a carnival, which is a form of institutionalized wandering. The novel seems to suggest that an end point is never reached. All that is left is the process and the searching.

Earthly Possessions
(1977)

Do not lay up for yourselves earthly treasures, where moth and rust consume and thieves break in and steal.

Matthew 6:19

Tighter and more compact in plot than some of the later novels, *Earthly Possessions* takes the form of a cross-country journey that begins and ends in the small town of Clarion. In the tradition of the classic American "road" narratives, from beat-generation writer Jack Kerouac's 1957 American classic *On the Road*, to the popular 1991 film *Thelma and Louise*, the novel's action is set in a series of nondescript towns that the characters pass through along the way.

NARRATIVE STRUCTURE

The story begins dynamically with Charlotte being taken on an involuntary trip after a foiled bank robbery. Like so many of the "on the road" narratives, the exterior journey is the occasion for an interior, psychological journey of self-discovery. As if to emphasize this, *Earthly Possessions* proceeds in alternating chapters to develop two lines of narrative: one external, the other internal. The first concerns the unfolding events as Jake Simms, the bank robber, flees across state lines with Charlotte as his unwilling companion. This forward-looking narrative is interrupted at regular intervals by Charlotte's backward-looking musings on a chain of memories leading from childhood to the day of her abduction.

The narrative alternation between past and present is a technique that Anne Tyler returns to and further develops in her later novel *Breathing Lessons*. Whereas in *Earthly Possessions* the past and present narratives are all narrated from Charlotte's point of view and are revealed in linear temporal sequence, with the alternation between them occurring in an orderly cadence, in *Breathing Lessons* the past reminiscences will be in no particular temporal order and will appear unpredictably in the text as part of a string of associations in the minds of various characters as the narrative point of view shifts from one to another.

On the most abstract level, then, the narrative in *Earthly Possessions* concerns time and its circular nature, coiling back upon itself snakelike in a spiral in which certain types of events repeat themselves in familiar variations. The points of intersection where the spirals overlap are like entrances or exits to the various levels. For example, the two parallel narratives—Charlotte's history up to the point of leaving Clarion, and the unfolding events after leaving—catch up with each other finally in the penultimate pair of chapters.

In Chapter 14, Charlotte's narrative of the unfolding past catches up to the point where the reader first entered the novel in Chapter 1: Charlotte has resolved to leave Saul and her children; she is about to go to the Clarion bank to get her money. A present variation on these past events is now mirrored in Chapter 15: Charlotte is again at a bank, but this time in some unknown town to which Jake has brought her. Just as the scene at the bank at the beginning of the book propelled Charlotte into a series of adventures traveling away from Clarion, her presence at a bank at the end of the novel propels a circular movement back to Clarion as she makes the resolution to leave Jake and Mindy. Chapter 16, which is written in the style of an epilogue, shows Charlotte back with Saul, by conscious choice.

This circular view of time is something that Anne Tyler began turning over in her mind at a very early age as a result of an insight she developed from reading a children's book, *The Little House*, over and over. She recognized a kindred spirit when she saw how South American writer Gabriel García Márquez actualized this view of time artistically in his famous novel *One Hundred Years of Solitude*. Encoded in *Earthly Possessions* is a teasing, ironic reference to García Márquez's novel: on their cross-country getaway, Jake's car is brought to a standstill by a small-town parade whose banner declares, "One Hundred Years of Progress"—a slogan that is debunked by the circular movement of the novel.

POINT OF VIEW

The novel is narrated totally from the viewpoint of Charlotte Emory, the reluctant wife of a small-town preacher. The subjectivity and unreliability inherent in the first-person narrative form is heightened by various devices that the author uses to subvert the reader's attempts to determine what is "real" in the naive sense. For example, after describing her memory of being kidnapped as a child, Charlotte states that her mother has narrated two alternative versions, so that now Charlotte does not "really know anymore" what happened (38). At the beginning of the novel, we are told that her mother did not believe that Charlotte was her real child, that there had been a mix-up at the hospital, but on her deathbed Charlotte's mother denies ever having believed such a thing.

PLOT

Charlotte grows up as part of a reclusive family in the backwater town of Clarion. Her father is a professional photographer, and her mother, an enormously fat woman, is an elementary school teacher. As a child Charlotte wins a beauty contest at the county fair. A strange foreign woman at the fair mistakes Charlotte for her long-lost daughter and kidnaps her. When returned to her parents, Charlotte feels estranged, as though she really belongs with the kidnapper.

When Charlotte's father dies, Charlotte takes over his photography studio. Hoping to be taken away from Clarion, she marries Saul Emory, a local boy who is returning home from the military. But he feels called to become a preacher and interprets his falling in love with Charlotte as a sign from God that he should remain in Clarion. He becomes pastor of Holy Basis, the local "total-dunking, hellfire" church (85). Charlotte vows to leave Saul and Clarion but remains when she discovers she is pregnant. She keeps a hundred dollar traveler's check in the secret compartment of her wallet to be used someday to make her escape.

In her early childhood Saul and Charlotte's daughter undergoes an identity change—she becomes swallowed up, so to speak, by her imaginary playmate, Selinda, with whom she trades places. Charlotte becomes pregnant again, has a miscarriage, and decides that this is a signal to leave; but Saul persuades her to stay and finds her an orphaned infant, Jiggs, to care for. Years later, depressed over the death of her mother and upset after being lectured about her passivity by Amos, her would-be lover, Charlotte finally resolves to leave. She goes to the bank to withdraw her money, at which point Jake Simms, who is robbing the bank, takes her hostage and kidnaps her. They travel in a stolen car to Georgia where Jake rescues Mindy, his pregnant teenage girlfriend, from a home for unwed mothers, then visits his reform school friend Oliver, who has gone straight and gotten married. Finally, in Florida, Charlotte finds herself again at a bank, where Jake has taken her to cash the hundred dollar traveler's check that was the symbol of her plans to leave home. After she turns this money over to Jake, she walks away, undeterred by his pleas of dependency upon her or his threats to shoot her. She returns to Clarion and to Saul.

Listed in this summary form, it seems that Charlotte's life is packed with dramatic events. Yet it feels as though very little "happens" in the narrative because everything is colored by the narrator's highly subjective and idiosyncratic mood in which confinement, tedium, and repetition are the elements that predominate. Things have a way of seeming unreal to Charlotte, and events flash by her like pictures on a television screen without seeming to have much impact. As Jake tells her, "You act like you take it all in stride. . . . You mostly wear this little smile" (212). But what the men around her take as a sign of inner strength, Charlotte experiences as really a kind of numbness.

CHARACTERS

Charlotte is the product of an unhappy childhood; and after marrying Saul, she fears she has traded one unhappy family for another. She watches herself from the outside, on family outings with Saul and Selinda, where each of them is forever "tugging and chafing," "irking," and "nagging" (147). When she has a miscarriage, she concludes that her body did it on purpose, rejecting the infant because a new baby would have encumbered her from leaving for several more years.

Like Anne Tyler, Charlotte is sensitive to omens and portents. She is confirmed in her resolve to leave home when she finds a prize in her cereal box: a medallion picturing a cartoon character with enormous feet and the motto "Keep on Truckin'," which strikes her as prophetic. Charlotte's dominant characteristic is her passivity. It is not the passivity of acquiescence, but rather a type of paralysis of the will caused by emotional ambivalence. As a child, her two major fears were that it would be discovered that she was *not* really her parents' true child and would be taken away and, alternately, that she really *was* their child and would never be taken away. Similarly, in the relationship with Saul, she is constantly preparing to take leave permanently but never quite manages to do it. Even on the day when she finally prepares to act, she is unable to do so on her own because fate intervenes in the form of Jake Simms's sweeping her away.

The hundred-dollar traveler's check that Charlotte carries around as escape money is her holdout, the hedging of her bets, the emblem of her inability to fully commit herself to "Yes!" even in the form of a wholehearted "No!" Instead she lives constantly in an uneasy compromise. When Jake finds the hundred dollars and takes it, in the next-to-last chapter, it signifies the removal of that safety harness, that thin layer of insulation that comes between Charlotte and the full experience of life. From now on, Charlotte has no choice but to give herself totally to her experience—one hundred percent. And in that very moment she is finally able to escape—and discovers that she was able to escape all along. This time the escape is fully hers. She is not snatched by fate in the form of a bank robber. Her resolve does not wither even in the face of a loaded gun. She has become the agent of fate, and she is now free to choose willingly that which destiny had earlier seemed to assign her.

Charlotte, like many of Anne Tyler's women (e.g., Mary Tell of *Celestial Navigation* and Fiona of *Breathing Lessons*), seems to need a mother more than a mate. She feels pulled toward the strange foreign woman who kidnaps her and toward Saul's mother, Alberta, who seems so "gypsyish" and free (66). In the end, Charlotte finds that the death of her own mother, Lacey, brings a much deeper sense of loss than she had anticipated.

Saul Emory, like all the other characters in the novel, is someone whom we see only through Charlotte's highly subjective eyes. Most of the time, he seems like just another literal-minded preacher who, as Charlotte says, can "rest back on his easy answers" (115). But sometimes a glimmer of something deeper slips through Charlotte's description. For example, when she accuses Saul of marrying her just to escape being alone, he surprises her with his existential reply: "There *is* no way not to be alone" (119). Or again, Charlotte resists taking in baby Jiggs, arguing that the foundling "isn't ours," so the birth mother could come to claim him at any time. Saul replies, "We could lose anybody at any moment. . . . Nobody's ours" (149). Saul also puts his finger squarely on the novel's theme of circularity: "I believe we're given the same lessons to learn, over and over . . . till we get them right. Things keep circling past us" (193).

How accurate, then, are Charlotte's unflattering impressions of Saul? Jake suggests that she has her husband "figured wrong" from the start (177). Just as her mother has some need to maintain the fiction that someone switched babies on her in the hospital, it seems that Charlotte needs to maintain a fixed image of her husband as a narrow, unchangeable individual, even though she sometimes glimpses his vulnerable side. Charlotte comes to see that there is no way she could "sum up" her husband. She intuits that he is not just a "fanatical preacher" but that underneath there are seismic rumbles, some "great substructure shifting and creaking inside him" (152–153).

Like one of Charlotte's studio portraits, frozen in time, any attempt to define Saul would be based on her past experience of him—and, therefore, "several steps behind" him (120)—not taking into account his existence as an open potentiality, re-creating himself daily. When Charlotte presses her ear at night against Saul's chest while he sleeps, there is a secret inner core of him that she cannot penetrate.

The central event in Saul's life was an abandonment: his mother Alberta ran off with her father-in-law, a retired actor, leaving Saul and his brothers behind with their alcoholic father. This left Saul with a gaping vulnerable spot whose pain he covers over with an unforgiving grudge. He is drawn to Charlotte, who has the aura of his mother, with her gypsyish longings, but whose passivity makes her a safer, stepped-down version.

Because of Saul's aforementioned weak spot, he seems incapable of admitting that Charlotte could leave him. Faced with any evidence of her leaving, he simply shuts his eyes and enters a state of denial. As a consequence, Saul disempowers Charlotte by refusing to hear anything she says that threatens his fixed view—thereby, in effect silencing her. Rather than reveal his vulnerability by telling Charlotte how much *he* would miss *her*, Saul comes across in an authoritarian fashion, telling her dogmatically, "Charlotte, you would never leave me . . . you love me" (147), as though he is trying to hypnotize or brainwash her with the force of his own conviction.

A vivid and important character, although she makes only a brief appearance in the novel, is the nameless woman who "kidnapped" seven-year-old Charlotte. She is described as very thin and starkly beautiful, in an unconventional manner, with "feverish" highlights of rouge on her high cheekbones (31). She speaks with a foreign accent. Everything about her manner bespeaks intensity, exoticism, and obsession. Like a gypsy, she lives in a trailer. The trailer has nothing "anchoring it down" (32); the sum of her possessions fits in one bureau drawer, and she says she loves to travel. Nothing very definite is revealed about her past. We learn that she was a refugee from some indeterminate country and that she tried to lead her children to a safe haven. They walked until their feet were bloody and were reduced to eating grass. The children died or were lost along the way, and only she survived, through sheer force of will, her existence reduced to the determination to continue putting one foot in front of the other even though everything of value had been lost. This woman seems to believe that Charlotte is her lost child.

In contrast to every other relationship that Charlotte will experience—with her mother, Lacey; her daughter, Selinda; and her husband, Saul—this encounter with the foreign woman is the only one where there is—at least momentarily—a sheer, intense, unambivalent expression of commitment. Although factually this woman cannot be Charlotte's real mother nor can Charlotte be the lady's lost child, somehow there is an inner correspondence that makes the relationship feel deeply true even while appearances say no. This is the determinative event in Charlotte's life. The eruption of a hitherto unknown and radically unexpected "other" into her existence. The secular equivalent of a call from God. In contrast to this, Charlotte's daily life pales and becomes unreal; it seems to Charlotte that her conventionally real parents are the kidnappers who steal her away from the heightened reality of this almost visionary moment of mutual fantasy. The very brevity and strange intensity of the encounter with the mad foreigner is comparable to Charlotte's being lifted momentarily into a mystical realm. From now on, the longing to return to this mystery becomes the inner compass of Charlotte's life. While her husband Saul is the conventionally religious figure in the novel, Charlotte is the true, unrecognized mystic. At the moment when she finally walks out on Saul and her children, she sees herself in the mirror, transformed into the image of that strange woman, "stark and high cheekboned" with "spots of color" on her cheeks that look "feverish" (204)—the same language that was used several chapters earlier in describing the foreign woman.

Like Drum Casey in *A Slipping Down Life*, Jake Simms's personality is drawn from Anne Tyler's youthful memories of summers working in the fields alongside the tobacco pickers, his speech laden with the same cadences and turns of phrase. Jake is a demolition derby driver. Although he has been to reform school, vandalized his brother-in-law Marvel's car dealership, robbed a bank, kidnapped Charlotte at gunpoint, and stolen a car, Jake bristles when Charlotte refers to him as a criminal, and he states instead that he is a victim, "a victim of impulse" (44). Indeed, Jake's life is full of self-defeating actions, like breaking an ankle while trying to escape from reform school when he had only one month left before being set free. Yet for all his bravado, Jake is afraid of the sharp tongue of his friend Oliver's mother.

Jake prides himself on being an outlaw and a kind of eternal free spirit, like one of the Lost Boys. He has nothing but contempt for the "soft life" of domesticity that Charlotte is running away from. But suddenly he finds himself saddled with a pregnant young woman who wants his opinion as to whether he would prefer to put up avocado or gold fiberglass curtains in their living room. As he says forlornly to Charlotte, "I'm going to end up married to her, ain't I?" (211).

LITERARY DEVICES

Anne Tyler has a highly developed visual sense and also a streak of deliciously ironic humor. She often links elements of a novel together through the poetic device of repeated imagery. For example, Tyler links together Charlotte's two abductors, the mysterious foreign woman of her childhood and the nonmysterious Jake, by a nearly identical visual image. Each of them is shown with their hands thrust "deep in pockets" (213) and staring intently at Charlotte, their concentrated fixedness suggesting a kind of trance and contrasting with the flux and movement of an environment that is "swirling" (31) or "swishing" (213). The odd resonance of these nearly identical images of two very dissimilar characters momentarily creates a kind of dreamlike structure whose hidden correspondences cannot be easily penetrated by waking logic.

Perhaps these two mirror images can be seen as portals or doorways through which the central character enters different states of mind. The mysterious lady, frozen in the pose of fixed staring, is the doorway that initiates Charlotte into the desire to flee from the uneasy compromises of her everyday reality. When Jake adopts the same pose, it marks Charlotte's opportunity to exit from that mad escapism, back through the doorway that returns her to the routines of mundane existence. Or, rather, Charlotte has the realization that there is really nothing to escape from or move toward, since it is all of one piece. After all, doesn't she find herself mothering her kidnapper and his "moll," just as she mothers Selinda and Saul? Where lies the escape for her, then?

An Anne Tyler trademark is to hold a mirror up to the banality of most of our thoughts. Even in the midst of disorientation and fear, the homely mental habits of everyday life still reassert themselves: Charlotte is glad that the robber let her have the window seat on the bus, even if he did not do so out of kindness but in order to prevent her from escaping.

Some of the funniest dialogue in the novel is a result of the exchanges between Charlotte and Jake. When Charlotte complains about being made to accompany him out of town, he protests it's not his fault. The gun-carrying citizen at the bank who loused up Jake's holdup was to blame. People like that, who didn't have any sense, shouldn't be carrying guns. "Guys like that ought to be locked up," Jake asserts (6). When Charlotte makes a sarcastic comment after Jake steals a car for the getaway, he indignantly states, "Bet you think I'm some kind of a criminal, don't you?" (43). He haughtily goes on to inform her that in fact he is not a criminal but a demolition derby driver.

Beyond the humor, there is a general tone of muted surrealism that is used to convey Charlotte's experience and that lends an air of unreality to her narrative. For example, the claustrophobia that Charlotte feels about possessions is conveyed in heightened, absurdist fashion when Saul moves his mother's furniture into Charlotte's house. They have to "double up" the furniture, each piece in front of its equivalent: a sofa behind a sofa, an end table in front of an end table, so that "every piece of furniture had its shadow, its Siamese twin" (106). On top of this multiplication of furniture is added Linus's miniaturized replicas, and his miniatures of the miniatures, like some genetic cloning experiment that has begun breeding out of control.

Another way in which the vaguely surreal atmosphere is created is through Charlotte's precise focus on odd details that upstage the standard emotional content of the moment. For example, when the surgeon comes out of the operating room to tell Charlotte that her mother has terminal cancer, the central focus of the scene is not Charlotte's emotional reaction but the way in which the vinyl couch, which her bare legs had gotten stuck to, makes a smacking sound as she stands up to speak to the doctor. At the same time that this irrelevant detail creates an absurdist tone, it also is reminiscent of a comment by Dr. Sisk, a physician, who associates his despair with the "Sppk!" sound the stethoscope makes when you pull it away from a chest smeared with Vicks VapoRub (155).

THEMES

Several recurrent Anne Tyler themes are present in this novel: the circularity of time, ambivalence about possessions and clutter, the horror of fatness, ambivalence about religion, art as an emotional necessity, and the way in which notions of personal identity break down when examined too closely. The first three themes have already been touched upon; the next three will be examined more closely here.

Throughout the book, Charlotte voices what are presumably Anne Tyler's objections to the unlovable aspects of institutionalized religion. The horrors of the Spanish Inquisition. The Bible stories featuring an irrational God who has jealous rages and demands that Abraham sacrifice his child. The multitudinous "rules, attitudes, platitudes" that govern the lives of the congregation (116). Expressing a characteristically modern sentiment, Charlotte says it's not so much that she doesn't believe—sometimes she does, sometimes she doesn't—but that she doesn't approve of her belief: it's against her principles.

But Tyler's attitudes to religion are not as unambivalently negative as might seem from reading just this novel. Having grown up in a Quaker household and having lived in various idealistic communes, Tyler has seen the value as well as the drawbacks of the religious impulse and balances the portrait in her later novel *Saint Maybe*, where much of the narrative is related from the point of view of a character who is in some ways like Saul. But even in *Earthly Possessions* there is an undercurrent of deep spiritual searching in Charlotte's behavior, although it is not explicitly acknowledged as such.

The novel provides multiple images of characters who are coping with their difficulties through an artistic outlet. Charlotte, like her father, is a photographer. While her father's photographs were naturalistic exercises in taking an "honest" portrait—akin to pinning a butterfly to a card—hers are more fanciful, yet perhaps in some way more truthful, too, since they evoke the mystery that is within her subjects. As mentioned earlier, these contrasting styles of photography suggest different ontologies: the beliefs about reality that are held by a psychoanalyst or detective versus those that characterize an artist or seer. Charlotte's father is a naive realist who believes there exists an eternal, monolithic stratum of objective truth that can be captured through prescribed methods. Charlotte has the soul of an artist, content to be merely recording appearances and admitting to uncertainty as to what is ultimately real.

Like the foreign mystery woman, Charlotte stares intently at her subjects, but only through the eye of the camera. She encourages her clients to live in a fantasy world by providing an outrageous assortment of garments and props for them to pose in, much like Morgan Gower's closet of costumes (*Morgan's Passing*). Charlotte's fanciful photography provides a temporary escape from the oppressiveness of her life. In this way she resembles the convicts Julian tells her about, who make little statues out of chewed up wads of bread, and Mindy, who uses her makeup artistry as a way to psychologically escape her "imprisonment" in the Dorothea Whitman Home. Saul's brother Julian, who had a nervous breakdown, has his outlet in the imaginative creation of doll house furniture. Eventually, he begins making superminiaturized doll furniture as accessories for the doll furniture. This suggests the artist's obsession with going deeper and deeper into increasingly refined levels of subjectivity until meaning begins to break down—a theme Antonioni explored in his film *Blowup* (1966). This parallels Charlotte's quest to increasingly cast off material and psychological possessions until there is no longer enough gravity left to hold her earthbound. But at the end of the novel, just as Charlotte has passed through her crisis and returned, so too Julian has abandoned his obsession with increasingly miniaturized *things* and has finally begun populating his miniature world with doll *people*.

The third thematic area in the novel concerns identity. The mutability of identity is a special case of the inherent slipperiness of experience—its fluidity, lack of permanence, and ultimate insubstantiality that Charlotte alludes to in her closing thought: "We couldn't stay in one place if we tried" (215). The text abounds in examples of this principle: Charlotte's daughter is absorbed by an imaginary playmate, her husband is transformed into a fundamentalist preacher, her kidnapper becomes her dependent, and the photograph she regards as revealing the identity of her mother's "true" child turns out to be only a childhood snapshot of her mother. Whatever she tries to grasp onto slips through her closing fingers like a dream. When she is able to consciously accept this elusiveness, she experiences the "grace things have when you know they're of no permanent importance" (121).

As Anne Tyler has observed in many of her novels, over time a couple's sense of being totally separate individuals begins to break down.

They begin to incorporate parts of each other. And they detect in the other person parts of themselves that they don't like. Eventually, it becomes clear that the images they have of each other are largely mental creations. For example, Charlotte sees Saul as a domineering, monolithically religious, unwavering true believer full of pat answers. But in actuality Saul is susceptible to the same doubts that Charlotte voices. He complains of having been unable to focus on a sermon he was trying to listen to because in the back of his mind he could hear Charlotte's voice cooly criticizing each of the preacher's statements. Clearly, it is Saul's own objections that are rising in his mind; but he imagines them in Charlotte's voice, and this projection onto her blocks his recognition of the doubting side of himself.

Charlotte comments on how the Emory brothers seem to be trading weaknesses, as though there were certain family traits that could never be eliminated or overcome but only "moved on to someone else" (157). This kind of psychological melding and exchange of personalities is reminiscent of Swedish director Ingmar Bergman's 1966 film *Persona* and is symbolized most starkly by Charlotte and Saul's daughter, whose identity is swallowed up by her imaginary playmate's. Catherine and Selinda are the same underlying person, just with different names and different seats at the dinner table.

A similar type of process is at work in the relationship between Charlotte and Jake. At the beginning, he appears to totally have the upper hand in the relationship. But by the end of the novel, it is clear that he has become psychologically dependent upon her and tries every means at his disposal to keep her from leaving. Tyler uses an interesting literary device to subconsciously communicate to the reader the gradual changes in the relationship between the bank robber and his hostage. In the early stages of the encounter, Charlotte's narration refers to him simply as "the robber." After she learns his identity from a news broadcast, she begins referring to him by his formal name, "Jake Simms." But soon she is using the shortened, familiar "Jake." Jake, in turn, at first uses no designation for her, then "Lady," finally "Charlotte," or "Miss Priss."

A close examination of the novel reveals that Charlotte and Jake share several points of similarity. Both of them seem prone to feelings of unreality. In an episode that is disturbingly humorous, Charlotte, looking through the newspaper, says, "We're not in here." Jake, momentarily uncomprehending, looks around the restaurant as if to reassure himself that they really are there (79).

Jake and Charlotte both have an ambivalence toward possessions and property. As a demolition derby driver, Jake is constantly destroying the cars he drives. As a housekeeper, Charlotte is slowly stripping her home of all its furnishings. Despite her best efforts at paring down to essentials, Charlotte still feels encumbered, wondering how she ended up with so many belongings even after she had "thrown so much away" (38).

According to Jake, everything he does in order to become "unencumbered" only draws him into more complications; every move he makes is worse than the previous one. There are so many ways that life has of "tying a person down" (100). Now he is encumbered with Charlotte, his hostage. Compare this to Charlotte's description of how her entanglement with Saul took place: "I should have said, 'I'm sorry . . . I never planned to take a second person on this trip.' But I didn't" (72).

Although Jake seems to be a man of action, he too experiences himself as being passively acted upon. He doesn't "know how" his destructive deeds unfold (99). He feels as though the violence just erupts and he has "no choice" whatsoever about it (100). This resonates with something deep within Charlotte. For despite her gentle nature, there are some unfathomed depths from whose recesses she can comprehend this kind of dangerous, fatalistic passivity. For example, she hopes that Saul will lose his religious faith and join a motorcyle gang so that he can carry her across country on the back of his cycle; she regrets Saul's lack of "recklessness" (71). Charlotte remembers once playing idly with Saul's hunting rifle, putting it to her shoulder, squinting down the sights, her finger on the trigger. She discovered she could easily picture herself shooting someone. Once having taken aim, there's the urge to complete the action, and Charlotte wonders how one resists "the pull to follow through" (84).

But despite this doubt of Charlotte's, the novel demonstrates that it *is* possible to resist the mechanical unfolding of events. In the final pages, Jake is sighting down the barrel of his gun at Charlotte, ordering her to stop. She continues walking. Certainly, he must feel pulled to follow through and shoot, yet he does not. Conversely, Charlotte, despite her fear, manages to make her move and break away. They both make a life-affirming choice, and yet they do not thereby become *externally* unencumbered in the sense they had imagined. Charlotte goes back to being tied down to Saul, and Jake presumably submits himself to Mindy and her plans to buy avocado curtains.

Perhaps this is an illustration of the paradox that Oliver put his finger on, "Your whole life is out of your control." In one sense, Charlotte's decision to leave and Jake's decision not to shoot stand out from the background of their lives as a momentary affirmation of freedom. But in another sense, the moment is not privileged. It is one of many moments in the intricate web of life, inextricably woven into everything that has gone before and all that will come after, as Ian Bedloe sees at the end of *Saint Maybe*.

A MYTHIC READING OF *EARTHLY POSSESSSIONS*

In the still young United States, with its expansionist, frontier mentality, taking to the road has often connoted an escape—going out West to start over or strike it rich. But for humankind in general the more universal significance of journey has been pilgrimage—inner journey, self-discovery, visiting the hallowed sites. Charlotte's travels with Jake can be read as a mythic journey. "Mythic" here means an emphasis on some timeless or universal element of the narrative. This type of analysis is particularly associated with the psychologist Carl Jung and his admirer Joseph Campbell, author of *The Hero with a Thousand Faces* (1949), both of whom felt there were certain constant themes, which they termed "archetypal," whose underlying essentials appear over and over again in countless variations in widely diverse cultures and epochs of history. For example, in religious myth the theme of the dying and reborn god is repeated in many different forms. Some works of art deliberately invoke mythic parallels, such as James Joyce's novel *Ulysses* (1924) or Marcel Camus's film *Black Orpheus* (1958).

Even when mythic parallels are not consciously part of the structure of the narrative, they can sometimes be latent since, as Jung would say, these mythic elements are part of the very fabric of our selves. In the case of *Earthly Possessions*, the mythic element may be said to appear when Charlotte enters into an altered state of consciousness.

As Charlotte is running from the bank, prodded by Jake Simms with his gun in his hand, she gets a new and disorienting view of the small town that had seemed so familiar to her. Charlotte and Jake pass the senile Mr. Linthincum, who has been put on the stoop to sit, and they pass her aunt's house where the old lady sits absorbed in the soap opera "Days of Our Lives." Charlotte goes down an alley she never knew existed, goes under a stilt-legged porch where she thinks she might have played as a child, then approaches the rear of an unkempt building surrounded by weeds that makes her feel very ill at ease. Her foot strikes an empty mustard jar that ominously seems "big enough to pickle a baby in" (4). Led to the front of the building, she is surprised to see that what had looked so unfamiliar and eerie from the rear is really just Libby's Grill, the local restaurant, pinball joint, and bus station. Jake Simms wants to make her travel with him on the first bus out of town. Charlotte is hoping some alert bystander will notice that something out of the ordinary is happening, but the waitress indifferently stamps the bus tickets without even glancing up, and the passengers on the bus are either asleep or preoccupied.

Charlotte's experience of these events is as if she has been suddenly set apart from her fellow creatures and is being led through a village of numbed-out sleepwalkers, entrapped in their mechanical routines. She feels as though she is moving in a dream. Like Scrooge being led through people's houses by the Ghost of Christmas, or like Jimmy Stewart being shown the future by his guardian angel in Frank Capra's *It's a Wonderful Life* (1946), Charlotte has become seemingly invisible to her fellow citizens. At the same time, her eyes have been opened to that which lies below the surface of everyday reality. The familiar begins to seem unfamiliar. As in David Lynch's *Twin Peaks*, even a reassuringly homey landmark like Libby's Grill can take on a sinister aspect when approached from this new angle. Superficially, Charlotte's state of mind could be taken as symptomatic of the state of shock of someone who has just been traumatized. But on another level, the nonordinariness of her experiences suggests someone who has just crossed over an invisible threshold and has taken a first step into the inner voyage of spiritual or psychological self-discovery. Later events seem to bear out this interpretation.

As the bus pulls out of Clarion, Charlotte watches Libby's Grill slip away. Next, she sees a child, then a drugstore with an advertising display in the window: a mechanized woman who repeatedly raises her arm to put Coppertone on it, "eternally laughing her faded laugh inside her dusty glass box." These images were not randomly selected by the author. They are repeated in slightly different form at the conclusion of the novel, when Charlotte parts company with Jake. She once again sees a child, then passes a "glass-boxed woman" selling tickets in front of a theatre (213). The image of the woman in the glass box recalls Charlotte's experience of existence, imprisoned by circumstances, mechanically going through the motions of living. Paired as it is, in both cases, with the image of the child, the image suggests being weighed down with the burdens and constraints of family life. When she leaves that life behind, on the lam with Jake Simms, the image of child and the woman vanish; when she consciously chooses to return to that life, they reappear. There is a slight change, though. The woman in the glass box is no longer a repetitive mechanical dummy in a store window, but rather a ticket vendor who tends the entrance to a magical imaginative display. If this image is a representation of Charlotte, it suggests a shift in Charlotte's inner view that now allows her to see life as a field of creative possibilities rather than just a numbing and crushing routine. The disappearance and reappearance of the child-woman imagery signals the beginning and end of the nonordinary reality that constitutes Charlotte's "trip."

This trip is like the Zen parable, "Taming the Ox," which describes a journey of several stages that leads to the maturing of wisdom (Suzuki 1960). At the culmination is a scene called "Entering the Marketplace," signifying that, having completed the interior voyage, the traveler seems to be back at the starting point. And yet something is different; the traveler is free. There is no need to journey any longer. No need to take concrete flight from external circumstances. These circumstances were never so solid or immutable as they once seemed. Charlotte now recognizes that the root of bondage and freedom is within herself. When Saul suggests that perhaps they should take a trip together, something she had always wanted in the past, she says she doesn't "see the need" anymore. After all, she tells him, they have been traveling "all our lives. . . . We couldn't stay in one place if we tried" (215).

Morgan's Passing
(1980)

"I write because I want more than one life. . . . It's greed, plain and simple."

Anne Tyler, "Because I Want More Than One Life"

Morgan's Passing is Anne Tyler's eighth novel, and her publishers had hoped this would be the book that could catapult her into the mainstream. Although it was nominated for the National Book Critics Circle Award and received the Janet Heidinger Kafka Award, the novel was treated unkindly by many of the critics, and sales suffered. The author had experienced some difficulty in keeping up her momentum while writing the novel. There were a number of crises that occurred during the summer that interrupted her concentration on the book, a situation that she describes in her essay "Still Just Writing" (1980).

Anne Tyler was very taken with the character of Morgan, having always been fascinated by impostors and their deceptions. This should not be surprising, since, in "Because I Want More Than One Life" (1976), she defines authorship in similar terms: "Mostly it's lies, writing novels," (45). And she told interviewer Margueritte Michaels (1977) that a novel "has to be an extremely believable lie" (40). The immediate inspiration for the book came from an article in the Baltimore newspaper about a local man who was discovered to be impersonating a doctor and who had previously pretended to be a clergyman (Croft 1995).

PLOT

Morgan's Passing is set primarily in Baltimore and covers a period of twelve years. Although plot is rarely a primary concern in Anne Tyler's novels, this plot seems even more shapeless than most. Clearly, it is primarily a character study of the central figure, Morgan Gower.

The primary narrative concerns the intersecting lives of two couples. Emily and Leon Meredith, a young couple, become involved with the older Morgan Gower and his family, which leads to the breakup of both marriages, Morgan eventually taking Leon's place.

The couples' encounter begins, improbably enough, when Morgan, who pretends to be a physician, delivers Emily's baby in a car when she goes into labor on the way to the hospital. Morgan becomes infatuated with the Merediths, idealizing them as the embodiment of a carefree, unencumbered, vagabond existence despite Emily's protests that he has "the wrong idea" about them (20). He is especially admiring of their streamlined stock of possessions, as exemplified by their plans to raise their baby in a padded cardboard box instead of acquiring a clunky crib. He begins shadowing the Merediths, wearing various outlandish costumes, observing them from a distance but avoiding contact. Like an anthropologist intrigued by an exotic culture, he is afraid that his intrusion could irrevocably alter the balance of this miniature world he admires. He does not realize that the Merediths have been aware of him the whole time, noticing him lurking in the shadows, and resenting it.

What finally propels Morgan to show himself openly to the Merediths is a kind of midlife crisis brought on by his daughter's marriage. Morgan is mourning the passing of his children's youth, the loss of his central place in their lives. Recalling his overprotectiveness as a young parent, remembering how afraid he was that one of his daughters would be stricken by a fatal illness or accident, he tells his wife Bonny that it's as though those "funny little roly-poly toddlers" died after all, only "more slowly" than he had foreseen (107–108).

Feeling lonely and depressed, he longs for the solace of some friend to talk to, but all of his acquaintances only know him through some role he plays for them—pretending to be a street priest, a refugee, a Greek shipping magnate. Lacking other options, he finally comes barging into the Merediths' apartment in his formal wedding suit, dropping his pretenses and confessing that he is not a physician but a hardware store manager. After their initial shock, the Merediths soften their attitude toward him. He begins to spend more time with them, vicariously satisfying his nostalgia by observing them with their elementary school age daughter, Gina. He introduces the Merediths to his family, trying to heal the cleavage between his two worlds, one of private disappointments and the other of public falsehoods.

Morgan invites the Merediths to join his family at the beach—a setting that marks a turning point in many Anne Tyler novels. He notices, as if for the first time, Leon and Emily's chronic bickering, which contradicts his cherished private image of them. Disappointed again, Morgan begins to fantasize about impersonating a wealthy collector in order to cultivate a relationship with Joshua Bennett, the antique dealer, whose velvet smoking jacket Morgan covets. But when Emily bursts into tears after a fight with Leon, Morgan impulsively takes her into his arms to comfort her and is startled to feel a kind of ache begin to stir within him. Gradually, he realizes he is in love with Emily. He flirts with her openly in front of Leon, making mock proposals of elopement, and they begin sneaking lovers' trysts. But he does not fantasize about having Emily all to himself. Instead, he imagines himself joining Emily and Leon's family unit, all of them living together.

When Emily suspects she is pregnant, she informs Morgan that she believes in abortion, but "not for me." She doesn't believe she could "go through with the actual process" (251). Confronted now with the potential for a radical change in his life—the kind of change he had thought he wanted—Morgan wavers, beginning to see his wife, home, and even his job in a more positive light. When he steels himself to announce to Bonny that Emily is pregnant, Bonny replies by throwing a wet sponge in his face (as Muriel does to Macon Leary in *The Accidental Tourist*) and dumps all his belongings on the sidewalk. She takes further revenge by having a fictitious notice of Morgan's funeral printed in the newspaper, knowing that he faithfully reads the daily obituaries.

Leon takes the news much more evenly, offering his small apartment and puppet troupe to Morgan. Since his conservative father's illness, it is as if Leon no longer needs to play rebel in his family. Moving to Virginia, he starts preparing to take a position in his father's bank and becomes so steady and conservative that his daughter Gina, now a teenager, chooses to go live with him.

By the end of the novel, Morgan has realized his original fantasy. Now *he* is the vagabond—an itinerant puppeteer living in rented rooms, unencumbered by teenage daughters or aging relatives. Even so, he is in the process of re-creating the familiar pattern of his life, now with Emily and their young child Josh. Morgan unrepentantly continues to escape in his same old ways, falling into the role of a postman when someone mistakes him for one, peeking into other people's private letters and drinking in glimpses of their hidden lives, continuing to drug himself with the illusion of limitless possibility.

A secondary narrative that runs through almost the entire book concerns Morgan's eccentric sister Brindle, and her high school sweetheart Robert Roberts. They each married someone else; but as a widow, Brindle now regrets having let her first true love slip through her fingers. Midway through the novel, Robert Roberts suddenly reappears in Brindle's life. They get married and move into their own place, to Morgan's great delight. It seems like the fulfillment of a romance novel fantasy. But Brindle becomes exasperated when she repeatedly catches Robert staring worshipfully at her high school photograph. She feels as though he is in love with his image of her rather than her real self. Brindle leaves Robert, who, in despair over her abandoning him, plunges fully clothed into the sea and has to be rescued by a lifeguard. No longer able to nostalgically mourn her lost love by dreaming of Robert, her childhood sweetheart, Brindle now takes to idealizing her dead husband and pining over him, although she did not appreciate him when he was living.

CHARACTERS

Like the puppeteers in her story, the author plays all the major parts in the novel. She has put much of herself into her two principal characters, Emily and Morgan. In Emily one can discern Anne Tyler's interest in Russian literature and bluesy ballads, her Quaker childhood, lack of religious sentiment, dislike of being photographed, and her aesthetic of starkness and simplicity. And, of course, Emily's relationship to her puppets parallels her creator's relationship to her characters. And in Morgan one discerns the author's lack of commercial instincts, her impassioned need to "live more than one life," and the way in which her imagination spins stories out of quirky newspaper articles and random glimpses into passing strangers' lives.

Like Macon Leary of *The Accidental Tourist*, Morgan tries to renew his life by leaving his wife and marrying a younger woman. But unlike

Macon Leary, whose personality is too rigid and circumscribed, Morgan's is diffuse and practically boundariless. He is like Jeremy Pauling of *Celestial Navigation* turned inside out—highly extraverted and social but equally obsessed with the unconventional logic of his own inner vision. Morgan's closet is crammed with costumes, as if he were the inheritor of the actor's wardrobe abandoned by Alberta's father-in-law in *Earthly Possessions*. He owns a Daniel Boone outfit and a safari suit complete with pith helmet, to name a few.

When Morgan first meets Emily, he is forty-two; and by the time they run off together, he is fifty-one, almost two decades older than she. Yet despite his age, Morgan is a perpetual adolescent. He likes to keep his options open, a sense of limitless possibility. Like Macon Leary's mother, Alicia in *The Accidental Tourist* or Justine's husband Duncan in *Searching for Caleb*, Morgan's life is littered with the remains of enthusiasms hastily adopted, then abandoned.

Morgan and his wife, Bonny, have seven daughters. Like Mary Tell of *Celestial Navigation*, Morgan kept wanting children because he was attracted to a certain stage in his children's development when they seemed so fresh and full of possibility. Each time he had such high hopes and was sure this time he and Bonny would "make no mistakes." But as their children got older, they stopped thinking their father was so wonderful, started doing "womanly things with their mother," went on crash diets, and became irritable (22).

In addition to his daughters, Morgan's aging mother Louisa and widowed sister Brindle also live with him. These two are more of a burden than a comfort. Louisa is losing her memory and spends her time nagging Morgan or bickering with his sister Brindle who lolls around the house all day. When Brindle's childhood sweetheart Robert Roberts reappears, Morgan is only too happy to see her go off to live with him.

Like Charlotte Emory of *Earthly Possessions*, Morgan feels oppressed by the complexity and clutter of his life, symbolized by his house that constantly needs shoring up and mending. He experiences his home as overflowing with a chaotic jumble of possessions belonging to his daughters, his wife, his mother, and his sister. In theory he longs for the kind of simplicity idealized by Henry David Thoreau, yet in practice he is too restless for this, his energy too manic to endure it.

The author seems to suggest that Morgan's lack of a strong sense of self is related to his absent father. Morgan's father killed himself for unknown reasons. Morgan fearfully speculates that his father killed himself out of no particular motive, simply that his interest in life had thinned to a trickle and dried up. Is this why Morgan keeps himself on a treadmill of novelties, throwing himself totally into each interest and then abandoning it as soon as his enthusiasm starts to wane? He keeps returning to his father's only legacy, an alphabetized file box full of instruction sheets for assembling and maintaining various pieces of equipment, searching in these impersonal words for some clue to what kind of man his father was.

Morgan treasures this file box as a child values its teddy bear. In fact, he resembles a young child who is trying through imitation to identify himself with ideal grownups. Lacking any felt sense of his father and without any other significant family member to model himself after, Morgan tries to patch together a soul from bits and pieces. He has a magical view of the world, like a tribesman who dances the movements of an animal in order to assimilate its power. In a similar way, Morgan tries infusing himself with the virtues of those whom he admires by copying external details. For example, when he becomes impressed by his doctor's matter-of-fact air of authority, he thinks he can appropriate it by growing a similar type of moustache.

Morgan has an overactive imagination. Purchasing a used Air Force jacket from which the prior owner removed all the insignia, Morgan likes to imagine that the decorations had been *ripped* off. He imagines himself in the scene—the drum rolls, the line of servicemen standing at attention, the commanding officer tearing Morgan's stripes off. At times Morgan resembles a postmodernist performance artist with his collection of platitudes like "Every situation has its difficult moments" (172) or television ad come-ons like "Have a cigarette. . . . Have a Rolaid. Have a cough drop. Have some Wrigley's spearmint gum" (172) or Robin Williams–type schtick complete with foreign dialects like "Nu. Vhere is de button? . . . Ah, so! . . . Naughty boy, Pinnochio! . . . Your nose has grown seven inches!" (227–228). In fact, Robin Williams might be a good choice to play Morgan in a movie version.

Morgan's vision of the world is slightly askew, and he is forever coming up with quirky ideas. He has an absurdist view of life, viewing the majority of the moods and events that affect him as essentially causeless, and our notions of predictability and safety as baseless illusions. Seeing passersby on the sidewalk who resemble deceased friends or relatives, he imagines that some of them did not really die but merely used the pretence of death to escape to a new life somewhere.

Through fantasies of this nature, Morgan is able to maintain a certain distance from life, feeling as though nothing *real* has ever touched him, as though this life is a rehearsal and he will have second chances, third chances, "the best two out of three" (226). He just can't take it all seriously. When a disturbing thought crosses his mind, he escapes it by taking off on an imaginative tangent. This coping strategy is similar to the one deliberately adopted by Jenny Tull in *Dinner at the Homesick Restaurant*—a way of getting through life on a slant, deflecting the frontal collisions, turning everything into some kind of joke.

Morgan's aptitude for imposture bears some similarities to the author's creative process. Anne Tyler (1976) has described her art as telling "an untrue story and you try to make it believeable, even to yourself" (45). Like his author, Morgan lives in two worlds: one in which imagination takes wild flight and another in which mundane details prevail.

Unlike *Celestial Navigation* where the two worlds of domesticity and artistic genius are incapable of being reconciled (as demonstrated by Jeremy and Mary's breakup), Morgan is trying to integrate the divided parts of himself. "I'm combining my worlds!" he says (155).

Emily Meredith, maiden name Cathcart, is one of Anne Tyler's country girls who moves to the big city. She was the only girl in her high school class who did not get married or take a job in the local factory immediately after graduation. Emily's widowed mother dies while Emily is still in college. Filling the void left by this loss, Emily drops out of school to run off with Leon, an aspiring actor with an explosive temper. Emily views herself as colorless, spiritless, and lacking in fire, managing at most "a little spark of delayed resentment" occasionally (76). When Leon's father, an anticommunist Virginia banker, goes into a ridiculous diatribe about Russian novelist Leo Tolstoy's being Lenin's right-hand man, Emily attempts a few mild protests, then politely declines to contradict him.

Emily lacks a solid sense of self, which is why she is able to sympathize with Morgan's statement that other people "push" him into giving a false impression. He hates to not be liked; and therefore if he senses that someone wants to view him in a certain role, he adopts the part. Emily explains to Leon that Morgan just "has to get out of his life, sometimes" (129). Emily experiences her marriage to Leon a bit like that. She compares their relationship to a car collision, where each vehicle transfers some of its paint color to the other vehicle's dent. She had hoped that more of Leon's extroverted energy would rub off on her and is disappointed that, instead, she has transformed him into a homebody. What she fails to do with Leon—to get outside of her own life—she succeeds in with Morgan. She wears her "new life" with him in the same way in which he tries on his various hats (290).

While Morgan's search for self involves trying on different identities, costumes, and hobbies, Emily's search at first consists of paring down, discarding, traveling light. Morgan's method is baroque and High Church, so to speak, while Emily's is austere and Puritan. As is true for many of Anne Tyler's women, childbearing enlarges Emily's sense of self, anchoring her to life in some deeper way. Her daughter Gina is the "whole point" of her life, overshadowing even Emily's relationship with Leon (96). To Emily no deed that her daughter could commit, no matter how atrocious, could sever the bond between them. In recognition of these mysterious claims of kinship, Emily resumes contact with her husband's family over his objections and despite their initial hostility toward her. Little by little, against her inclinations, Emily finds herself drawn out of her austere, simplified existence into the world of complexity that Morgan is seeking to withdraw from. Having made contact with her in-laws, Emily finds that they now insist on buying nursery equipment for their granddaughter. One day, a fancy crib arrives and, little by little over the course of several days, Emily finds herself assembling it, almost without thinking.

The complications of child rearing make themselves felt in other ways too. Going out for an evening with Leon is no longer a carefree affair. When they leave Gina with the baby-sitter, the child cries heartbreakingly. Throughout the movie or dinner, Emily's mind is on Gina, and she is unable to concentrate upon the present moment. Leon notices her preoccupation and becomes angry. They have a fight and waste the evening. But when Emily and Leon return, Gina is smiling and playing with the baby-sitter and hardly notices her parents are back.

As Margaret Gullette (1990) has pointed out, there is typically very little ferocity or ruthlessness in the appetites of Anne Tyler's characters. With the exception of Cody Tull in *Dinner at the Homesick Restaurant*, the usual Tyler character expends more energy in trying to figure out what he or she really wants than in struggling to get it. Morgan and Emily are no exception. Like many other Tyler characters, Morgan and Emily seem to get more pleasure out of parenthood than out of physical passion. While they willingly run the risk of hurting their spouses through their love affair, the actual damage done is relatively minor.

In the wake of their marital breakups, Leon and Bonny both grow to resemble the spouses whom they used to live with. Bonny begins smoking, like Morgan. She joins "strange philosophical societies" and women's groups, takes up macrobiotic cooking, begins unpromising jobs and resigns them almost immediately, and calls up Emily at all hours to talk interminably (283). It is as if in Morgan's absence she has somehow had to become like him. A similar process occurs with Leon. It seems as if she and Leon have "switched sides," Emily reflects. It used to be that Leon was complaining about Emily's tying him down to a domestic lifestyle; but since his separation from Emily, Leon has begun working in a bank and now preaches to Emily that she is leading "an unstable life" (296). These developments reflect Anne Tyler's view of relationships, ideas that she expounds in a similar way in *The Accidental Tourist*: namely, that husbands and wives construct each other's personality to a degree, like the gravitational fields of planets exerting a mutual influence in order to maintain each other in a steady orbit. Because of this effect, a divorce is not a final rupture, but only "another step" in a marriage, since each of the partners has been irrevocably altered by their years of extended contact (298).

THEMES

The primary theme of this novel is the mutability of identity and the blurred boundary between authenticity and play acting. Mutability is the key word for understanding Morgan. He is a shape shifter, like Proteus of Greek mythology or the Trickster of Native American lore, adopting a multiplicity of forms according to the needs of the moment. At his core, Morgan seems to lack any solid nugget of irreducible selfhood. He is perpetually in search of someone or something to define him. His initial attraction to his wife Bonny stemmed from her "definiteness" (31) and moneyed sense of self-assurance, a quality that he hoped would magically rub off on him.

Leaving Bonny, Morgan eventually adopts another identity wholesale. When Durwood Lithincum from Tindell, Maryland, comes to recruit "Mr. Meredith" to join the Holy Word Entertainment Troupe, Morgan pretends to be Leon and joins the troupe.

Morgan's characterization is not intended solely as an oddity or a case study in abnormal psychology. Although Morgan is an extreme example, he represents a widespread tendency of the modern soul that Anne Tyler has explored in other novels. Witness, for example, Olivia of *Celestial Navigation*, a vacancy searching to be filled, or Delia of *Ladder of Years*, who drifts from one life to another and back, with very little sense of decision, letting herself be defined primarily by circumstances.

Other characters in the novel share Morgan's dilemma to some degree.

Living with Leon and his troupe of actors, Emily senses that to them all of life is a play. Even a simple card game is an occasion for histrionics and dramatic gestures, groaning and tearing their hair if they lose, or flinging the cards in the air and trumpeting "Tataa!" if they win (81).

When Emily tries to persuade Leon to marry her, she affects a spunkiness that she does not possess. She wonders whether Leon is really taken in or if he just is playing a prescribed part, knowing that "this was what the audience expected": when a girl chases you outrageously you're supposed to laughingly "throw your hands up and surrender" (73–74).

Similarly, Morgan sometimes adopts a role purely in response to the momentary demands of the situation. When Leon calls out, "Is there a doctor in the house?" Morgan obliges (7). When a fellow customer in a shoe repair shop mistakes him for the owner, he accepts her broken high-heeled pumps and delivers her a zany lecture about how Italian shoes are often hollow heeled because they have been used to smuggle drugs into the country.

Morgan's mother, Louisa, who seems to be developing Alzheimer's disease, is an extreme example of the loss of a context for identity. Louisa's disorientation at times is quite profound. When Morgan deposits Louisa's granddaughter in her arms, she asks Morgan in surprise, "What *is* this?" Morgan informs her that it's a baby; "Is it mine?" she asks him (240).

Related to the mutability of identity is the predominance of image over reality. Several minor incidents in *Morgan's Passing* allude to the distortions created by images. For instance, Morgan's mother complains about the cooking program on television, how they make the food preparation look so simple and don't show the cook trying to scrape the tomato paste out of those tiny cans.

Then there is the family photo album. Some of the photographs are so widely spaced in time that whole generations flash past, then it moves in slow motion past fifteen solid pages of Morgan's infant daughter, taken by Morgan in "the first proud flush of fatherhood," before time speeds up again, traveling through several years' worth of summer beach photographs, as though the remaining years had been "an endless stream of vacations" (27–28).

Finally, there is the entire episode with Robert Roberts, who seems so fixated on Brindle's image in her high school photograph that he is unable to relate to the flesh-and-blood Brindle. Emily voices similar complaints: various men have seemed to be attracted to her; but as she gets to know them, she sees that what they really like is "their idea of her"

(91). Emily avoids having her photograph taken because the objectified image does not correspond to her internal sense of herself: she dislikes "being seen from outside" (92).

One begins to wonder: in the end is there anything solid about identity? Is it all misleading images and play acting? If you answer no, how can you be sure? After all, you can be deceived by your own play acting. In Emily's words, if you act like a certain type of person for long enough, "you become that person" (77). On the other hand, you don't construct yourself completely out of thin air. For one thing, there is a generational continuity that suggests some genetic substratum of selfhood—but can we really call it *self*hood if it is something that is merely passed on unconsciously rather than chosen? This is illustrated by the scene where Emily returns to Virginia to attend her great-aunt Mercer's memorial service.

Emily believes she has distinguished herself from her Quaker background through her unconventional lifestyle. But she learns that great-aunt Mercer used to daydream about joining the gypsies and becoming a fortune-teller (as Justine, also from a staid Quaker family, does in *Searching for Caleb*). Then, Aunt Junie shows Emily an antique marionette, a relic of Aunt Junie's long-ago fantasies of giving puppet shows in a painted wagon. Emily feels oppressed by these revelations, feeling robbed of what had defined her as unique. She wonders whether she had glimpsed this marionette in her childhood and whether this glimpse had subconsciously planted the seeds of her future puppetry, or whether the impulse was somehow mysteriously in her blood: something "passed down in the dark through the generations." How naive she had been to think she had escaped her origins and now lived "such a different existence" (221).

A MYTHOLOGICAL READING OF *MORGAN'S PASSING*

As discussed in Chapter 7, a mythic reading deals with the timeless and universal aspects of a text, comparing the text to motifs found in myths and fairy tales.

Some critics complained about the unbelievability of Morgan's character. But this novel signals early on that it is not intended as a psychological study. Its fantastic nature is hinted at in the opening paragraph where we are told of a six-foot-tall rabbit passing out jellybeans and where the smell of confectionery sugar blends synethesically with the wisps of music in the air.

The novel opens with a "play within a play." In the heart of the carnival is a puppet show in which the illusion of reality is created so perfectly that when the puppets dance it is easy to forget they are really only "two hands clasping each other" (7). The puppet play is *Cinderella*, a story of magical enchantment and illusory transformation. Cinderella and the prince dance on mirrorlike floors, an image that suggests the illusory quality of the fictional work, in which by some mystery the author and the reader can simultaneously see their own reflections.

Suddenly, something goes wrong, the spell is broken. The enchanted ballroom is seen for what it is—a huge cardboard carton with the front cut away. There has been a medical emergency. One of the puppeteers, Emily, has collapsed. Her partner Leon calls out for a doctor. Suddenly, there appears Morgan, dressed in a shaggy suit that looks as though it were "cut from blankets" (7), as Emily might do when constructing a costume for one of her puppets. On his head is a pointy red ski cap with a pom-pom—a distant relation to the cap that an elf might wear. He really looks like someone from a fairy tale, as Emily later says.

"Doctor" Morgan drives Emily and Leon to the hospital, humming "After the Ball Is Over," which is simultaneously a reference to the Cinderella play itself and to the breaking of the enchanted illusion when Emily collapsed. Perhaps he subliminally picked up the tune at the carnival where the carousel was playing it. Morgan is no real doctor; he is playacting. So the theme of illusion and theater is carried over from the puppet show into real life, where Morgan with his bushy eyebrows and wild beard fits the profile of Emily's favorite folk story, "Beauty and the Beast."

In that tale, the Beast's fate is dependent upon how the heroine sees him. Here again, as in *Celestial Navigation* and *The Accidental Tourist*, the type of person that the male protagonist sees himself as can be transformed by the attitude of the female protagonist. Other allusions to this principle in the text include the description of Morgan as having a jaw "as clumsily hinged as a nutcracker," a reference to the Christmas fable and popular ballet in which a wooden nutcracker is magically transformed into a prince (25). On another occasion, Morgan feels like a repulsive "toad" (58), which could be taken as an allusion to the story of the Frog Prince, another character who is transformed by love.

Fairy tale references are scattered through many of Anne Tyler's novels, but *Morgan's Passing* is especially rich in them. It should be remembered that one of Tyler's favorite authors is Gabriel García Márquez, the South American magical realist who blends the fantastic with the ordinary. *Morgan's Passing* also interweaves the fabulous and the realistic, though on a much more subdued scale.

However, Anne Tyler does not feel slavishly constrained by the archetypal plots of fairy tales but uses them as a springboard for her own imagination. In *Celestial Navigation* (200), Mary True reads fairy tales to her children while silently making up new endings "beyond the endings": the prince stops loving Rapunzel after she cuts her hair; the king keeps nagging the miller's daughter to spin more gold.

And in *Morgan's Passing*, when Emily and Leon stage their first children's puppet show, they misremember the ending: Beauty marries the Beast without him ever turning into a prince. When the mother who hired them draws their attention to their omission, Emily covers up their mistake by telling her their play is based on a "more authentic version" of the tale (88).

As Anne Tyler (1976) wrote in her book review of a psychoanalytic text about fairy tales, *The Uses of Enchantment*: "By forming a true interpersonal relation, one escapes the separation anxiety which haunts him." This is the real lesson of "happy ever after" (21).

Dinner at the Homesick Restaurant
(1982)

"The pain within the millstone's pitiless turning is real, for our love for each other ... is real, vaulting, insofar as it is love, beyond the plane of the stones' sickening churn and arcing to the realm of spirit bare."

Annie Dillard, Holy the Firm

Anne Tyler's ninth novel received the P.E.N./Faulkner Award, was nominated for a Pulitzer Prize, and was reviewed on the front page of the *New York Times Book Review*. It appears to be John Updike's (1982) favorite among her novels because of its "darker," somber tone.

PLOT

The novel is ambitious in scope, covering substantial stretches of time from multiple points of view. It focuses on Pearl Tull and her three children—Cody, Ezra, and Jenny—and extends forward to her grandchildren, Becky and Luke. The narrative begins in childhood when the Tull children are abandoned by their father and follows them through to adulthood, until shortly after the death of their mother, Pearl. Each of the four central characters is developed in quite a bit of detail.

As in *Earthly Possessions* and later in *Breathing Lessons*, Anne Tyler experiments with the sense of time, unfolding it in a circular fashion. This attitude toward time stems from an insight she first experienced in reading *The Little House* (see Chapter 2), and she alludes to this by including a scene where Jenny Tull has a déja vu flashback to childhood as she watches her daughter listen to Pearl reading *The Little House*.

The novel opens with the dying Pearl Tull, who is reminiscing while her youngest son Ezra sits by her side. Subsequent chapters look back on significant events in the history of the Tull family. Toward the final chapter, the chronicle of past events catches up with the opening scene, and we find ourselves again at the side of the dying Pearl, this time viewing the scene from Ezra's viewpoint.

The novel is written with a narrative voice that seems personal, yet is not totally identified with any one character. But it is not a godlike narrator, in a privileged position of omniscience. The narrator is a kind of floating awareness that assumes the coloring of whichever character it is speaking through at that moment.

The novel operates somewhat like a series of interconnected short stories, any one of which could stand alone if need be. To the extent that there is a central plot stringing them together, it focuses around the conflict between Cody Tull and his younger brother Ezra.

Their relationship is a bit like that of Cain and Abel. Ezra can do no wrong in their mother's eyes, and Cody is perenially jealous. He views himself in competition with Ezra, but he's the only one keeping score. It irks him that Ezra seems to be successful without even trying. During an archery contest, Ezra manages through sheer dumb luck to split Cody's arrow in twain, duplicating Robin Hood's legendary feat. To even up the score, Cody is perpetually tormenting Ezra, constantly playing cruel practical jokes.

After high school, Ezra is drafted into the army but gets an early discharge because of his chronic sleepwalking. He resumes his job as a cook in Scarlatti's restaurant. This proves to be another example of Ezra's charmed life, for he ends up being all but adopted by the owner, Mrs. Scarlatti. She puts Ezra in charge of the restaurant and deeds it to him upon her death.

Meanwhile, Cody, who moved away from Baltimore, has developed a lucrative career for himself as an efficiency expert, doing time-motion studies at factories. A handsome, elegantly dressed bachelor with plenty of cash, he has many attractive girlfriends but develops no lasting ties to any of them. When Ezra announces he is in love with a plain country girl named Ruth and intends to marry her, Cody becomes feverishly obsessed with having her for himself. Ezra is blind to Cody's intentions and is absolutely stunned when the inevitable elopement of Ruth and Cody occurs. Crushed, Ezra devotes the rest of his life to tending the restaurant and his ailing mother, who is going blind.

Cody is not unscathed by his ill deed. He remains constantly insecure about Ruth, fearful that she will return to Ezra. Later, he begins to also fear that their son Luke will fall in the orbit of Ezra's influence. Cody's irrational suspiciousness finally causes Luke to run away.

A second narrative involves Jenny, the third Tull child. She is involved in a series of marriages. Sleep deprived under the strain of a grueling medical residency, she begins physically lashing out at her tiny daughter Becky, as was done to her by her own mother, Pearl. This generational cycle of abuse is halted when Pearl comes up for two weeks to nurse Jenny and mind Becky. Subsequently, Jenny sets up a practice in pediatrics and inherits six step-children when she gets married for the third time.

The third narrative involves Pearl Tull and her husband Beck. The novel begins with a flashback to Beck's desertion, Pearl's attempt to conceal it and her stubborn refusal to admit it. In the final chapter, this narrative is completed from Beck's side as he explains to Cody how he remained emotionally entangled with Pearl and the children even after he physically escaped them.

These three principal narratives are framed by Pearl's death, which occurs in the first chapter and culminates in the final two chapters. Overarching these subnarratives is the metanarrative of the family as an organism with a life of its own, whose members are forever pulling together and pushing apart. The central metaphor for this phenomenon becomes the family dinners that Ezra organizes at his restaurant. They are meant as ritualistic affirmation of family cohesiveness, but, like Sisyphus's boulder that never quite reaches the summit of the mountain, some quarrel or emergency always disrupts the family meal. It is only in the final pages of the novel that this perpetually interrupted meal is finally brought to closure.

In the course of the novel, each of the Tull children has some momentary, individual experience of epiphany (if such experiences are ever truly individual) that have prepared the way for this final communal affirmation. The enactment of the meal is the visible sign of an enduring bond between the family members that persists mysteriously beneath all the rancor and misunderstanding.

There is also a fourth narrative that lies somewhat outside these three. It is the story of Luke, Pearl's grandson, who adds a new layer of meaning to the old conflicts by seeing them through the eyes of another generation. While the final resolution of the novel comes with the death of Pearl and the return of Beck, who are from the first generation, the way for this resolution is prepared or anticipated by Luke, who sees how Cody has selected and distorted events in order to erect a psychological wall that separates him from Pearl and Ezra.

CHARACTERS

Cody Tull, the oldest child, is unforgiving of his mother's failings, so that she wonders if there shouldn't be a "statute of limitations" on complaints about one's childhood, feeling that her middle-aged son has no right to hold her responsible anymore (21). Cody is a study in ambivalence. His seduction of Ezra's fiancée, Ruth, is both a hateful attempt to deal a deadly blow to Ezra and a twisted expression of his love for Ezra—as if to absorb Ezra's envied qualities by sympathetic magic. Cody seems to be trying to redress the lack he experienced in his youth, to win from Ruth the love that he felt Pearl bestowed exclusively on Ezra. But he ends up recreating the same old fear, namely, that like his mother, Ruth has always "loved Ezra better than me" (231).

Competition is essential to Cody's enjoyment of life. For him happiness is a limited and measurable commodity, like time. He cannot be satisfied with the simple, unconstructed pleasure of the moment and is eternally irritated with Ezra's "goddamn forgiving smile" (231) and his success in being liked "without even having to try." Unable to feel happiness from within, Cody looks for some external indicator of success—some competitor to measure himself against. His successes have no intrinsic value except as momentary trophies of victory. He must vanquish his rival again and again in order to fill an inner void that can't be filled. Throughout Cody's life, his chief rival has been Ezra, who is not interested in competing. If Ezra occasionally got the better of Cody, as in the archery contest, it was purely through luck. In order to sustain the illusion of their rivalry, Cody has had to mentally distort Ezra's image, re-creating him as a competitor who always "stole" Cody's girlfriends.

When Cody finally succeeds in "winning," in stealing away the one girl Ezra has ever loved, it is a very ambivalent victory since it destroys the beloved competitor and leaves Cody with the taste of ashes in his mouth. When Cody is on the train, successfully carrying Ruth away forever, the screech of the wheels momentarily sounds like a melody on Ezra's wooden flute—a sound that had always irritated Cody, but which at this moment pierces his heart with grief.

Ezra is completely the opposite type from Cody. Where Cody is analytical, strong willed, and unforgiving, Ezra is dreamy, intuitive, and placid. Cody is the archetypal realist, Ezra a visionary whose "radiant, grave expression" Cody misreads as smug (61). Above all, Ezra is an innocent; and as Dorothy Day once remarked, in literature such a person can only be portrayed as a bit of a comic fool.

Ezra is "adopted" by his employer, the elegant Mrs. Scartlatti, who conceals as fierce a heart as Pearl's beneath her European stylishness and reserve. Ezra's first great loss is when Mrs. Scarlatti becomes terminally ill. He reacts to her impending death with a bewildered, grieving frenzy, suddenly tearing down the restaurant's drapery and knocking down its interior walls as though he were angry at Mrs. Scarlatti for dying on him. But there is also an ambivalence: the spectre of Mrs. Scarlatti's death frees him, allowing him to fully express his own unique vision of how the restaurant should be run. This impulsive frenzy is the only violent emotional reaction Ezra displays throughout the book. He mutely absorbs the subsequent tragedies—the betrayal by Cody and his fiancée, Ruth, and the illness and death of his doting mother, Pearl. In the latter half of the book, we see Ezra taping squares of cardboard to the broken window panes in Cody's uninhabited farmhouse, an abandoned dwelling which symbolizes the Tulls' unrealizable ideal of family living. With each square of cardboard decreasing the light that enters, the farmhouse becomes increasingly tomblike, as though he were sealing himself in, "windowpane by windowpane" (173).

Pearl Tull is a proud and willful woman, bitterly frustrated because things haven't gone the way she believed they should. Tyrannized by the image of the ideal family, she feels that hers doesn't measure up. She wavers between blaming herself and blaming the children. Periodically, Pearl goes "on the warpath"—she trashes her daughter's room, dumps food over Ezra's head, throws a kitchen utensil at Cody's face, and wishes them dead, then locks herself in her room. Yet, in Beck Tull's opinion, Pearl was a better parent than he because she could endure being wrong, whereas Beck couldn't stand the "grayness of things; half-right-and-half-wrongness of things. Everything tangled, mingled, not perfect anymore. . . . Your mother could, but not me. Yes sir, I have to hand it to your mother" (308).

Pearl dotes on Ezra because he is the only one of the children that lets her get close to him. But being the favorite has its disadvantages since Pearl's feelings, like those of all the other characters, are ambivalent. The negative side of her love is her jealous possessiveness. When Ezra announces that Mrs. Scarlatti has made him a partner in the restaurant, Pearl is far from pleased. She is jealous of Ezra's relationship to the aristocratic Mrs. Scarlatti, nervous at its intrusion into the closed and defensive circle of her family, and upset that Ezra will not be pursuing the teaching career she had wanted for him.

Though Ezra is Pearl's favorite, in her prickly ferocity she has more in common with Cody. As she tells Cody: "You and I are more alike than you think" (64). They are both strong-willed, both survivors. And on the rare occasions when Pearl pulls Cody aside and confides in him, she unwittingly encourages him to act out the destructive side of her love toward Ezra.

Pearl deliberately sabotages Ezra's surprise engagement announcement at the restaurant. Like King Henry II—sending Archbishop Thomas à Becket to his death with an idle phrase—Pearl plants a deadly idea in Cody's mind without either her or Cody's consciously realizing it. "I wouldn't hold Ezra back for the world, if he's so set on marrying that girl—though I don't know what he see in her. . . . I've never been one of those mothers who tries to keep her sons for themselves" (143). She resents Ezra and Ruth's romantic illusions that "they'll live happily ever after," as if they were reproaching her for her failed marriage (143). When Cody begins trying to seduce Ruth, Pearl sees what he is up to but does not bring herself to interfere. Yet, in her ambivalence, she grieves for Ezra when she sees how Ruth's betrayal has broken him.

Jenny Tull has less space in the novel than her brothers—but after all, the middle child is usually neglected. She has a string of failed marriages, flirts with anorexia, and has a nervous breakdown in the middle of her medical residency when she begins treating her child as brutally as Pearl treated her. Even as an adult, Jenny can be cowed and thrown into a panic by her mother's disapproval when Pearl once again discovers that her daughter is befriending Josiah Payson. So devastating are these emotional assaults that, after one of them, Jenny glances at her reflection in her compact mirror as if "making certain that she was still there" (141). But a healing of their relationship occurs when Pearl nurses Jenny through her nervous collapse. After she recovers, Jenny decides to modify her intense and driven style. She decides her childhood wasn't so bad: "We made it, didn't we? We did grow up." She begins using whimsical and offbeat humor to deflect some of the intensity of life's problems, like Anne Tyler herself, whose novels blend heartache with a sense of the comic and absurd.

LITERARY DEVICES

As in *Breathing Lessons*, the title of this novel suggests a very homely, everyday activity—in this case, eating. The central image is of Ezra the cook, in his restaurant, serving up food that is not just utilitarian but medicinal, curative, alchemical, with unique dishes whose recipes emerge from his inner world, and whose "depth of flavors" (131) is restorative to the soul. Ezra is cook as artist; Anne Tyler is novelist as cook; this novel, her banquet, with its various courses, bitter, salty, and sweet.

The colors, textures, and feel of food in the mouth and the delicious smells wafting through the air are an essential component of the sensory experience of both cooking and eating. And this novel is particularly rich in olfactory images, beginning with Pearl whose other senses take on a new vividness as she loses her vision. Even in her youthful memories, she doesn't visualize her friends' faces but rather remembers the sounds of their voices, the way they smelled of "pomade and lavender water," and the crisp texture of their clothing (4).

These sensory images continue all the way through, as when Jenny visits with Slevin's teacher and is amazed that even these modern classrooms still have smells that are the same as her old grade school—an odor whose ingredients are "book glue," "cheap grey paper," and "what's that other smell? . . . Radiator dust" (198). In this way the texture of the novel reflects its central metaphor in a circular and self-referential fashion.

THEMES

A central theme of this novel is that life is a complexity whose texture is built out of multiple layers. The novelist sets out to bind up the reader's wounds with a healing balm that imitates the multilayered texture of real life, like the meal Ezra longs to make for Mrs. Scarlatti, a "complicated" meal "with a depth of flavors" (131).

The characters too are multilayered. The reader is continually presented with conflicting viewpoints on each of the main characters, each of whom is driven by some fundamental ambivalence, as has been discussed earlier. A fundamental example of this ambivalence is Pearl's relation to Ezra. He has always been her most beloved child. When he wrapped his little arms about her she would think, "This is what I'm alive for," his chirpy voice "ringing through the house like a trill of water" (175). When Ezra would leave for school in the morning, Pearl would sometimes feel a pang in her heart, a presentiment that this was the last time she would ever see him. Yet, when he would return full of talk about the day's events, "how solid, how commonplace—even how irritating—he seemed" (175).

The multilayered complexity of events is most clearly illustrated by the archery incident when Pearl is wounded by an arrow. This is the crossroads at which several of the characters' narratives meet. Like the four gospels, there are four different versions. Cody's is the most detailed. He aims an arrow at Ezra, fantasizing about shooting him. Ezra becomes alarmed and takes a flying leap at Cody, knocking him over so that the arrow flies out of control and hits their mother. Pearl is unsure exactly how the accident happened, but blames Beck and Cody. Ezra places all the blame upon his own clumsiness. He wanted his mother to forgive him for causing her wound, but instead she placed all the blame on his father and brother, which only intensified his guilt. Finally, to Beck this was the last in a series of disastrous family outings in which his plans for a little fun always went awry. After this incident, Beck decided to abandon Pearl and the children.

The archery incident is also a central metaphor for the nature of the family. In this novel the dream of the perfect family at times becomes a tyrannical ideal before whom the living members' blood is sacrificed. Set amidst the author's references to fairy tales and legends, the archery incident naturally calls to mind Cupid's arrows. The arrow is both an image of cruelty and an image of love. As a symbol it captures the ambivalence, the destructive as well as the fulfilling sides of the family's love-hate relationships. This interpretation is confirmed in part by the description in Cody's narrative: Cody turned the bow toward Ezra and fantasized shooting him; seeing the arrow aimed at him, Ezra rushed at Cody, arms open wide "like a lover" (38).

AN EXISTENTIAL READING OF *DINNER AT THE HOMESICK RESTAURANT*

As discussed in Chapter 4, an existential analysis concerns itself with the fundamental categories of human experience, of which death is a primary one. And integrally related to death is the experience of time, which has long been a central thematic preoccupation for Anne Tyler. An existential investigation explores the different textures of time as a lived experience, rather than as an abstract, scientific concept.

In a sophisticated analysis of *Dinner at the Homesick Restaurant*, Joseph Voelker (1989) suggests that the arrow, traveling through the air in the archery incident, is "Zeno's arrow," referring to a time paradox developed by the Greek philosopher Zeno. This image has also been used by Kingsley Amis for the title of his novel *Time's Arrow*.

Voelker distinguishes between two notions of time in ancient Greek philosophical thought: *"chronos* and *kairos"* (138). Chronos is linear, quantifiable, standardized clock time; it is time in its quantitative aspect. Kairos is time in its qualitative aspect, as the auspicious opportunities that are present at propitious moments. Chronos is concerned with surface, kairos with depth. Chronos is historical, profane time; kairos is ahistorical, sacred time. In some respects this dichotomy mirrors Martin Buber's (1970) notion of two alternating and complementary modes of experiencing life, the *I-It*, in which one experiences oneself standing outside a world of objects, and the *I-You* (sometimes translated "I-Thou") in which one feels oneself connected to a world apprehended as wonder and mystery. Time as chronos is necessary for the manipulation of things to achieve a limited goal. Time as kairos is necessary to infuse meaning into the deepest levels of existence.

Cody and Ezra embody the opposed attitudes toward time. Cody experiences time as fleeting moments that one wants to possess but that keep receding, so that his emotional life is entirely made up of "memories and anticipations" (Voelker 139): catalogs of childhood wrongs and a striving for goals that lose their savor as soon as they are within his grasp, "as if anything you can have is something it turns out you don't want" (169). In contrast, Ezra, who is always tooting on his pipe like Pan, has an instinctive "pagan piety" and "cosmic locatedness" that enables him to find comfort in the depths of the eternal present (Voelker 1989, 146).

Ezra's ease of access to that 'now' is the source of Cody's envy: "It is not Ezra's 'luck' or his appeal to women, it is his maddening ability to stay blind to the segmenting of moments, to slip inside any single one and take a nap with his cat" (Voelker 1989, 140).

These different senses of time relate to the way in which Anne Tyler uses epiphany in *Dinner at the Homesick Restaurant*. Epiphany in literature is the equivalent of what Martin Buber has defined as a "confirmation of meaning" that is a "presence" rather than a "content." In Buber's words, "You do not know how to point to or define the meaning, you lack any formula or image for it, and yet it is more certain for you than the sensation of your senses" (158–159). In no other Anne Tyler novel do so many characters have epiphanies; the central epiphany is experienced by Pearl as a young girl. As her death approaches, Pearl instructs Ezra to search her old diary to find the description of that afternoon in the garden when she suddenly realized that "at just this moment I am absolutely happy." In that still point, the "Bedloe girl's piano scales were floating out her window . . . and a bottle fly was buzzing in the grass, and I saw that I was kneeling on such a beautiful green little planet" (284).

This instant of insight was transformative: "I don't care what else might come about. I have had this moment" (284). Pearl and Ezra both fall silent before the magic of that moment re-evoked. She tells Ezra he can stop reading now, as though this moment is what she had been searching for amid all the trivia of her diaries. The chapter ends here, and on the next page it is announced that Pearl has died.

The motif of Pearl's epiphany is repeated for Cody on the last page of the book. He too remembers a moment of his boyhood when the sky was "clear and blue." The famous archery trip. Now he remembers a new version: his mother's hair "lit gold" and the arrow sailing gracefully through the air. And in the sky above, he seems to now recall, there had been a little airplane, "almost motionless, droning through the sunshine like a bumblebee" (310).

The image of the bumblebee droning through the sunshine provides a structural association with Pearl's moment of wholeness, in which a bottle fly was buzzing in the grass. The "little airplane" with its aerial view, taking in the whole pattern, and its seeming stillness even though in motion, also evoke the qualities of a moment of deep seeing. Looking back with this motif as a key, the reader can see that in Jenny's story there is also a moment that bears some structural resemblance to Cody's. It occurs after her nervous breakdown. Through some kind of grace, she develops the inner freedom to laugh in the midst of the problems. This new resiliency is punctuated by the appearance of a little toy helicopter that "buzzed across the waiting room," landing in Jenny's hair (219) and calling to mind the plane buzzing overhead in Cody's moment of insight. Ezra too has a moment of viewing the interconnectedness of life as if from an aerial perspective: small figures, mysteriously linked to one another, steadfastly "traversing the curve of the earth" together (284).

What is an ephiphany? Just an isolated moment that passes or an abiding assurance of some deeper level of meaning? For Pearl it is a foretaste of what she experiences on her deathbed: that it is a great relief to simply "drift," at last (33). She wonders why it has taken her so long to learn how. The sounds of the traffic outside her sickroom mingle indiscriminately with vivid sensory memories from the distant past: the feel and smell of the wind, the weight of a baby on her shoulder. As she accepts death, her orientation in time is momentarily suspended, and she rediscovers the simple pleasure of sheer experience.

Pearl had hoped that on her deathbed she would "have something final" that she could tell her children (29). But when the moment of death arrives, she realizes that nothing is final. There is nothing to be said. The "secret," she now sees, cannot be objectified into a graspable answer but consists in that unmanipulated openness to life that she experienced in her youthful moment in the garden and again in the act of dying as she returns "home" to this moment and merges again with the broad stream of time.

The promise inherent in Pearl's epiphany also graces those left behind. She is present in her absence at the family's now completed sacramental meal at the Homesick Restaurant. Her instructions to Ezra to invite Beck to her funeral constitutes a final act of unselfish forgiveness that opens the door to Cody's healing of his tortured childhood memories.

The Accidental Tourist
(1985)

"The real sin of pride, in a Tyler lexicon, is that of thinking one has all the answers."

Linda Wagner-Martin

The Accidental Tourist won a National Book Critics Circle Award and was nominated for a Pulitzer Prize. It is the story of a man who writes travel guidebooks for people who hate to travel. Anne Tyler (interview by Bail 1997) has stated that she feels "exactly the same about travel" as Macon Leary, the protagonist," namely, "I like to stay in one place and just examine it more and more deeply, rather than skimming across the surface of a whole bunch of places" (interview by Bail 1997). The theme of travelers who insulate themselves from new experiences was explored earlier by Tyler (1967) in the short story "The Feather Behind the Rock."

When it was made into a feature motion picture, movie critic Pauline Kael carped in the *New Yorker* over the selection of Geena Davis to play Muriel, but the Motion Picture Academy of Arts and Sciences disagreed and gave her an Oscar for Best Supporting Actress. Although Anne Tyler refrained from commenting publicly on the movie, privately she indicated that she was especially pleased with William Hurt's interpretation of the character of Macon Leary.

The film brought Anne Tyler's work to the attention of a broader audience. Between the handsome figure paid for the movie rights and the benefits of being a Book-of-the-Month Club Main Selection, the book brought in a tidy sum, finally compensating the author and her publisher for decades of laboring diligently for meager earnings.

PLOT

Displaying the short-story writer's talent for getting the essentials across quickly, Anne Tyler conveys on the first page of *The Accidental Tourist* the estrangement between Sarah and Macon Leary. Driving back from a vacation at the beach, Sarah and Macon look as though they have been on separate trips: Sarah is tanned and casually dressed, Macon is pale and wearing a suit. Within the next four pages, we are introduced to Macon's penchant for order, Sarah's perception of Macon as cold and unempathic, the fact of their son Ethan's death, and Sarah's sudden resolve to get a divorce—essential themes that will be developed more fully throughout the remainder of the novel.

The basic conflict in the marriage is between Macon's obsessive, superior, intellectual style and Sarah's more passionate, feeling nature. The structure of this novel is simple and straightforward. The unfolding events are viewed totally from the perspective of Macon, although he does not narrate it to us in the first-person voice. The plot proceeds in a straight-ahead fashion without the circularity of some of Anne Tyler's more structurally complex novels. Time proceeds linearly with few flashbacks and no giant leaps forward.

The reader is barely introduced to Sarah in the short first chapter before she leaves. The next three chapters show Macon alone, gradually drowning in his loneliness. He cannot sustain the loss of his wife on top of the unresolved grief over his son Ethan's death. By Chapter 5, Macon moves back in with his family—two brothers with broken marriages and a sister who never married. Their kitchen cabinets are arranged alphabetically, so that allspice is stored next to ant poison, and in the evenings they play Vaccination, a card game of their own invention with such complex rules that no outsider (such as their ex-wives) ever succeeded in mastering it.

Macon brings along Edward, a temperamental dog that bites people; even so, Macon refuses to give up Edward since the dog belonged to Ethan. In Chapter 7, after much urging by his siblings, Macon hires Muriel the dog trainer to teach Edward obedience. Although Muriel takes a personal interest in Macon from the moment she meets him, Macon does not consider Muriel anything but an animal trainer until Chapter 9 when he finds himself going into a full-fledged agoraphobic anxiety attack in the men's room on top of a skyscraper. Unable to reach his family or his estranged wife by telephone, he calls Muriel, who is able to calm him down. After this, their relationship develops quickly. Macon becomes Muriel's lover, moves in with her, and plays surrogate father to her son. Like Delia in *Ladder of Years*, he is able to recapture the coziness of family life without having to pay the price of permanent commitment. And like Delia, he finds himself mysteriously returning, almost by inertia, to his estranged spouse in Chapter 18. In Chapter 20, the final chapter, Macon takes a business trip to Paris, the city of romance. There he finds himself unexpectedly joined by his ex-girlfriend Muriel and wife Sarah, both of whom have flown to Paris on their own initiative. He feels himself torn between them. Like Morgan Gower in *Morgan's Passing*, Macon realizes that whatever course of action he takes he cannot avoid hurting one of the two women. Although he feels he will always remain married to Sarah in a sense, the opportunity for joyousness in his life lies with Muriel, and he decides finally to cast his lot with her.

The main plot of the novel is extremely simple, but it is enriched by the author's richly detailed and convincing characterization of Macon that is calculated to evoke a pang in the reader that is midway between laughter and heartache.

The subplot of the novel is the burgeoning relationship between Macon's sister Rose and his publisher Julian—a match as improbable as the one between Macon and Muriel. Julian is a jaunty, self-assured businessman who enjoys sailing his boat. Rose is a colorful eccentric who takes care of her brothers and fixes the plumbing for the elderly people in the neighborhood. Their relationship traverses a course similar to Macon and Muriel's: they marry and live together for awhile, then Rose moves back with her brothers, and finally she and Julian are reunited. But there's a twist. The way in which they get back together is that Julian moves in with Rose and her brothers, becoming assimilated to the Leary lifestyle and learning to play their strange clannish game of Vaccination every night.

CHARACTERS

Macon Leary is Anne Tyler's most poignant male character since Jeremy Pauling in *Celestial Navigation*. In his early forties (like Anne Tyler at that time), Macon makes his living writing travel guidebooks even though he himself hates to travel. He is a good-hearted but frightened person with an old-fashioned sense of propriety and genteel fairness. He is also a hypochondriac, plagued with fussy worries about being poisoned by lead leaching into the canned orange juice and about Muriel's "unsanitary" habit of licking her finger to turn the magazine page.

Macon is so fastidious that when he breaks his leg he refuses to let anyone autograph his cast. Instead, he whitens it with liquid shoe polish to keep it neat. He fantasizes about having a cast that would cover his whole body, like the cocoon that he could travel about in, insulating himself from the outside world.

Macon, like his whole family, has a kind of "geographic dyslexia" (111). He has difficulty with directions and gets lost easily when navigating in the car. His theory is that because he and his siblings were moved around so much as children they never developed a stable point of reference. The reason for all these dislocations was that Macon's widowed mother, Alicia, an expansive woman of many short-lived "enthusiasms," was leaping from one relationship to another with a series of men, each of whose obsessions she entered into as passionately as Morgan Gower (*Morgan's Passing*) playing his various roles.

Macon is the sedately boring opposite of his flamboyant mother, eating the same dish at every restaurant he travels to in France (Salade Niçoise) and dining at the same stodgy establishment (The Old Bay) whenever he goes out to eat in Baltimore. Everything about Macon is restrained. Even the way in which he grieves over his dead son Ethan is restrained, so that from the outside it looks more like indifference. When Sarah unfairly accuses him of not really having loved Ethan very much and stalks out of the restaurant in the middle of their lunch, Macon gathers his dignity and forces himself to finish his plate. He makes his way "conscientiously" through his shrimp salad, eating his cole slaw "for Vitamin C" and making himself eat "every last one" of his potato chips, in a heartbreaking attempt to carry on as though nothing devastating had happened (136). But we have witnessed him at home earlier, involuntarily crying out in the bewildered guilt and grief of an abandoned child: "I'm all alone. . . . Where is everybody? Oh, God, what did I do that was so bad?" (55).

Macon's estranged wife Sarah is his temperamental opposite. Where he is predictable, methodical, orderly, she is mercurial, haphazard, cluttered. In marriage their complementary polarities exerted a moderating influence on each other. But after their separation, Macon's behavior becomes increasingly frenetic to the point of breakdown, while Sarah descends into a profound torpor where she often sulks in her bathrobe all day amidst the unsorted clutter of her new apartment.

Unlike Macon, Sarah was highly popular and social in her youth. What attracted her to Macon was his aloofness, which posed a challenge. Macon quickly realized that he needed to feign a degree of indifference in order to keep Sarah's interest. But the very thing that attracted Sarah to Macon became the undoing of their relationship after Ethan was killed. In reaction to Ethan's brutal death, Macon withdraws further and holds an even tighter rein on his emotions, whereas Sarah feels a need to express her feelings of grief and rage.

Sarah would like to confront Ethan's murderer. She would get the murderer to realize the enormity of his deed and then would shoot him point blank. Macon, who is uncomfortable with passionate feeling, tells Sarah, "We can't afford to have these thoughts." She snaps back: "Easy for you to say . . . pretend it never happened. Go rearrange your wrenches from biggest to smallest instead of from smallest to biggest; that's always fun" (24).

Sarah and Macon are stifled by patterns of relating that have become mechanical. On the one hand, Sarah thinks she has Macon all figured out, an attitude summed up by the phrase she addresses him with: "The trouble with you is . . ." On the other hand, they have a little dance they do in which Macon is only able to win Sarah's attention by withdrawing. Caught between these two pincers, their relationship no longer has any room for growth or change. In contrast, when Macon is with Muriel, he is free to discover new facets of himself.

Muriel Pritchett, the dog obedience trainer, is angular and bony with legs like sticks. She dresses in a highly individualistic style, costuming herself in flamboyant secondhand outfits garnered at thrift stores. When Macon and Muriel first meet, it is the collision of two radically different styles of being in the world. For relaxation, Macon studies the metric conversion table at the back of his date book, while Muriel prefers reading about makeup tips in women's magazines.

Muriel's penchant for instant intimacy baffles Macon, with his stuffy reserve. She babbles nonstop throughout Edward's first obedience lesson, then rushes off, promising, "Next time I'll stay and talk," to Macon who is reeling with verbal overload. Whereas Macon and his siblings choose their words with pedantic exactitude, Muriel uses language as a kind of background music. During the initial few lessons, Muriel tells Macon her entire life story in installments. She reveals that during her high school years she developed a reputation for being "easy." The boys were eager to take her to the drive-in movie on the weekend but would pretend they didn't know her in front of their peers at school.

With an unconscious seductiveness (or perhaps it's conscious), Muriel tells Macon about the behavior of her high school dates, the boys inching an arm around her shoulder "like they thought I wouldn't notice" and then letting their hand slide down "lower and lower ... all the while staring straight ahead at the movie like it was the most fascinating spectacle they'd ever seen" (102).

That night Macon dreams he is back in his high school years, parked in his grandfather's Buick with some unidentified female. She takes control of the situation, removing his keys from his hand and putting them on the dash and then sticking her hand deep into his trousers. He awakens with a start, realizing that Muriel is the girl in his dream.

As Muriel burrows her way into the deeper layers of his heart, Macon realizes that, with her colorful outfits and scent of bruised flowers, Muriel bears a certain similarity to his mother, Alicia. Macon's coming to terms with his feelings about Muriel means, on some level, making peace with his suppressed feelings about Alicia—that "vain, annoying woman"—and a shocked recognition that she "might have the right answers after all."

Coming from less-privileged social circumstances than Macon's, Muriel has a different consciousness of money. First, Muriel tells Macon that she will charge him less than her usual fee because, as she says to him, "you're my friend" (although they've only met once). Then, when Macon doesn't have the exact change for the dog lesson, Muriel tells him he can make up the four-cent difference next time. And sure enough, she remembers to collect those pennies when she comes for Edward's next lesson.

Muriel is no pushover. She is the type of character whom Anne Tyler describes as blending "sweetness with an iron backbone" (Tyler and Ravenel 1996, x). When Edward springs at Muriel's throat during a lesson, she chokes the dog until it is practically unconscious in order to assert her dominance. Macon is angered by this incident and breaks off the lessons for a while. But Muriel's strong will is a quality that Macon lacks and desparately needs in order to keep from gradually fading away into lifelessness.

Muriel is a bit like those weeds whose endurance and survival abilities Macon admires—the way some weeds survive by releasing seeds just as they are picked and other weeds survive by allowing themselves to be easily broken off at the stem, leaving their roots behind. Another image that reminds Macon of Muriel is the stubborn persistence of the cat, which tried to enter the house by working her way down the exhaust vent of the clothes dryer, her eyes *"pressed into slits*, her ears flattened back by the lint-filled gale. . . . What persistence!" (italics mine) (57). Much later, Macon sees a childhood photograph of Muriel and describes it in terms reminiscent of the cat, admiring Muriel's "spiky pugnacious fierceness as she fought her way toward the camera . . . her eyes *bright slits of determination*" (italics mine) (219).

Muriel's fierce core is most clearly made manifest when a mugger accosts Macon and Muriel in the street late at night and she hits him square in the jaw with her purse without missing a beat. Her nonchalant mastery of this situation carries a particular charge for Macon whose son was murdered by a robber. Macon has the feeling that he *should* somehow have protected Ethan and is doubly burdened by his belief that Sarah faults him for not having been able to control the situation. In contrast, Muriel relieves Macon of this sense of burden: "Macon, don't you know Muriel can always take care of herself?" she tells him (268).

Macon is not romantically "in love" with Muriel. Too much of his heart is still involved with Sarah. And he sees Muriel's flaws too clearly—her "shrewish tongue," fits of self-loathing, and inconsistent mothering that alternates between overprotection and neglect (225). But he chooses to be with her because he realizes the relationship is good for him. He likes her surprises and the way in which he surprises himself when he is with her.

Part of the healing that Macon obtains with Muriel comes from his relationship to her preadolescent son Alexander, a nail biter and mouth breather whose gestures are all stingy. Alexander is constricted in his smile and in the way he walks; his glasses are always smudged with fingerprints, and Muriel has transformed him into a fussy hypochondriac, afraid to eat pizza because he thinks he is "allergic." Macon takes Alexander under his wing; he debunks Alexander's allergies, instills a sense of self-confidence by teaching him how to do home repairs, and buys him more relaxed, boyish clothing. Alexander is Macon's mirror image; by helping Alexander, Macon is restoring himself and re-creating his role as a father, which was interrupted by his son's death.

Holding Alexander's hand as he walks him to school, Macon feels "a pleasant kind of sorrow" spreading through his body. His life has "resumed all its old perils" (246). Affection has made Macon feel vulnerable again—not only for himself but for this little boy exposed to the risks of existence in the world.

Of Anne Tyler's clannish families, the Leary siblings are the most eccentric, engaging in interminable, ritual discussions whenever any minor decision has to be made. Their idiosyncracy is reminiscent of J. D. Salinger's precocious Glass family children. In addition to Macon, the siblings include Rose, Charles, and Porter. Charles is good at repairing machinery; Porter is good at handling money. Together, Charles and Porter manage to make the family bottle cap factory a profitable venture. It is typical of Tyler's penchant for the quirky detail that she comes up with a bottle cap factory as a family business.

Rose Leary is an example of the type of Anne Tyler character who fits the conventions of neither feminism nor femininity. Middle-aged and never married, Rose has the kind of obsessively logical mind stereotypically associated with males. Although she cooks, she does so in a nonconformist fashion, coming up with odd experiments such as baking the Thanksgiving turkey at extremely low heat. Like Elizabeth of *The Clock Winder*, Rose is more comfortable playing handyman than fussing about the kitchen. Her elderly neighbors frequently call upon her to fix their plumbing.

Rose has been a caretaker all her life, taking care of her senile grandfather and then her brothers. But like many of Anne Tyler's women, Rose enjoys soap operas and accepts the pop-culture images of love and romance. When Macon's publisher Julian becomes enamored of Rose, she accepts his proposal. But a change seems to come over her with marriage. She no longer seems quite herself. She seems "more graceful, but also more self-conscious," (278) as if she were trying to fit herself into some mold that doesn't really suit her. Perhaps this change comes from trying to accommodate herself to Julian, who is an opposite type to the Learys with his athletic, jaunty, and casually self-confident manner. Julian is, in Macon's phrase, the type of person who "would make a purchase without consulting *Consumer Reports*" (81). When Rose, who has an innate mechanical aptitude, protests that she cannot work Julian's expensive German camera because it is too complicated, one suspects she is trying to "dumb down" for her mate, the way the women's magazines used to advise.

However, Rose is too strong a character to play this kind of false role for long. Almost in spite of herself, she gravitates back to her family home to take care of her brothers, who have taken to staying in their pajamas and eating "gorp" (298) in her absence. It is as though she had "worn herself a groove" at the old house and is powerless to avoid "swerving back into it . . . like she was just gliding past helpless" (308). The improbable match of Rose and Julian mirrors the romance between Macon and Muriel Pritchett and is resolved when Julian moves in with Rose and his brothers-in-law at the Leary family residence.

LITERARY DEVICES

Imagery in Anne Tyler's novels sometimes functions on multiple levels of allusion. For instance, at a pivotal point in Muriel and Macon's relationship, Muriel cajoles Macon into joining her at a thrift shop by reciting to him an imaginative litany of magical items for sale there: a silent hammer with which you can pound nails in the dead of night and a cracked magnifying glass that, when you peer through it, makes broken things seem to turn whole again.

Within the story the cracked magnifying glass, of course, is Muriel, or Macon's relationship with Muriel. Though appearing to be a flawed and tarnished mismatch to the uninitiated, it has the power to alchemically restore wholeness to Macon's damaged life.

At the self-referential literary level, the broken magnifying glass's magical properties symbolize poetic vision and the creative illusion of fiction itself. This self-referential aspect functions like a "dream within the dream" or a mirror reflected in a mirror. Muriel coaxing Macon with the hand puppet is a figure of Anne Tyler's inviting the reader to enter into the story with her. The character of Muriel, of course, is Tyler's hand puppet. The second-hand shop, with its magical objects, is Tyler's imaginative world. The magical glass one looks through is the process of engagement with the novel itself.

Finally, on the most generic level, the magical glass could be taken to represent the healing potential or spark of primordial wisdom inherent in every individual. This is what George Fox and the early Quakers referred to as "The Inner Light." The eighteenth-century Quaker writer L. Violet Hodgkin (quoted in Renfer 1995, 348) explicitly used the image of a broken glass as an analogy for the portion of spiritual vision alloted to each individual at birth:

> Imagine that ever since the beginning of Time there has been a great big looking-glass with the sun shining down upon it. Then imagine that the looking glass has been broken up into innumerable fragments, and that one bit is given to each human soul, when it is born on the earth, to keep and to hold at the right angle, so that it can still reflect the sun's beams.

Having said his goodbye to Sarah and the baggage of the past, and having experienced a moment of heightened, almost mystical, reconnection with his departed son, Macon is now able to begin a new life with Muriel. As he directs the cab to where she is waiting, surrounded by suitcases and shopping bags representing the exuberance of life, a "sudden flash of sunlight hit the [taxi's] windshield, and spangles flew across the glass" (342). Although these are nothing more than old water spots, they are so "bright and festive" that for a moment Macon thinks they are being bombarded by confetti. And with that sentence the novel ends. In this final paragraph, Anne Tyler evokes marriage, life as a carnival, and the transformative vision that extracts poetry from the banal. With the magic of her language, she succeeds in matching the kind of lyrical visual effects that the best films achieve.

THEMES

A notable feature of this novel is its treatment of evil, which here takes the form of brutal violence. Violence in Anne Tyler's novels is typically psychological. In a few of the novels there has been physical violence—child abuse (*Dinner at the Homesick Restaurant*), suicide (*The Clock Winder, Saint Maybe*), attempted murder (*The Clock Winder*), armed robbery and kidnapping (*Earthly Possessions*)—but it always occurs in an understandable context and there is a human face to it. *The Accidental Tourist* treats the presence of evil in a different way. Because the killer remains faceless to the reader, the deed takes on a quality of impersonal, radical evil. We see it only in terms of its aftershocks, the psychological wreckage of Macon and Sarah's lives.

Since Ethan's death, Sarah has come to the conclusion that people are basically evil. It's as if the scales have fallen from her eyes and she suddenly sees the evidence of depravity all around her—on television, in the newspapers, and even in the faces of the students whom she teaches: "They're so ordinary, but they're exactly like the boy who killed Ethan" (133). Increasingly, she shrinks away from people and wonders whether she can live in such a world anymore. She realizes this is how Macon has always viewed the world.

If evil is that which causes people to shrink into themselves, what is the process for breaking out of this condition? This seems to be the main theme of the novel. In Macon's case, it can come only if he begins facing his pain. When Sarah leaves him, he is exposed to naked, squirming pain and tries to block it out by occupying his mind with complex schemes for "simplifying" the housekeeping, similar to the outlandish inventions of his senile grandfather.

In order to avoid making the bed, Macon sews the sheets together into a kind of improvised sleeping bag that he thinks of as "a Macon Leary Body Bag" (10), forgetting that a "body bag" is something that is used to store a corpse in. Indeed, these "methods" of his have a deadening effect, further isolating him from life just as his guidebooks are designed to insulate travelers from their journeys.

Though Macon's inventions are supposed to organize his life along more "logical" lines, the more he tinkers with them the more the arbitrariness and pointlessness of them becomes apparent. Cut off from Sarah's moderating influence, his schemes become increasingly bizarre, culminating in his phone call to the grocery store to ask that someone deliver the "perishables to the back . . . the dog food next to the coal chute . . . and the upstairs items at the front of the house" (55). It makes perfect sense if you understand the inner logic of it, but at face value it sounds totally crazy. Macon suddenly realizes he's on the verge of a nervous breakdown. At this point, he accidentally breaks his leg, thanks to one of his inventions, and the resulting immobility brings him one step closer to finally facing his pain.

This motif is repeated again in the final chapter of the novel when Macon's back muscles go into spasm in his hotel room in Paris. Sarah brings him pills to lull his pain; but they cloud his mind with an artificial haze, and he decides to stop taking them and endure the discomfort. Macon's decision to face his physical pain symbolizes his willingness to confront his psychological pain and his deep-seated fear of life. His decision at that point to commit himself to Muriel is seamlessly connected to his rejection of dulling himself with pain medication.

One step in Macon's process of change is to recognize how he unsuccessfully uses his disembodied intellect to fend off his pain. Another is his recognition of the unexplored emotional depths that he is estranged from. This nonrational side of Macon is represented by the dog Edward. The hidden correspondence between Macon and Edward is first glimpsed at the end of Chapter 3. While on his trip abroad, Macon fantasizes that Sarah has changed her mind and has moved back into the house in his absence. His disappointment at finding her still absent is mirrored by the dog's puzzled expression over the missing rug, which Sarah has taken to her new apartment.

This parallelism between the dog and Macon is unmistakable in the scene at the top of the skyscraper in a grottolike restaurant whose spacious darkness flickers with candles, where an intense, unreasonable feeling of panic suddenly floods Macon's body, causing his heart to pound and his legs to disobey him. Feeling out of control, his first reaction is to shut himself in a bathroom cubicle. After some minutes, he ventures to a phone and calls his family for assistance but discovers that his brother Charles has cloistered himself in the pantry in fear of Macon's barking, disobedient dog who, like Macon, has gone out of control.

Macon's evolving character is incomprehensible to his brothers. Macon is not acting like himself, Charles tells him. Macon counters, "I'm more myself than I've been my whole life long" (237). To Charles this statement doesn't make any sense. Charles is identifying "self" as some static bundle of habits that remains unchanging over time. Macon is beginning to identify self with something deeper, an *élan vital*, an exuberant life energy, that cannot be reduced simply to sexual attraction.

Gradually, Macon's senses begin to reawaken. Coming home from the airport, he opens the car's windows and remarks upon the distinctive fragrance of the breeze. This marks a new level of immediacy in the narrative, which thus far has been primarily intellectual and visual. He notices spring with its signs of awakening life: babies in strollers and crocuses pushing their way up through the hardened dirt.

Another image of the process of change is conveyed in a scene between Macon and Sarah at the Old Bay Restaurant. The stodgy Old Bay is symbolic of Macon's stagnant, self-contained way of life. It was his grandfather's favorite restaurant, and Macon boasts that the same unchanging recipes are still being served there. But the restaurant on this occasion has an odd assortment of patrons, not the usual Old Bay crowd. A priest in his black suit is offering a toast to a woman dressed in tennis whites. Macon fantasizes that the woman wants to join a convent and that the priest is discouraging her, telling her everyday life can be just as holy. At another table, a young man dressed in the orange robe of the Hare Krishna sect sits dining with an elegantly suited woman. Like a movie director visually composing a frame, Anne Tyler has made the outer world act as a reflection of Macon's inner state.

Macon's favorite bastion of the unchanging is suddenly populated by these exotic, mismatched couples who signify the potential for radical change in one's life. Also present are some schoolgirls who are cheerfully heaping their potato chips onto a little boy's plate. They represent the possibility for spontaneous, uncomplicated joy.

As the novel progresses, young people increasingly appear on the scene at critical points—a row of children bumping into Macon at the airport and causing him to laugh, a young couple dancing in the rain on Singleton Street, a starry-eyed teenage pair who laughingly precede Macon back into the sky top restaurant after his panic attack has subsided. They represent the forces of rejuvenation. One almost senses that they are emanations of Ethan, acting like guardian angels, appearing to encourage Macon in his process of inner renewal. This is most explicit in the critical last scene when Macon is rushing to catch a taxi so that he can overtake Muriel.

As Macon races down the street, he is burdened by his overnight bag, which represents the accumulated baggage of his life. Realizing there is nothing essential in it, he leaves it behind on the sidewalk. Now unencumbered by the deadweight of the past, he can catch up with a cab. A French boy, seeing Macon's efforts, calls to the taxi to halt, then assists him into the seat. As Macon drives off, he sees that there is something familiar about the boy's shaggy blonde hair, his "sweet, pure face," and his stiff-legged gait that closely resemble Ethan's (341).

In the film version of *The Accidental Tourist*, the encounter with the boy is a pivotal moment, clearly an epiphany of sorts, as underlined by the camera movement swooping in on Macon (William Hurt). This particular segment is a rare instance in which the visual medium of cinema was able to condense more emotional meaning into the moment than the book's prose could convey.

A POLITICAL READING OF *THE ACCIDENTAL TOURIST*

A political analysis of a piece of fiction concerns the way in which the fiction influences the social consciousness of its readers. Novels tend to embody a variety of social assumptions that have political consequences in the real world. The creator of fiction can either implicitly accept these assumptions or can examine, question, or challenge them in some way. Novels that bring current social and cultural assumptions into question are often seen as more politically engaged and progressive. In the United States, two of the more common cultural assumptions have been to value individualism over collective action and to expect fulfillment primarily in the private rather than the public sphere of life.

Susan Gilbert (1990) is one of several critics who have taken Anne Tyler to task for the apolitical quality of her novels and has gone even further to suggest that by default Tyler's novels serve the cause of political and social conservatism. Gilbert reads Tyler's admiration for her characters' endurance as implying that "toward really changing things there's little to be done" (144) and lampoons the underlying philosophy of the novels as "only meddlesome, silly people try to change things. The wise see to the unchanging heart of things and accept" (142).

Picking *The Accidental Tourist* as an example, Gilbert faults the author for raising such topics as handgun violence, crime in the streets, and the poor quality of the public schools, but then ignoring "the application of human intelligence and energy to organizing society to provide for the common safety or promote the general welfare" (141).

Gilbert fusses about Macon Leary's volunteering to pay for Muriel's son to attend a private school, feeling he will get a better education there. Gilbert criticizes Macon's proposal as a politically reactionary impulse to settle for private solutions instead of struggling for social change. However, it is absurd to think that Anne Tyler is holding Macon up as an ideological model for the reader. His action is a reflection of his character, which is one of avoidance. One could point to Morgan Gower's opposite reaction in *Morgan's Passing*, which is also in character. Emily is disgusted with the overcrowding in the local public school and its unsafe surroundings. She is accepting her in-laws' offer to pay for her daughter's education at a private school. Morgan is opposed to the idea of a private school and urges Emily, "Don't forsake your principles" (137).

From Anne Tyler's perspective, her role is to be a storyteller rather than an agent of social change: "Much as I would love to think that a novel could make a positive political change, I've never seen it done, and I believe it is always a mistake to aim for anything more than pure storytelling when writing fiction" (interview by Bail 1997).

As Doris Betts (1990) has commented, alluding to the novels of Jane

Austen: "One might as well insist that *Sense and Sensibility* take a stand on Napoleon, that *Emma* be more forceful about the War of 1812, or that *Persuasion* concern itself with the 1817 riots in Derbyshire over low wages" (10).

However, even this observation is not quite on the mark. Anne Tyler is not primarily a comedian of manners like Jane Austen. She is less concerned with getting her characters married off to the right persons than she is about their interior condition, the quality of their being.

It is not that Anne Tyler discounts politics, which was her parents' mode of discourse, but that she specializes in a different grammar and concerns herself with experiences whose subtlety is easily eclipsed by the vividness and urgency of political struggle.

Anne Tyler's awareness of how these private concerns can pass unnoticed in the clamor of social realities is voiced by her alter ego Emily in the novel *Morgan's Passing*. Emily lives in an inner-city neighborhood. When the social worker at a community clinic asks her if she has any problems, Emily wants to talk about her feeling of separateness, but "she knew that wasn't a serious enough problem. In this neighborhood women were getting murdered." Emily feels she must seem "frivolous" to the social worker (75).

It is clearly not the case that Anne Tyler is politically unaware or indifferent. When the film version of *The Accidental Tourist* premiered in Baltimore, Anne Tyler agreed to attend only on condition that the event be used as a benefit for a worthy cause. As a result, $20,000 was raised for the Juvenile Diabetes Foundation (Croft 1995). Witness also Tyler's unabashedly political article "Trouble in the Boys Club" (1977). She does not lack a social conscience. What she lacks is an ideological programme for fiction.

Breathing Lessons
(1988)

"Sisyphus is in love with the rock. . . . He talks to it, sings to it."
Stephen Mitchell, "The Myth of Sisyphus," in *Parables and Portraits*

Breathing Lessons was published in 1988 on the heels of Anne Tyler's prize-winning *The Accidental Tourist*. Her intent was to show that "an ordinary, run-of-the-mill marriage has in many ways a more dramatic plot than any thriller ever written" (Croft 81). *Breathing Lessons* was a Book-of-the-Month Club main selection and was made into a television movie of the same title, starring James Garner and Joanne Woodward, in 1994. An excerpt from the novel was published in the *New Yorker*.

STRUCTURE

The primary story line concerns Maggie Moran's maneuverings to establish a connection with Leroy, her young granddaughter whom she has not seen for several years following her son Jesse's unamicable divorce from Fiona, Leroy's mother. Maggie's plan is to try to arrange a reconciliation between Jesse and Fiona so that she will again have access to Leroy. This is the central motive that sustains the action in the novel.

Threaded around this narrative line is the ongoing story of Maggie's push-and-pull relationship with her husband, Ira, who is as stubbornly hardheaded and matter-of-fact as Maggie is fanciful and sentimental. Their comical bickering permeates the novel. There is a complex dance in which it gradually becomes clear that Maggie and Ira's seemingly distinct personal styles are complementary and interpenetrate each other.

Subordinate stories involve the mixed signals and ambivalence in Fiona and Jesse's relationship, the quarrels and reconciliations that occur in Maggie's relationship to her girlhood chum Serena, and the encounter with the elderly Mr. Otis on the highway. There are also a number of flashbacks dealing with Maggie and Ira's courtship, Ira and Maggie's relationship to Ira's family, Maggie's job at the nursing home, and her relationship with Serena's mother.

PLOT

Maggie is the central character of the book, around whom all the other plot lines orbit. Maggie's central preoccupation is dramatized in the opening scene where she has an auto accident because she is distracted when she imagines hearing Fiona's voice on a radio talk show. Within these same few opening pages, we are quickly introduced to the essentials of Maggie's married life: Maggie's scatterbrained qualities, Ira's cool sarcasm, and Maggie and Ira's conflicting views about their son Jesse whom Ira belittles and Maggie defends.

In Chapter 1, Ira and Maggie set out for the town of Deer Lick to attend the funeral of Max, Maggie's friend Serena's husband. Maggie sees this excursion as an opportunity to make a side trip to Fiona's house in Cartwheel on the way back. Maggie hopes to persuade Fiona to let seven-year-old Leroy come with her and Ira for a visit. These simple plans become increasingly complicated as a result of unforeseen events. These events include a fight with Serena when she discovers Maggie and Ira smooching in her bedroom at the close of Max's funeral and a time-consuming detour to bring old Mr. Otis's car to his nephew Lamont's garage. Finally, the trip unintentionally escalates into a scheme to transport both Fiona and Leroy back to Ira and Maggie's house where Maggie will try to engineer a reconciliation between Fiona and Jesse. The plans for reconciliation backfire, of course. Fiona and Jesse exchange words, Maggie and Ira quarrel, and Fiona disgustedly sneaks out with Leroy, without even saying goodbye. Maggie is left feeling foolish and hopeless, although she quickly recovers and begins plotting her next move to stake her claims on Leroy.

Stuck right in the middle of the novel, like a self-contained and separate short story, is the time-consuming encounter with Mr. Otis on the highway. Mr. Otis's car accidentally cuts theirs off as they are motoring down the highway. Ira, the voice of reason, tells Maggie the near-accident was as much their fault as the other driver's. But Maggie in her fanciful fashion, declares that the driver is probably drunk and a menace to the public. She persuades Ira to overtake the car; and as they pull alongside, Maggie shouts out the window to the other driver that his wheel is coming loose—a lie that she has concocted for revenge. But she immediately regrets this spiteful prank. She sees that the "public menace" her imagination concocted is really an elderly black man, who acknowledges her warning with a courteous tip of his hat. The hat reminds her of her grandfather. Now her imagination goes into reverse gear. She pictures the old man pulling his car over to the side of the road and sitting there helplessly, afraid to drive further because of the tire. She persuades Ira to turn the car around and go back to check on him.

At first, Maggie tells Mr. Otis that she was mistaken about the tire, not wanting to admit that she outright lied, because then Mr. Otis might think she and Ira tricked him because they are racists. Ironically, nothing that Maggie tells Mr. Otis can shake him from the newly developed belief that his wheel is about to fall off. Even when Maggie finally admits that she made it up, Mr. Otis refuses to believe that she lied. Calling Maggie an "angel of mercy," Mr. Otis reasons that God was using Maggie to warn him (144) and that she must have been "moved" to say what she did, without really understanding why (147). Hoping to prove that the wheel is fine, Ira test drives the car while Mr. Otis and Maggie look on. But, sure enough, the wheel now looks as though it might really be loose! So they take the car to a service station that belongs to Mr. Otis's nephew Lamont. But the reader never finds out whether the wheel was really defective or not, since the Morans drive off before Lamont has inspected it. Even though it seems completely tangential to the plot, this incident does enrich the reader's overall understanding of the characters. The absurdity and strangeness of this episode opens up an additional dimension to the otherwise fairly straightforward narrative.

The novel is structured in an interesting and complex fashion. The action takes place in a single day. But with her skill at making time malleable and bending it back upon itself, Anne Tyler succeeds in loop-

ing in and out of Maggie and Ira's past several times in the course of
that one day, covering such prior events as a teenage Maggie's sending
Ira's family a note of condolence because she had mistakenly thought
that Ira was dead. Or an adult Maggie's rescuing her future daughter-
in-law from a pack of demonstrators outside the abortion clinic and,
against her better judgment, talking the girl into keeping the baby.

Like a complex symphony, themes are repeated with slight variations.
The book is divided into three parts, the first covering the trip to Max's
funeral, the second the encounter with Mr. Otis, and the third the encounter with Serena and Leroy. In the first part there are a number of
flashbacks to Maggie and Serena's high school years and Maggie and
Ira's courtship. The last section deals with Jesse and Fiona's courtship.

Repeatedly in the novel, Maggie comes to the conclusion that life is
circular: you could seek a new relationship, but find yourself repeating
the same situation. "You could change *who* but not *what*," she muses
(48). This thematic content is echoed and reinforced by the very structure
of the narrative itself, which is also circular and winds in upon itself in
a series of spiraling layers that gradually disclose deeper and more comprehensive layers of meanings in the repeated events. For instance, in
the first chapters of the novel, the kitten that Maggie bought for her
granddaughter is mentioned by Ira as an example of Maggie's poor judgment, since Leroy turned out to be allergic to cats. The kitten comes up
again, from Leroy's perspective, in the final chapters of the novel. Similarly Jesse's arrest for drunkenness, the episode with Serena's mother in
the nursing home, Ira's dream of being a doctor, and several other events
keep reappearing from different perspectives at various points in the
narrative.

And the characters make the same mistakes all over again too. In a
flashback we see how Ira contributed to the original breakup of Fiona's
marriage by letting Fiona know that Jesse was seeing another woman.
He immediately regretted having meddled in this way. And yet at the
end of the novel, Ira again meddles in exactly the same way, giving the
final blow to Jesse and Fiona's shaky reconciliation by revealing that
Jesse is living with a woman. Similarly, the disastrous outcome of Ira's
family's outing at Harborpoint is repeated when Ira and his relatives
gather at the Pimlico Race Track for his father Sam's birthday. *Breathing
Lessons* is like a Greek tragedy where characters seem incapable of alter-
ing their fates. Serena's funeral for Max is also circular. It feels more like
a high school reunion than a burial; and instead of the standard funeral

hymns, Serena tries to do a "rerun" of her wedding program, using all the same songs, like "Love Is a Many Splendored Thing."

CHARACTERS

The two central characters in this novel, Maggie and Ira Moran, are presented as polar opposites, and yet there is a hidden correspondence between them that enables them to act in a complementary fashion. For Anne Tyler, personality is fluid and certain aspects of one's self become accentuated due to the particular constellation of one's intimate relationships. Ira can freely be as he is because he has Maggie to keep him in check, and vice versa. Maggie makes it clear that she looked for a husband who was *not* "pliant" so that she would not be forced to play the heavy in the household, as her mother did (73).

To a large extent, then, Maggie's style of being can be defined as the opposite of her husband's. Ira has a logical and linear mind; Maggie thinks in associations, zig-zagging in a ricocheting flow of thoughts that Ira finds baffling. As he says, Maggie is not a "straight-line" type of person (168). Ira operates solely by daytime logic. When Maggie tells him about her night dreams, it always makes him feel "fidgety" and unsettled (134). Maggie can also unnerve him with her ability to read his private thoughts. She uses the tunes he absently hums to give her clues to what he is thinking.

Maggie with her persistent optimism is a bit of a Mary Poppins figure. Like many Anne Tyler characters, she has a reputation for being a klutz; but at the nursing home where she works, she feels valued and competent among the elderly people, just as Elizabeth does in *The Clock Winder* when she is tending the aging Mrs. Emerson. Maggie gets a crush on one of her patients, Mr. Gabriel, and even fantasizes running off with him, until she realizes that he is just an older version of Ira.

Maggie is everyone's mother. She is warm and expansive, opens her heart to strangers, and collects strays. Ira, in contrast, wants to set strict boundaries around everything. He even resents his children as "outsiders" sometimes (153). Like some other Tyler men, he at times feels shut out by the mother-child relationship.

Maggie is a meddler who tries to tinker with her children's lives. Anne Tyler doesn't usually approve of meddling, although we sense that she has a soft spot for Maggie. Even so, Maggie gets her comeuppance at the end when Fiona tells her off and leaves. Although Tyler is no moralist, there certainly seems to be a moral there. And yet, maybe Maggie is a visionary, not just a deluded sentimentalist. Perhaps her heart intuits the truth hidden under the surface. The heart is Maggie Moran's great asset. It is this asset that keeps Ira spinning in her orbit, even while he is taking sarcastic potshots at her.

Ira is Maggie's husband. He rations his emotional life, a bit as Macon Leary does in *The Accidental Tourist*. He doesn't like the way in which Maggie can involve him in her dramas and get his feelings all worked up for nothing. He feels it is "wasteful" to continue to care about Fiona or Leroy when Fiona obviously doesn't care about him and Maggie (132). He even resents wasting energy by worrying about his own children, now that they are more or less fully grown. There are days when he speaks less than a dozen words, spending his spare moments absorbed in playing solitaire—a game that folds him back in upon himself—or reading books about solitary men who have voyaged alone across the ocean.

Ira has a way of souring things for people. Deep down he feels he is a failure because he gave up his youthful dreams of going to medical school and discovering a cure for some major disease. In self-defense he cloaks himself in an air of perfectionism, and those around him feel intimidated by what they sense to be disapproval. He particularly berates Jesse for not growing up, feeling reproached by Jesse's unwillingness to give up his youthful dreams of stardom. But at some deeper level, Ira feels an absence of joy in his life and intuitively understands that his fussy standards of right and wrong do not bring him any closer to joyfulness. Since childhood he has envied those "jolly, noisy families" that are so unlike his own (162). We see here a reflection of Anne Tyler who, as a youngster, used to envy the big, rollicking, traditional Southern families she saw around her.

Ira is a carefully measured person; compared to him, Maggie laughs too much and cries too much. He is a methodical person who likes to plan ahead, and he dislikes surprises. Ira is uncomfortable with amibiguity and likes to categorize everything. He dislikes the mild feeling of disorientation that he gets during the transitional seasons of fall and spring because sometimes he realizes with a start that he cannot immediately remember whether winter or summer is coming next.

Ira supports not only his own nuclear family but also his father Sam and his two stay-at-home spinster sisters Dorrie and Junie. Dorrie is mentally retarded. Her pathetic treasures, that she lugs with her in a little suitcase, stand for everyone's. They are the equivalent of Ira's car, whose dents he fusses over, or the intact family that Maggie fantasizes about. Junie is agoraphobic, like Jeremy Pauling in *Celestial Navigation*. Maggie gets Junie a red wig that allows her to go out in public for the first time. As with Morgan Gower (*Morgan's Passing*), when Junie is in costume she feels it is "not she" who is going out (169). It was because of the premature retirement of his father—a worn-down, defeated man—that Ira had to abandon his dream of going to medical school and go to work instead. Ira's clannish family members, who still consider Maggie an outsider, are reminiscent of the Emersons (*The Clock Winder*), the Pecks (*Searching for Caleb*), and the Learys (*The Accidental Tourist*).

Ira and Maggie's two children, with their opposite personalities, mirror the polarity between their parents. Jesse is a dreamer like his mother and Daisy is a sober perfectionist like her father—serious and practical, always color coordinated and and well organized, a bit like Justine Peck's daughter Meg in *Searching for Caleb*, but more driven, biting her nails and getting migraines. The children are like mirrors for Ira, who deals with aspects of himself through them. In Jesse he sees himself as a young man, with grandiose ambitions of becoming famous. He sees Jesse as a failure, yet secretly resents Jesse for not having had to give up his youthful dreams in order to support a family. And he imagines that Jesse judges him as a failure: a shopkeeper plugging away at his banal tasks. In his daughter Daisy, Ira sees the side of himself that accepted excessive responsibility prematurely. He worries that she is "missing out on her own youth" (162). He wishes Daisy wouldn't always have that "pinch-faced" expression of disapproval that so closely resembles his own.

Jesse, the older child, is a high school dropout in his twenties who won't hold a steady job but aspires for stardom with his rock band. Maggie is partial to him, feeling that he is at a disadvantage with a perfectionist father and super-organized sister. But even Maggie admits that Jesse has a short attention span. Jesse can't understand why someone would still hold a grudge about something that he did "hours ago." Yet Maggie remembers his tenderly nursing her when she had the flu. He doesn't have a malicious bone in his body, but his feelings are easily hurt. In fact, he and Fiona are both very proud and too sensitive, so that they are constantly clashing, always at "cross-purposes" (250).

Although Jesse is primarily his mother's child, he does resemble his father in one way. During Fiona's pregnancy, Jesse tries to master the anxiety that this female event arouses by obsessively reading about the technology of childbearing. He demonstrates his male competence through intellectual discussion of the relative merits of various theories of infant rearing—the pros and cons of pacifiers versus thumbsucking, and so forth. He tries to wrest control of the delivery process from Fiona with the male technological gadgetry of a special stopwatch that he has bought for timing her contractions. He intrudes into the rhythms of Fiona's body and tells her that she is not breathing "right." She, in turn, tells him to leave and asks to have Maggie in the delivery room with her.

Fiona is first glimpsed in Maggie's memory as an unremarkable girl who follows Jesse's rock band. When Fiona gets pregnant, her sister arranges an abortion for her. Jesse tries to talk Fiona into getting married instead, but she doesn't take him seriously. So he begs Maggie to be his go-between. Reluctantly, she gets drawn into this role, and is never able to break out of it. At the abortion clinic, Maggie simultaneously argues with Fiona's sister, who is insisting that Fiona get the abortion, and with the picketers who are shouting at Fiona not to. Finally, Maggie convinces Fiona to come home with her to see the (nonexistent) cradle that Jesse is supposed to be building. Maggie sees that she has interrupted the momentum of Fiona's resolve and that it will be too late now for Fiona to muster the will to go back to the abortion clinic. "Oh, tell me I didn't do wrong!" she begs Fiona, as she realizes the enormity of what she has just done (253).

Maggie searches for Jesse's Doctor Spock baby-care book, or the plans for the cradle that he said he was going to build, as tangible proof for Fiona that Jesse cares. Finally, Maggie seizes a bundle of doweling rods that Ira had bought for another purpose and, waving the rods before Fiona, says that they are the spindles for Jesse's cradle. This "white lie" is the beginning of Maggie's pattern of improving upon the facts in order to convince Fiona of Jesse's intentions. Fiona moves in with her in-laws. As with Mary Tell in *Celestial Navigation*, it seems that Fiona covets a mother at least as much as a husband. When it is time to enter the delivery room, Fiona chooses to have Maggie assist her in labor rather than Jesse. Yet there is something fragile about her relationship to Maggie nonetheless.

Fiona and Jesse's daughter Leroy is a wiry, tomboyish seven-year-old. Leroy hasn't seen Maggie, her grandmother, for so long that she has difficulty understanding who she is. To help her remember, Maggie reminds Leroy about the kitten they had when she was three. Leroy is, naturally, more interested in learning about what happened to the kitten than about why Maggie stopped visiting, the realization of which causes

a momentary comic shift in Maggie's perspective on her own importance.

Serena Palermo, Maggie's lifelong best girlfriend, and recent widow
of Max Gill, is the type of gypsyish, vital eccentric that Anne Tyler loves
to write about. She is one of a long line of such characters—Alberta of
Earthly Possessions, Muriel of *The Accidental Tourist*, and Daphne of *Saint
Maybe*—each so different from what is known of Tyler's own persona.
For her husband's funeral, Serena wears a bright red dress with a black
shawl, and the memorial service features the song "I Want You, I Love
You, I Need You" and a reading from Kahlil Gibran's poetic *The Prophet*,
which was a best-seller in the nonconformist culture of the 1960s. Serena's deceased mother, Anita, remembered by Maggie as a middle-aged
single parent with skin-tight, red toreador pants, represents the same
principle of tenacious vitality. Another of this character type is seen in
Mary Tell's mother-in-law in *Celestial Navigation*. But in *Breathing Lessons*,
we are forced to witness the crucifixion of Anita as a type, once so
spunky in her vulgar tastes, reduced in old age to the common denom-
inator and revealed heartbreakingly as a sad-faced clown (332). In the
few brief strokes with which Anita's character and tragic outcome are
drawn, we see a connection to the simultaneously pedestrian and por-
tentious figure of the Fat Lady, as developed by J. D. Salinger. In Salinger's *Franny and Zooey*, one of the Glass brothers explains: "Don't you
know that goddam secret yet? And don't you know—listen to me,
now—don't you know who that Fat Lady really is? . . . Ah, buddy. It's
Christ Himself" (202).

STYLISTIC DEVICES

This novel is a masterpiece of comic writing. There is more comedy
in the various dialogues, descriptions, and interior monologues than can
be cataloged here. But, to take one example, Anne Tyler gets almost
endless comic effects out of the opening incident of the auto accident.
The day starts with Maggie picking up the newly repaired car from the
auto body shop and promptly crashing it into a Pepsi truck just as she
is driving it out the door. Tyler seems to be caricaturizing herself, with
her often confessed fears of merging on the freeway

To compound the irony, Maggie has managed to hit the one spot on
the car that has never yet been dented. Next, we witness Ira's nonverbal
reaction to the damage. Inspecting the car with a pleased look, he sud-

denly spies the bruised fender and fixes Maggie with a sorrowful gaze. Finally, there is the verbal reaction to Maggie's lame excuse that she accidentally hit the gas pedal: "How could you mix up the brake with the gas pedal? . . . I mean a brake is more or less *reflex*" (8).

Another very comical image occurs when a thief snatches Maggie's pocketbook in the dead of winter and tries to escape on the treacherously icy sidewalk. The thief moves along at a "snail's pace" with Maggie inching behind in pursuit, the two of them resembling "those mimes who can portray a speedy stride while making no progress at all" (134).

Anne Tyler also reworks the comic premise of Abbott and Costello's "Who's on First?" routine during the family's disastrous outing to the horse races where the one spectator asks the other about what Maggie said during the family argument:

> "What'd she say?"
> "Nothing."
> "She did say something. I saw her lips move."
> "She said, 'Nothing.' "
> "But I thought I saw—" (281)

Storytelling, mimicking the rhythms of oral history, is the predominant mode of exposition in the novel. There is some straight-ahead narration, but mostly the characters tell each other stories or reminisce to themselves. Some of the stories are layered, like Ira's story about the disastrous family outing to Harborplace with his mentally retarded sister, Dorrie: the thread of the story is dropped, then picked up again later, and a deeper layer of meaning is unravelled. At first, Ira can only remember that Dorrie's feelings "somehow" got hurt (171), so that the outing turned out badly, just as he had predicted it would. But later, the mists of memory part, and Ira realizes it was he who had ruined it for Dorrie by deflating her fantasies with his usual ill-timed note of soul-killing "realism."

Stylistically, Anne Tyler can often express a complex idea in an economical turn of phrase. She writes that the Morans overslept and had to drink "faucet coffee" (3). Those two words immediately evoke the atmosphere of Maggie madly rushing about and Ira making do with a tasteless cup of instant coffee fixed with hot water straight from the tap. Later, she describes a subtle shift in the nonverbal atmosphere of a conversation as "a kind of alteration of rhythm" in the room (197).

Certain images recur in the text. For example, a red wig serves as a symbolic element that binds several characters together: Ira's sister Junie; Maggie; and Serena's mother, Anita. Maggie gets the wig for the agoraphobic Junie, to enable her to overcome her anxieties and go out in public. Later, when Ira decrees they should no longer visit Leroy, Maggie borrows the wig to wear on her "spy trips" to Cartwheel so that she can watch her granddaughter without being recognized. Finally a different wig, made out of red yarn, is made by Maggie as part of a clown costume for Anita to wear on her first night in the nursing home. But Maggie's plan backfires, and Anita ends up looking foolish and pathetic.

The wearing of the wig is also an image of the author, Anne Tyler, who wants to "live more than one life" and who camouflages herself among her various fictional creations each of whom contains a scrap of her identity. This theme of disguise is developed in more detail in an earlier novel, *Morgan's Passing*, where the central character keeps a closetful of costumes, goes on spy trips to watch a young woman and her baby, and engages in elaborate role playing with various assumed identities.

THEMES

There are two fundamental themes in *Breathing Lessons*. One is whether some kind of linear progress is possible in life and in relationships. The second, related theme, is whether there is some objective and realistic perspective by which one can get a handle on in life, or whether one is left trying to grasp at an irreducible core of mystery and subjectivity.

Concerning the first theme, the notion of progress, the very title *Breathing Lessons* is wonderfully evocative, encompassing multiple layers of meaning. At face value the notion of "breathing lessons" is an absurdity. After all, breathing is the most fundamental activity of life. Who would seek a curriculum for an activity so thoroughly natural and spontaneous? The very notion conjures up an image of trying too hard, of adding an unnecessary layer of activity that clutters up the transparent simplicity of life's basic functions.

But at another level, the idea of breathing lessons makes a certain kind of sense. Though the breath is purely reflexive at birth, by maturity one becomes more conscious of its pulse. In its constantly changing rhythms, breathing reflects the play of the emotions and of variations in the body's vitality and health. For some people, patterns of anxiety and tension greatly distort the natural flow of breathing. And when they notice their difficulty in breathing, it can compound the problem by generating even more anxiety and tension. Such people need corrective lessons in breathing. Yet, paradoxically, the "lessons" involve unlearning—freeing the breath rather than imposing an "ideal" pattern on it, as Jesse tries to do during labor and delivery, when he tells Fiona she is not breathing "right."

Breath itself can be a metaphor for a much larger set of exchanges between the person and the world. Breathing represents an impulse to live. The act of taking in a new breath expresses some sense of hope that is built into the body at a cellular level. Whether it be emotions, relationships, or any other level, there is a dance of taking in and letting go, occurring in a particular rhythm. Often Anne Tyler's characters get stuck on one side of this cycle. They fixate on inhaling through the accumulation of clutter, or alternatively they long to exhale and jettison everything that has been accumulated. They impose upon themselves ideal pictures of how things should be, thereby distorting the natural flow of events.

One final element of the breath, which is particularly relevant to Anne Tyler's view of the world, is its circularity. Ira notices this about his marriage, the same "affectionate passwords" and "gestures of support" but in addition "the same old resentments dragged up year after year" (163). In Tyler's novels time tends to be circular, and characters often seem to end up more or less where they started, although there is usually some inner change that has occured. Similarly, the breath is essentially repetitive, despite minor variations in its rhythm. And yet, despite this circularity, each inhalation can be experienced as vital, fresh, and new.

Anne Tyler recounts a series of parables for us. There is the parable of the dog, which is a bit like Plato's simile of the cave, only homelier. Mr. Otis's dog, Bessie, the "smartest" dog he ever owned, loved to play ball. But if the ball landed on the kitchen chair the dog would stick her snout through the spindles of the chair back and whine, never realizing that it could just come around the chair and grab the ball from in front (177). Similarly, we readers, like Maggie and Ira, Jesse and Fiona are caught in repetitive patterns that obscures our view of our own freedom, like the mist obscuring the view at Harborplace during Ira and Dorrie's family outing. If only the characters could see the situation clearly. But what is clarity? Is it that disconnected sense of strangeness that Serena describes as stepping "outside your own life" (55)? Is it Ira's cramped, cautious "realism"? Is it Maggie's optimism that always seems to get ahead of itself?

"I mean think if we all did that! Mistook our dreams for real life," (158) Maggie exclaims, unconscious of the irony in her speech. For this is, in effect, what Maggie does. Like Don Quixote, she projects her fantasies onto life and tilts at windmills. At first, Maggie seems deluded, but gradually we see that Ira's lack of dreams is just as false, if not more so. By some strange, intuitive logic, Maggie's fictions are true and Ira's realities are false. Even Ira must admit that Maggie gets along in the world better than he. She collects strays who are attracted to her warmth and openness.

The parable of Mr. Otis's tire seems to confirm that Maggie's fantasies may be more real than Ira's realism. Although Maggie falsely yelled to Mr. Otis that his tire was loose, it seems she may have unintentionally hit on the truth, since his wheel does appear to wobble when Ira test-drives it. The reader is left in uncertainty about this, however, suggesting that ultimately no objective verification is possible, and we must live with a sense of mystery at the limits. Do Jesse and Fiona still love each other? Does it make sense for them to get back together? Would it be possible? Ira the realist says no; Maggie thinks yes. But we simply don't know. The fact that Maggie's attempt at a reunion failed does not necessarily mean that she sees wrongly or that Ira is right. The situation is more complicated than that.

Maggie, more than any of the other characters, represents the truth of the heart. She does not embody it completely, but she is closer to it than anyone else. Ira has a moment of revelation of this truth. He confronts his darkest vision of his family, as hands dragging him down "the way drowning victims drag down whoever tries to rescue them," and he feels trapped and unable to be free of them (172). Shortly after this bleak moment, he has a memory of the outing at Harborplace when he felt "pierced" by his sister's sadness and realized that the "true waste" was not the energy he spends on supporting these people but his "failure to notice how he loved them." In the next instant, "the feeling had faded," and he forgot his insight, which would no doubt be repeated and forgotten again in the future (180–181).

AN EXISTENTIAL READING OF *BREATHING LESSONS*

As discussed in Chapter 4, existentialism has as its starting point a concern with the human experience as lived in its concreteness and immediacy and a valuing of the authenticity that comes from consciously acknowledging the ultimate sources of human anxiety: the enormity and uncertainty of life, the inevitable shadow of our death, and the inescapability of choice. According to existentialism, each individual must creatively shape a meaning in life—a meaning that is lived and felt and that cannot be reduced to a set of platitudes or an abstract system of certainties. The accent is on *being*, which is an activity of the total person, rather than on an objectified knowing or possessing since these modes of activity can be misused as distractions from the central challenge of existence.

At first glance, Anne Tyler's comedic storytelling shares nothing with the bleak atmosphere and extreme situations of the prototypical existential novels. But a closer examination shows that in its own fashion Tyler's storytelling does engage the central questions of the human condition. *Breathing Lessons* shows how characters establish provisional, makeshift meanings because ultimate meaning is ungraspable. It demonstrates that meaning is not something apart from life but is inherent in the circular and seemingly absurd patterns that form the fabric of one's life. It is the clear seeing of this tissue of absurdities and contradictions that creates the preconditions for meaning to arise, through a spontaneous act of self-awareness. While such clear vision may not arise for the characters, it is a possibility for the reader who sees his or her own expectations and disillusionments mirrored in theirs.

The characters confront failure, old age, and the inevitability of death without the consolation of the gratuitous epiphanies enjoyed by Pearl Tull while working in her garden (in *Dinner at the Homesick Restaurant*). Maggie, as with Camus's *Sisyphus* (1955), overcomes her disappointment simply by beginning once again to roll the boulder up the mountain, as we see her doing at the end of the novel.

Yet the possibility of epiphany peeps tantalizingly out from behind the backdrop after Max's funeral. There is a moment when Maggie gazes at an old stone house, and it seems to shimmer momentarily, dissolving in "a gentle radiant haze" before it "regrouped itself and grew solid again." Maggie concludes that it was some "trick of light or heat" (126), but in fact it is a hint of freedom: the freedom of stepping out of one's usual life, of what Annie Dillard (1975) calls "another way of seeing," the secret of seeing "truly" (33–34), a tantalizing glimpse that passes almost unnoticed, the way Mr. Otis's dog fails to see that nothing really prevents it from getting the ball.

According to her husband, Maggie is not taking life seriously, regarding it as some kind of rehearsal that offers "second and third chances to get it right" (129). But Maggie does take it seriously. She is well aware of death, and it reminds her that she's "living a real life" (69). Ira seems to evade the awareness of death. He doesn't understand how Maggie can tolerate the impermanence of her work with the elderly patients in the nursing home—the absence of "permanent results" (133). He apparently has the illusion that there is some project that one can work on that isn't impermanent. Ira criticizes Maggie for operating moment to moment though all of his long-range planning has come pretty much to naught, starting with his teenage plan of going to medical school. Without some moments of authenticity, some moments of stepping out of the pattern of one's life, death reduces the person to what Max is at his funeral, namely, "a walking suit" remembered in the eulogy as a booster of the Church's furnace fund.

The novel deals with one day in the life of Maggie Moran. This may seem to be an overly confined canvas on which to paint a portrait of Maggie's life. But remember that Anne Tyler is a practitioner of the art of looking deeply into one thing, rather than scattering one's attention over many things. Just as breathing can be a metaphor for all the processes of giving and receiving in life, so too this single day is a microcosm of the whole of Maggie's span of years. And Maggie is, in a sense, Everywoman. Although the specific content may be different, her ups and downs mirror mine and yours. In the course of the day, Maggie cycles from elation to depression and back again several times. She faces unpleasant truths about herself and flees from them again. In her memory she revisits many significant moments in her life, and imaginatively she projects herself into the future. She deals with friends and family members across the span of generations, representing every station of life's progress, from the portals of childhood to the anteroom of death. In the course of the day, a complete cycle is traversed that portrays in miniature the cycle of the months and years, like a grownup version of Anne Tyler's favorite children's book, *The Little House* (see Chapter 2).

Three interrelated themes in *Breathing Lessons* reflect the existential sensibility: the presence of the absurd in life, the ungraspability of meaning, and the inevitability of failure, old age, and death. The absurd permeates the novel in many ways. The incident with Mr. Otis's tire and the episode of Maggie at the abortion clinic are two of the more obvious examples, which have been discussed earlier in this chapter. As for the ungraspability of life, the novel demonstrates this elusiveness in two ways: the impossibility of stopping time, and the uncertainty of meaning. The fleeting nature of time is represented by the funeral for Serena's husband at which Serena unsuccessfully tries to recapture the past, and by Maggie's failed attempts to undo the damage that has been done to Fiona and Jesse's relationship.

The ungraspability of meaning points to the fact that there are no fixed meanings to events. Each character's interpretations are relative and provisional constructions of truth and are not ultimate. For example, is Jesse a self-absorbed deadbeat? or a caring, vulnerable person? Whose view captures the "real" Jesse? Maggie's? Ira's? Mrs. Stuckey's? Jesse's view of himself? Though each of these views has a certain validity from the frame of reference of the person who holds them, the views say as much about the person who holds them as they do about Jesse. None of them represents the ultimate or final truth—not even Jesse's view of himself. Why? Because Jesse is an open-ended subjectivity and therefore cannot be completely summed up solely by the history of his deeds or reduced to an object capable of precise classification.

Even one's own opinions are not graspable, because they are not stable, unless the person chooses to impose stability by ignoring the actual fluctuations in his or her views. Fiona's view of Jesse is constantly changing throughout the events narrated in the novel. Fiona is unable to hold onto one fixed, unchanging interpretation of Jesse's actions. Similarly, Ira cannot maintain ownership of the insights that come to him. When recovering certain forgotten memories about Harborplace, he is struck with a sudden realization about his love for his family, but then forgets it. Since he doesn't "own" this momentary insight, it can be swept away again in the flow of mental events. These experiences escape memory; they cannot be retained intellectually as a living experience. They can only be lived and thus integrated with one's concrete existence.

Similarly, one cannot hide from one's freedom with such notions as "falling in love" or "destiny." This is reflected in the conversation between Maggie and Serena shortly before Serena's wedding. Maggie asks how she can be certain she's chosen the right man. Serena replies that she's had other boyfriends before that she loved just as much as Max, but she hadn't felt it was "time" to marry before. Maggie is surprised. She thought each person has only one soulmate whom they are destined to recognize and fall in love with. But now she sees that she is not "in the hands of fate" as she had imagined, but can wrest herself free at any time (113).

All one's constructed meanings are threatened by the central fact of existence—the inevitability of one's own death. The characters have varying reactions to death. Maggie, who works in a nursing home, is relatively comfortable with aging and, by implication, death. With Ira it is a different case. When he sees the elderly Mr. Otis's bumbling behavior, Ira feels "utterly despairing" (149). He appears to fear old age and consequently does not face the truth of his own aging. Even though Ira notes that Mr. Otis is not so much older than he is himself, the implications of this do not register emotionally. His own aging and death still seem relatively remote to Ira. In the same way, the late middle-aged mourners at Max's funeral reassure each other that they all look so much younger than their parents did at the same age.

This is not uncommon, the existentialists say. Most of us try to dull the awareness of death because of a sense of dread. Yet the awareness of fragility, vulnerability, and death is the one thing that gives urgency and poignancy to living. When Maggie thinks of Max's death, she is suddenly grateful for the sights and sensations of the present moment, even the feeling of the "sticky vinyl upholstery plastered to the backs of her arms" (15). Moreover, it was death that hastened Maggie's courtship. When she mistakenly thought Ira had been killed, she realized for the first time that she cared for him. Again, at the funeral, confronted with Max's death, she feels herself falling in love with Ira again and tries to seduce him in Serena's bedroom.

Near the end of the novel, after Fiona and Leroy have again abandoned her, Maggie feels utterly without hope. This is an emotional state of negation and feels like the equivalent of a death. But by confronting these painful feelings and passing through them to the other side, Maggie regains her sense of life and hope. Similarly, after Ira fully experiences his claustrophobic sense that his family is killing him, he is momentarily free to experience his underlying love for them.

At the end of the novel, Maggie sees that the approach of death is like the endgame of solitaire. So many options have already been spent. There are fewer choices left, and one is more conscious and present when making them. (Although it was probably not the author's intention, Ira's solitaire game in this scene could be seen as a parody of the knight's chess match with death in Ingmar Bergman's film *The Seventh Seal*.)

Maggie's strategy is to persist in trying to reestablish a lost dream. Ira's strategy is not to get involved. Serena's is to give up—"Let it all go! . . . What a relief! Discard, discard! Throw out the toys in the basement." (83)

Mr. Otis responds to death in a different way from all of these. His nephew Lamont tries to persuade him to apologize to his wife by arguing that one of them will eventually die and the survivor will regret that they acted "so ugly," throwing themselves away on spitefulness. Mr. Otis replies, "Could be what you throw away is all that really counts" (175–176).

Saint Maybe
(1991)

"Anything I've ever written I've wanted to know how much dependency is allowed between people, how much right people have to want to change other people."

Anne Tyler, "Olives Out of a Bottle"

Saint Maybe, published in 1991, was a *New York Times* Notable Book of the Year and a Main Selection of the Book-of-the-Month Club. Chapter 5, "People Who Don't Know the Answers," appeared as a short story in the *New Yorker* (26 August 1991).

Anne Tyler has commented that the Middle Eastern graduate students in the novel who are so disastrously fascinated by American gadgets were inspired by an Iranian in-law of hers.

POINT OF VIEW

As in *Celestial Navigation* and *Dinner at the Homesick Restaurant*, the narrative events are related in a neutral, authorial voice from several distinct points of view. Ian's father Doug has a chapter. Lucy's three children—Agatha, Thomas, and Daphne—each have a chapter. And there is a chapter that seems to be from the combined view of the three children. Ian's narrative understanding dominates the remainder of the book.

Lucy's story is narrated primarily through Ian's eyes but also in part through Agatha's. Within Ian's narrative several other characters express their divergent views about Lucy. Ian's brother Danny and sister Claudia; his girlfriend, Cicely; his parents, Doug and Bee; one of Lucy's friends Mrs. Myrdal and Lucy's ex–mother-in-law, Mrs. Millet—each has his or her own particular view of Lucy. In fact, the two topics about which the greatest number of opinions are expressed in the novel are the nature of Lucy and the enigma of God.

PLOT

As with its predecessors, *Saint Maybe* is set in Anne Tyler's home town of Baltimore. In the opening pages, we are introduced to the Bedloes, an "ideal, apple-pie household" with "golden"-hued children (1–2). The older son, Danny, was captain of the football team, and the younger son, Ian, is dating Cicely Brown, the sweetest, prettiest girl in his class. Tyler explicitly compares the Bedloes to an idealized television family. But there is a difference. Unlike "Ozzie and Harriet" of the 1950's situation comedies, the Bedloes do not live in a homogeneously white middle-class neighborhood. The house down the street is inhabited by an ever-changing procession of foreign graduate students from the Middle East whose ongoing mishaps and ethnic antics provide a kind of running gag, "I Love Lucy" style.

The Bedloes' picture-perfect view of their existence is based on matriarch Bee Bedloe's well-practiced capacity for denial of the flawed and tragic dimensions of life. Under her tutelage, the family philosophy is that everything about their life is wonderful and things will always turn out fine. Of course, such a filtered experience of life cannot be successfully maintained over time. Sickness and death cannot be perpetually denied access, and once admitted, they undermine the illusion of seamless continuity at the surface level of life. The first visible chink in the family myth occurs on the day when Danny presents his new girlfriend and fiancée, Lucy Dean, to the family. Danny, the golden boy, the all-American high school athlete, has somehow become engaged to a divorced woman who has two children and who waits on tables at the Fill 'Er Up Café. Bee and Doug have barely digested this shocking piece of news, before their son and this divorced woman have arranged a hasty marriage. The reason for the haste becomes apparent when their new baby, Daphne, is born a wee bit earlier than propriety would allow.

Although Danny's brother, Ian, has a girlfriend who is his own age—Cicely—Ian is nonetheless fascinated by Lucy's womanliness and glamor. Following an awkward incident in which his passion is aroused, Ian begins avoiding Lucy and increasingly finds fault with her and tears her down in his mind, never acknowledging any lurking sense of guilt or shame within himself. He begins to imagine that every time Lucy asks him to babysit it is so she can go out on some secret tryst with her lover, who Ian imagines has been supplying Lucy with her beautiful new clothes. Only much later does he learn that she shoplifts her clothes.

When Lucy is out on one of her excursions, Danny suddenly appears, feeling happy after a few beers with his buddies. Ian, who is baby sitting, as much as tells him he's a cuckold and a fool. Minutes later, Danny accelerates his car into a stone wall and is killed. Although Bee and Doug believe it's an accident, Ian knows it to be a suicide and blames himself. The tragedy is compounded when Lucy begins descending into a deep depression. Finally, Lucy dies of an overdose of tranquilizers.

Now the three children are completely orphaned. Unable to trace down Lucy's family of origin or her ex-husband's family, Bee Bedloe seems saddled with two youngsters and an infant—a task she is ill suited for now that her oldest son's death has broken her spirit and arthritis has begun to set in to her joints.

Ian is distraught and confused about what to do, when he stumbles into the Church of the Second Chance, a store front ministry founded by the gangly, gentle Reverend Emmett. He moves back into his parents' house, becomes an apprentice to a highly skilled furniture maker, leads a celibate and single lifestyle and occupies himself with the children and the church. After several years of bearing this burden, Ian secretly begins to explore avenues of escape. He impulsively hires a private investigator who discovers that the children have no living relatives with whom they could be placed. The investigator also enlightens Ian as to the secrets of Lucy's difficult and deprived early life.

The novel could easily have been ended here—in Chapter 6—now that Ian has cleared up the mystery of Lucy's origins and realizes that her infidelity to his brother was a figment of his overheated imagination.

At the end of Chapter 6, Ian angrily asks Reverend Emmett how much longer he must wait before he will be forgiven. The plain-spoken pastor startles Ian into silence by telling him he's got it all backward: it is not that Ian has to be forgiven; rather it is that Ian has to forgive. He must learn to forgive Lucy and his brother Danny. Rather than end with this revelation, the book goes on for another four chapters. The children grow up and move out, and in the process try various schemes to find a wife for Ian, who has increasingly become an eccentric, aging bachelor. After his mother, Bee, dies, the house falls into disrepair until Agatha hires a Clutter Counselor, Rita diCarlo, to organize the household. She falls in love with Ian, marries him, and bears him a son. As the novel closes, Ian feels spiritually connected to Danny and Lucy, as though they are some-how celebrating the birth of this child with him.

As was mentioned earlier, the final third of the novel seems less tightly constructed than the first two-thirds. Critic Joseph Voelker (1992) is of the opinion that Anne Tyler was experimenting here with a new type of fictional narrative—"the chronicle"—that tries to be more faithful to the shapeless manner in which the flow of events is experienced in everyday life. Yet there does seem to be a certain pattern that can be loosely dis-cerned under the surface.

Consistent with Anne Tyler's interest in a circular or spiraling notion of time, some of the key events of the first two-thirds of the book are echoed in the last third. For instance, Chapter 7 opens with the intro-duction of Ian to Miss Ariana Pennington, whose old-fashioned glamor echoes Ian's first impression of Lucy in Chapter 1. In Chapter 8, as in Chapter 3, Ian must again make a life-changing decision about his com-mitment to the church—in this case it is whether he should train to become the new pastor. And in Chapter 9, after Ian's mother's death the household descends into a level of chaos similar to what occurred in Lucy's house in Chapter 2, shortly before Lucy's death.

Chapter 9 also revisits the diminished family Thanksgiving and Christ-mas celebrations, which was a feature introduced in Chapter 3. Finally, Rita's pregnancy and the birth of Ian's son in Chapter 10 are clearly meant to recall the events following Danny's wedding, and the Christ-mas celebration in this chapter reestablishes the state of affairs at the very beginning of the novel, with its elaborate holiday get-togethers.

HUMOR

The novel is seasoned with various forms of humor. Some of it is subtle. Cooking her first meal for Ian, Cicely has stuffed every menu item in an attempt to make it fancy: "Flank steaks stuffed with mushrooms, baked potatoes stuffed with cheese, and green peppers stuffed with . . ." (elipsis in original) (43).

There is generational humor. Daphne, a post–baby boomer, considers rock groups like Led Zeppelin and the Doors to be "classical" music.

The loaded minefields in relationships can be funny. When Cicely gets upset because Ian doesn't seem sufficiently interested in the fancy dinner she is preparing, he hastily assures her that he has been looking forward to the meal all day long. But this also turns out to be the wrong response: "Don't say that!" Cicely replies, "I'm afraid you'll be disappointed" (44).

Wordplay is funny, as in the name Mac McLintock, or when church member Sister Clara introduces a family member as "my brother, Brother James" (335).

Some of the humor is ruthless, biting irony. On the eve of Danny's unforeseen death, Ian considers it the "biggest night" in his life because he hopes to have his first sexual encounter with Cicely (48). He is right. This will be a "big" night. In fact, it will be determinative of his future—but in an entirely opposite direction from what he imagined.

There is also humor in the way in which children subvert parents and other authority figures. A tiny vignette of Anne Tyler's illustrates this subversion: at the church's summer Bible camp two boys circumvent the pedagogical intent of the camp; they utilize the plastic Bible figurines for their own purposes, designating some of the figures as ranchers and others as cattle rustlers.

Some of the humor is simply slapstick. First, the foreign students accidentally set the car on fire by faultily installing a radio. They are reluctant to call the fire department because they don't want to "keep disturbing them" (186). Later, the car is crushed in the middle, like a discarded beer can, by the newly installed electronic garage door closer.

In the most emotionally charged scenes, Anne Tyler generally plays the pathos straight, but in one instance she dips into a kind of parody reminiscent of the black humor of David Lynch. Perhaps she is trying to signal, through a hint of irony, that she is not writing a soap opera. In the depressing chapter in which we watch Lucy's emotional disintegration veer toward suicide, the author inserts some over-the-top dialogue into Lucy's mouth: "You think I enjoy this? Watching my weight . . . never letting my guard down, always on the lookout for split ends?" (70).

STYLISTIC DEVICES

In Chapter 2 of *Saint Maybe*, Anne Tyler uses the device of letting the reader see Lucy's depression through the children's eyes. This is one of the most effective devices in the novel. The children's limited comprehension of Lucy's mood swings only increases the pathos of this section as we sense the gulf between our own understanding of Lucy's actions and the children's frightened bafflement. It is as though we are inhabiting two spaces at once: the wide-eyed vulnerability of early childhood as filtered through the bittersweet wisdom of a mature sensibility. The reader observes, through Agatha's eyes, the ups and downs of Lucy's moods: her nervous pacing as her mind struggles to find a way out of her dilemma, her perking up as a new idea comes to her, a burst of energy as she rallies her determination. When her new idea also turns out to be a dead end, Lucy is thrown back into a deeper dejection. The children must navigate these sudden changes in the emotional weather as best they can. Agatha is the most aware of her mother's moods, though not always comprehending the causes behind them. She knows when it is time to lay low and represses her own needs at those times. As she lies in bed at night, listening to her mother move about the house, every sound she hears has meaning. The sound of a match being struck and of her mother exhaling a cigarette: Agatha has learned that her mother only smokes when she is upset. Or the sound of her mother's pacing back and forth, which makes Agatha long for the sound of the cover being popped off the pill bottle. At least when her mother takes the pills, she isn't so restless. And Agatha has learned to gauge the depth of her mother's unconsciousness after she has exhausted herself with pacing and smoking and has drugged herself with sleeping pills. She can differentiate between a "two-pill nap" and a "three-pill" one and knows how to wake her mother with a Coca-Cola into which she has stirred a spoonful of instant coffee.

Dreams are woven into the narrative to reveal the unseen and mysterious interconnections among the characters. Shortly after Danny's death, Agatha has a nightmare in which Ian rattles the Parcheesi dice and then rudely flings them straight into her face. Upon awakening, Agatha realizes that the stimulus for the dream was the sound of her mother rattling her pill bottle. Agatha does not know that it was Ian's words that sent Danny to his death. Yet her dream encodes the fact that it was Ian who launched their bad luck through what he himself characterizes as a "handful of tossed-off words" (96). Danny's restless spirit seems to be trying to send Ian cryptic messages in dreams until the day when Ian joins Second Chance and decides to take care of Danny's orphaned children. That night, Ian dreams that Danny is helping him carry a very heavy load and is smiling into Ian's eyes the whole time. From that moment on, he stops dreaming about Danny.

Anne Tyler often lets minor observations carry a larger significance. An example is the way in which Ian, now in his forties, constructs the cradle for the child he is expecting. This is the first time, in all his years in the wood shop, that he has departed from working with straight lines. Until now, he has avoided making pieces with curves that required "eye judgement, personal opinion" (347). This is a metaphor for Ian's philosophy of life after Danny and Lucy's death: stick to the straight and narrow way mapped out by the church and avoid the risks of anything that might take him off that course. As Daphne said, he had become, "Mr. Look-Both-Ways" (291). But now, first with Rita, then the baby, he bows to the necessity of going off-road and abandoning himself to uncharted territory.

Anne Tyler seems to be stringing her novels together loosely, as if they were stories within a larger framework. There is a symbolic tie-in between *Saint Maybe* and *Breathing Lessons*, in which Jesse Moran was supposed to make a cradle for his baby daughter but never completed it. The unfinished cradle becomes a central symbol for Jesse's irresponsibility. The symbol of the cradle persists in *Saint Maybe* where Ian accomplishes the self-transformation that Jesse couldn't. He finishes a cradle that is so lovingly constructed that it will endure for several generations.

Other examples of the intertextual connections between the novels include the Bedloes' eating dinner at Ezra Tull's Homesick Restaurant (330) and Ian's hiring of private detective Eli Everjohn, whom the Peck family employed in *Searching for Caleb*. Moreover, in *Dinner at the Homesick Restaurant*, Ruth is a boarder at the Paulsen's rooming house described in *Celestial Navigation*. (The astute reader may also notice that minor characters with the family name Lithincum appear in three of Anne Tyler's novels, although it is not clear whether that was intentional.)

HISTORICAL CONTEXT

Anne Tyler is sometimes criticized for being apolitical and ahistorical. However, in *Saint Maybe* the historical context is glimpsed through the background of the novel. The Vietnam war, for instance, is alluded to several times. A woman at the church asks for prayers because her son was just killed in a military accident. Bee expresses concern that if Ian drops out of college he will be drafted into the service. The war flashes past the corner of the reader's eye again, almost subliminally, during an episode in which Ian is talking to his parents. His mother looks up from the evening news. The television is showing a sky filled with bomber planes. There is almost a full page of dialogue, and then Ian notices that the images of the bombers have been replaced by a moisturizer commercial. There is no further comment on this; the images on the television are not identified as war footage; nor is the war named. However, in typical Anne Tyler understatement these two simple sentences could provoke many ideas about viewer desensitization, commercialization of violence, an insular preoccupation with the private sphere over the public, and the connections between capitalism and war. As usual, Anne Tyler leaves it for us to sort out.

The era is also one of countercultural fads and trends. Daphne becomes a vegetarian, Agatha eats cruciferous vegetables and sprouts, Cicely substitutes organic honey for sugar, Thomas buys a special healing crystal for his sister, Lucy sometimes goes to a palm reader, Ian gets involved in a storefront church. Mrs. Jordan expresses the opinion that so many new alternative religions are sprouting up that she's afraid she'll fall "hopelessly behind" (191). This interest in the alternative fringe is another recurrent area of novelistic examination for Anne Tyler. And here again, as in her references to political events, it can be difficult to discern her intent. Beginning with *Searching for Caleb*, where Justine Peck is a fortune teller who tries casting the *I Ching* by using uncooked spaghetti as a substitute for divining sticks, to *Ladder of Years*, where Eliza constantly talks about reincarnation and burns healing herbs around the house, Anne Tyler has a habit of presenting these nonmainstream activities in a manner that appears to be affectionately tongue-in-cheek.

CHARACTERS

Ian Bedloe is the protagonist of the novel. At the beginning of the novel, he is seventeen, and by the end he is in his forties. The novel is about his odyssey to overcome the guilt that binds him in a very intimate sense to his deceased sister-in-law, Lucy Dean. Long after her death and throughout most of the novel, Ian is haunted by both his attraction to

Lucy—which he pushes out of his awareness—and his condemnation of her.

During the course of Ian's long bachelorhood, he finds himself stirred by women who physically resemble Lucy: the children's teacher Ariana Pennington who looks "brightly colored" (251) like Lucy and a dark-haired foreign woman who wears the type of seamed stockings that he found so attractive on Lucy (11). In each case, Ian immediately shuts the door on his feelings of attraction.

Even near the end of the novel, over twenty years after her death, Ian still feels drawn to Lucy and tries to distance himself by analyzing how out of date her sixties clothing seems. Looking at an old picture of Lucy from the vantage point of his forties, she now seems "preposterously young" to Ian. In the end, he has to admit that he is still no wiser as to "what Lucy's meaning had been in his life" (355).

As he enters his forties, the combination of impending parenthood and middle age fosters new perspectives for Ian. He begins to see life through a longer, transgenerational time span. For the first time, he comprehends Mr. Brandt's prejudice against using nails, preferring a dovetailed joint that will remain tight "for a century" (348). In the construction of his child's cradle, he elevates his craftsmanship to a new level with his seamless joints that will "contract and expand in harmony" no matter what the weather.

Similarly, Ian's religious understanding evolves over time. As a child he sees an illustration of an armored Roman soldier and a bearded old man in a religious storybook. Identifying God with power, he assumes at first that God is the soldier. When Ian joins Church of the Second Chance, he sees God as a severe judge who requires acts of atonement before he will grant forgiveness. It is only much later that he is able to comprehend Reverend Emmet's statement to him that the healing he is seeking is internal.

In the final stage of his religious pilgrimage, Ian is not so much seeking something specific for himself but rather beginning to appreciate the overall pattern of the totality, picturing the world as a "spinning green planet" safely in God's hands, with Ian and his family "small trusting dots among all the other dots" (293).

Lucy Dean Bedloe, Danny's bride, is a small-town girl from the wrong side of the tracks who came searching for a better life in the big city. The child of alcoholics, she was orphaned at a young age (like Daphne) and was reared in a shack by her eccentric aunt. An attractive girl whose aunt was unable to afford the things she needed, Lucy learned to shoplift to fill out her wardrobe, so she was always perfectly color coordinated and accessorized when she went out. In order to camouflage her dirt-poor origins, Lucy always strives for elegance: meals are by candlelight, the food artfully arranged on the plate, the napkins folded into decorative shapes.

Lucy first impresses Ian as a "brightly feathered bird" in the midst of Bedloe drabness (4). She has learned to use her personality and good looks to attract men, but men have a habit of leaving, especially if she gets pregnant. When she met Danny, she was down on her luck and already pregnant, but not yet showing.

With the quirkiness that is Anne Tyler's trademark, Lucy snares Danny's attention when she comes into the post office to mail a bowling ball. Lucy's legacy of advice to her daughter Agatha consists of such maxims as to always prepare red meat for a man's dinner because "it shows you think of them as strong" (80). Although Lucy has a certain spunkiness at times, she lacks the boundless reserves of vitality of a Mary Tell (*Celestial Navigation*) or the "won't take 'no' for an answer" resourcefulness of a Muriel Pritchett (*The Accidental Tourist*), and so is finally unable to endure the repeated blows of life. When her attempt at financial independence through a secretarial career fails, she falls back on trying to attract the attention of a man to support her.

But Lucy tires of expending so much energy to cultivate and perfect an alluring surface. After Danny's death it seems as if some inner core has crumbled away. During the months before Lucy's death Agatha gets the creepy feeling at times that her mother "wasn't there behind her face anymore" (58). What lies in the depths finally emerges to destroy Lucy: a bone-weary depression fueled by memories of an unhappy and poverty-stricken childhood and repeated victimization by men. There is an image of Lucy, just before her death, that symbolizes the contradiction between her image and her inner self. As she finishes mopping up the water from the overflowed toilet, she is standing in Danny's gigantic shoes, her body looking "thin and fragile" in contrast to the enormous shoes she is trying to fill (85).

Daphne Bedloe, Lucy's youngest child, is the one who tugs at Ian's heart the most. Ian rears her practically from infancy, and she bears a stronger physical resemblance to her mother, Lucy, than her brother and sister do. It is she who insists on hanging Lucy's picture on the living room wall, over Agatha's objections. Daphne is Ian's "birthmate," born on the same birthday as he. When Daphne is first presented to Ian as a newborn baby, he feels something deep inside him give way as the baby eyes him with a "thoughtful, considering stare" as though "she *knew* him" (24–25). It is Ian who blinks.

This passage clearly underlines the significance of the relationship between Daphne and Ian, both from the coincidence of their birthdates and the intensity of their first eye-to-eye encounter. Whether the author is suggesting anything beyond that—whether, for instance, she is again toying with the notion of rebirth—is left ambiguous. The phrase "It seemed she knew him" *could* be read as implying that Daphne remembers Ian from a previous incarnation. Or it could simply be a dramatic way of asserting that there is some mysterious, inexplicable sympathy between them, such as exists between Charlotte and the enigmatic refugee woman in *Earthly Possessions*.

The uniqueness of the connection between Ian and Daphne is underscored again in another passage about Ian's tendency to fall asleep in the rocking chair while cradling the infant Daphne. When he awakened, she would be "cooly studying his face," giving him the eerie feeling that it was she who was rocking him (116).

Daphne is one of those Anne Tyler characters who has a sense of clothing as costume, gypsylike in her "tatters and gold thread" (249) She is a risk taker who prefers things to be unfamiliar and enjoys the thrill of not knowing how it will all turn out. She rushes ahead, deliberately exposing herself to falling flat on her face in her headlong attempt to live life to the full. Since early childhood, she had been a strong-willed child who was unshakable once her mind was made up about something. Although she doesn't adhere to the church's no-alcohol rule and is not averse to one-night stands, Daphne in her teens and twenties nevertheless seems to enjoy church services and continues to pitch in for the Saturday Good Works projects. It is Daphne who introduces Ian to Rita, the Clutter Counselor. After Ian and Rita marry and have a baby boy, Daphne becomes Rita's partner in the Clutter Counseling business.

Agatha is Lucy's oldest child from her first marriage. When Lucy plunges into depression, Agatha, age seven, is forced into an early maturity as she tries to fill in as caretaker to both Thomas and Daphne and has to provide reassurance to her own mother: "No, Mama, *you* didn't do anything wrong" (86). Agatha, even at this young age, has moments of seeing things all too clearly—almost through adult eyes—as when she is suddenly struck by the signs of her mother's neglect after Danny's death. With a precocious self-awareness, Agatha notices that she has begun to speak to Thomas in her mother's exasperated tone of voice. When Agatha wishes on a star, it is not a child's self-centered prayer for a new toy but rather for things to "turn out" right and for them all to be "safe" (74). Then, after Lucy's death, when Ian and his parents have taken the children in, Agatha continues to guard the secret of her biological father's identity, hiding all of Lucy's essential papers from the grownups in order to forestall any possibility of being sent away.

In her later years, Agatha bears the marks of having wrestled with the absurdity of her mother's death. A studious, no-nonsense teenager, Agatha becomes a freethinker who can't reconcile the notion of a benevolent God with the existence of tragedy in the world. She also has no use for prettiness, having seen in childhood how her mother's reliance on her charms got her nowhere. For Agatha, such appearances seem inconsequential, although she is mindful of her physical environment and is the one who insists on hiring a clutter counselor to clean up the neglected Bedloe home. True to her childhood character, Agatha remains a take-charge kind of person who generally gets her way. She is married to Stuart, an unusually handsome man, and Daphne suspects it is Agatha's imperviousness to physical attraction that made Stuart fall in love with her. Stuart and Agatha are both physicians, making fistfuls of money in Los Angeles and flying back to Baltimore to be with the family for major holidays.

Thomas, Lucy's middle child, starts life as a scrawny youngster, perpetually starved for affection, wearing the "drugged, veiled gaze of a dedicated thumbsucker" (43). In middle childhood, Agatha is always rolling her eyes in exasperation at Thomas's ignorance and naivete. But by his teenage years, Thomas has a leg up on Agatha socially and feels free to point out her ignorance. Nevertheless, he remains attracted to managerial type of women who boss him around as Agatha did. Still the perpetual boy, he makes a career out of developing educational computer games for children. In other ways, too, his childhood has left its indelible mark on him. He dodges conflict and shrugs off serious questions. This may be a self-protective device left over from the sometimes volatile household he grew up in.

Rita diCarlo, the Clutter Counselor, is twelve years younger than Ian and is a strikingly attractive woman, almost six feet tall, with long, frizzy black hair and a bold manner. A "tough cookie," she likes to wear boots (those symbols of male fearlessness in Lucy's eyes), jeans, and logging shirts and drinks Pabst beer. Rita is an angel of destruction and renewal, preaching the gospel of impermanence. As Ian puts it, her mission is informing people that "their lifelong treasures belonged in the nearest landfill" (344). She helps Ian to realize that people change each other's lives "every day of the year," and consequently such change was nothing to make a "fuss" about (373). This thought, which is the closing line of the novel, echoes the final paragraph of *Earthly Possessions*: "We have been travelling for years. . . . We couldn't stay in one place if we tried" (215).

Reverend Emmett, founder of the Church of the Second Chance, works as a counselor in a girl's school during the day and is a minister on nights and weekends. The son of an Episcopal minister, he followed in his father's footsteps, hoping to earn the elder man's approval. But his reading of the Bible led him to a personal vision of Christianity that ultimately alienated his father from him. Reverend Emmett is an unmarried and lonely man. After his heart attack, he hopes to persuade Ian to train to take over the ministry. He looks forward to having someone working beside him who will call him "Emmett" rather than "Reverend." But Ian ultimately refuses the offer.

THEMES

The larger themes of the novel have to do with impermanence and change, loss and continuity. At the center of the novel is the loss of loved ones through death. More broadly, the narrative covers almost three decades in the life of a multigenerational family, so that loss is constantly occurring through growth and change.

Impermanence can be experienced as threatening and chaotic. People will sometimes grasp at anything that will impose order. Ian feels psychologically dislocated by Danny and Lucy's deaths and their devastating effect on his parents and on the children. He deals with this dislocation by accepting responsibility for the deaths, which creates a kind of orderliness in the situation. Even with the help of Daphne and Reverend Emmett and his own life experiences, it takes Ian over twenty years to come to the realization that his actions did not determine Danny and Lucy's death in any final or ultimate way. His words and deeds were but one small part in a complex, constantly shifting, multidimensional web of causes and effects. Everything is interconnected. It is like the educational computer game that Thomas develops which shows how changing one historical event could affect a hundred others, even ones that seem totally unrelated. People are constantly changing each others lives, and there's no need to make a "fuss" over it (373).

Near the beginning of the novel, in a chapter entitled "The Man Who Forgot How to Fly," a woman tells about her paratrooper son who accidentally jumped out of an aircraft without his parachute. Ian imagines that the parachutist had jumped so often that unconsciously he had begun to assume that it was he who was responsible for his being able to float through the air—and that when he started falling, the parachutist felt "betrayed" by what he had always taken for granted (128).

In a sense, Danny crashed his car because he too "forgot how to fly." The function of this anecdote seems to be to represent the way in which human beings take for granted the world that seems to be presented to them, not realizing that their particular phenomenal reality is ultimately a construction and that life is essentially a high-wire acrobatic act. This echoes Ian's experience in which the supposed reliability of reality fails him: his brother suddenly disappears into a void, his adolescence is shattered, and his family is unalterably transformed as a result of opinions that he expressed which he later learned were false.

One way to deal with the fear of transitoriness and change is to accumulate possessions—a theme that Anne Tyler has explored in other novels, such as *Morgan's Passing* and *Earthly Possessions*. The Bedloes find it hard to ditch the accumulated junk in their house: old letters, unused clothing, and so forth. This dead debris of the vanished past is a kind of illusory safety net that gives the Bedloes a false sense of permanence and stability. But allowed to pile up indefinitely, the belongings eventually fill up all the space and choke off the possibility of anything fresh and new. In addition to the material clutter, there is the psychological "junk" that characters hoard, as with Mr. Kitt who blames all the problems of his life on his fifth-grade teacher. Reverend Emmett calls these the people who "hug their problems to themselves" (247). Rita diCarlo revitalizes the Bedloes by helping them deal with their stale emotional and psychological fixations whose tangible sign is the accumulated physical debris that she clears out of their lives.

Another way of dealing with impermanence is through religion. But to the extent that religion becomes ossified into rigid forms and doctrines, it is susceptible to becoming a form of spiritual clutter. The novel explores the many faces of religion, from the more judgmental and exclusivist creed of the Holy House of the Gospel to the more communitarian beliefs of the Church of the Second Chance. The fundamental orientation of the Church of the Second Chance is humanitarian in contrast to the more judgmental and exclusivist type of doctrine represented by Eli Everjohn of the Holy House of the Gospel. Scratching his head in wonderment over Ian's willingness to raise another man's children, Eli proclaims that he "hates" those deadbeat dads who don't pay their child support. Then, noticing the tone of self-righteousness in this stance, he dresses it up in religiously acceptable language: "Or, no, not hate. Forget hate. The Bible cautions us not to hate. But I . . . pity them, yes, I surely do" (207).

Whereas Eli's church commands him to go out and preach to others, Ian states that the Church of the Second Chance feels that the believers' charitable manner of living constitutes their missionary activity. Ian's position reflects a historical tendency among many Quakers to express their faith through social service and social reform as opposed to the more evangelical, fundamentalist churches who focus on the conversion of unbelievers. The sympathies of the author, herself of Quaker background, clearly lie with Ian in this exchange.

Despite the genteel social connections of Reverend Emmett's mother, the Church of the Second Chance occupies an essentially marginal position in society. An example is its summer Bible Camp, which Ian's parents call the "Holy Roller" Camp. The "camp" is in Sister Myra's house and backyard, and the number of "campers" is so small that all the age groups are mixed together. Its swimming pool is the corrugated plastic kind you fill with a hose. The children are terrified of the lifeguard, Sister Audrey, a teenager who is making amends for having abandoned her newborn baby in a dumpster.

In the novel, Anne Tyler refuses to side completely with the believers or with the secularists. But she simultaneously points to the untenability of refusing to take sides. The marginalization of authentic religious belief is underscored. The majority of the population consists of the frankly secular, or those who belong to churches requiring only nominal adherence. This marginalization of religion is contrasted with the pervasiveness of modern consumerism, which has become the unofficial "religion" of the United States; the populace focuses on the consumption of entertainment and of tangible commodities.

Television, the symbol of passive consumerism, has become so much a part of American culture that it cleaves deeper than belief or nonbelief in a Supreme Being. Reverend Emmett confesses to Ian that when he founded the church he toyed with prohibiting television but did not do so because he was afraid he wouldn't get any members. In contrast to commercialized entertainment are the more enduring works of individual creativity as symbolized by Ian's furniture making that goes beyond the merely utilitarian.

Despite the allusion to sainthood in the title of this novel, Ezra Tull (*Dinner at the Homesick Restaurant*) with his churchlike restaurant is probably closer than Ian to the usual notion of a saint. However, both of them are creative persons who lift their crafts into art forms. And in an age of unbelief, the artist may be the closest stand-in for the saint.

A FEMINIST READING

Feminist literary criticism began with the publication of Virginia Woolf's *A Room of One's Own* (1929), which attacked the prevalent male prejudice against women writers—attitudes that had forced George Sand and George Eliot to adopt masculine-sounding authorial names. Woolf defended the concept of "difference" in women's writing: "it is obvious that the values of women differ very often from the values which have been made by the other sex. . . . Yet it is the masculine values that prevail. . . . This is an important book, the critic assumes, because it deals with war. This is an insignificant book because it deals with the feelings of women in a drawing-room" (76–77).

Feminist literary criticism gained impetus in the United States from the development of the women's liberation movement in the 1960s, one of whose germinal texts was *The Second Sex* (1949) by the French existentialist Simone de Beauvoir. Betty Friedan's popular and accessible book *The Feminine Mystique* (1963) was also influential. In the wake of its publication, there was the formation of the National Organization of Women (N.O.W.), the founding of the feminist magazine *Ms.* edited by Gloria Steinem, and the grassroots formation of women's consciousness-raising groups for discussion, self-help, and political action, culminating in the unsuccessful attempt to pass an Equal Rights Amendment (ERA) to the Bill of Rights of the Constitution. This burst of activity inspired a global movement that has resulted in international women's conferences, the passage of United Nations resolutions on the rights of women and children, and indigenous movements against female genital mutilation and other practices that affect the status of women in other parts of the world.

Feminist literary criticism is one aspect of this broad spectrum of activity. As an American phenomenon, such criticism burst into public view with the publication of Kate Millett's *Sexual Politics* (1970), which attacked the sexist stereotyping of women in works by such male authors as Ernest Hemingway, Henry Miller, and Norman Mailer. Next, the history of women's writing began to be seriously reconsidered as female authors previously considered "minor" by male academics were promoted to first-class status and a gynocentric theory of literature was developed. Some of the important initial explorations were Patricia Meyer Spacks's *The Female Imagination* (1975), Ellen Moers's *Literary Women* (1976), Elaine Showalter's *A Literature of Their Own* (1977), and Sandra Gilbert and Susan Gubar's *The Madwoman in the Attic* (1979).

Then came the reclaiming of "lost works"—by authors whose novels had been totally forgotten, or dismissed as sentimental, trivial, and uninteresting, such as Harriet Beecher Stowe. This led to a reconsideration of the effects of devaluing some literary forms as "popular," which has resulted for so long in an all-male canon of "classic" authors. A further development in this area has been the reclaiming of unpublished works. Recent feminist scholarship (Ezell 1990) suggests that the women participated in pre–nineteenth-century literary culture to a higher degree than was previously imagined. Much of their literary output was overlooked because the genres prevalent at that time included the unpublished, privately circulated manuscript, the diary, and the religious essay. Currently, much energy is going into reclaiming works by women of color as feminism integrates its focus on gender into a larger political context of understanding the disempowerment of women along class and color lines.

An important concept in most feminist theorizing is the notion of "patriarchy" as a complex of legal, social, and cultural practices characteristic of many different types of societies, economies, and political systems throughout history that limit and suppress the potential of women and concentrate power in the male-dominated institutions, including the state, the church, and the patriarchal family.

Saint Maybe can be analyzed from a feminist perspective on two levels: first, what Lucy's life reveals about the tendency of women to become commodities in typical gender relations, and second, what Ian's attitudes reveal about the deep-rooted negative images of women in the culture that are encoded to some degree in popular religious practice.

Underneath its religious themes, this novel is a tragic love story that begins with the fateful encounter between a teenage boy and a woman who deep inside is as frightened and confused as a teenager. Lucy's death is largely the result of her internalization of certain social attitudes about women. Lucy accepts the notion that socially she is a commodity whose value depends upon her desirability to males. She treats herself as commodity, always conscious of her surface image and what it will fetch on the market. When dealing with men, she is an actress on stage. Agatha notes with amazement how quickly her mother can change her apparent mood. Lucy is able to produce "her best little husky-throated laugh" the moment an eligible man appears in view, regardless of whether the man was "even listening yet" (63). In accepting that she is a commodity, Lucy treats others in an equally alienated and deliberate fashion. When "on stage," Lucy's gestures are not spontaneous but are parcelled out to achieve certain ends. Her children have intuited this. When accompanying her mother, the young Agatha learns to smile at men on cue, trying to look appealing, because she can never be entirely certain whom she "had to be nice to" and whom she didn't (73).

Raised in poverty and second-class social status, Lucy aspires for more. Her unwillingness to resign herself to her fate appeals to a certain American sympathy for the "go-getter." But the means that she chooses to lift herself up the next rung of the ladder are not forthright. She shoplifts a wardrobe that will enhance her appeal, and she marries Danny presumably without telling him that she's already pregnant. Although she can be partially forgiven because she tells these lies for survival, ultimately they are her undoing because Danny is particularly sensitive about deception and becomes emotionally unhinged when Ian persuades him that Lucy has lied to him.

Ian—who loves Lucy and who indirectly slays her—is a product of the transitional gender relations of the '60s. Unlike his father, he can mop the kitchen floor and can change a baby's diaper without vomiting, and he doesn't find his masculinity threatened by rocking the infant Daphne to sleep. But his beliefs about women's roles in society are inaccurate, attributing to women much more power in the scheme of things than they truly had in the '50s and '60s.

Consider some of the opinions of the youthful Ian concerning Lucy: women hold "the reins," and men are forced to submit to women's "reading" of events (26); and Lucy had things "her way" every moment of her life, because a woman as beautiful as she never has to consider the feelings of others (45).

But everything we learn about Lucy's life belies Ian's snap judgment of her. It is men who have called the shots in Lucy's life—when it wasn't fate, in the form of the accidental death of her parents or husband. Ian's generalization about attractive women always getting their own way is clearly an inaccurate male stereotype, based on resentment. To the extent that being attractive means experiencing yourself as a commodity, attractiveness can be burdensome.

In actuality, the most pervasive feeling that Lucy experiences is vulnerability and fear—emotions to which she believes men are immune.

Lucy's fear makes her struggle to preserve appearances, even after appearances have worn hopelessly thin. She avoids alcohol because it threatens to break down her facade of control and could lead her to say things that would betray the depths of her helplessness. Unlike Pearl Tull (*Dinner at the Homesick Restaurant*) whose fear causes her to lash out in rage, Lucy's fear ultimately leads her to shrink into herself and withdraw.

Even in adulthood, Ian's attitudes about women remain distorted. He continues to project onto Lucy the unacceptable sexual impulses that he harbors within his own heart, and he replicates this with other women he meets. He considers a buxom young woman co-worker to be a "juicy morsel" (214) and wonders if perhaps she is "the Devil" sent to plague him with doubts and tempt him from the righteous path (234).

This ancient tendency to mythologize woman as the temptress and the devil's servant is one of the key issues that a feminist theology addresses. The feminist critique of religion concerns itself largely with the way in which religious experience is assimilated to patriarchal ways of thinking. A central issue is the way in which males deal with their ambivalence about sexuality by projection of the dark side of their feelings onto women, who are then seen as the corrupters of men. This projection can be seen in the way in which Eve is blamed for Adam's fall from grace, leading to the expulsion of humans from the Garden of Paradise.

Examples in the novel of negative or limiting attitudes toward women include Eli Everjohn's disapprovingly stating that in his church they would never let women wear "the raiment of men," such as blue jeans (205), and at Lucy's funeral Mrs. Jordan's asking one of the foreigners about an ancient Indian custom of the widow throwing herself on the funeral pyre.

In Christianity, particularly during the medieval period, religious ambivalence about sexuality limited its legitimate role to procreation, making all other forms of sexuality sinful. Such a narrow band of acceptable sexuality causes many feminists to view traditional Christian thought as promoting many sex-negative attitudes. In the United States, with its Puritan heritage, such negative feelings seem to be a deep-rooted tendency in the culture. It is only to be expected, then, that when an awareness of sinfulness first erupts into Ian's consciousness, it expresses itself in a feeling of shame concerning sexual frivolity. Glimpsing his backlit silhouette in the mirror, it seems to him as though he is seeing his dark side personified. He throws away his *Playboy* magazine and a sexually provocative greeting card that his college roomate sent him.

Throughout the remainder of the novel, Ian's guilt over his own sexuality seems to be the primary reason that he avoids involving himself in a relationship with a woman. His forbidden attraction to his brother's wife accounts for a large part of this sexual guilt. Sex, in the form of Danny's concerns about sexual fidelity, is also implicated in Danny's suicide. And part of the reason that the fatal accusation of infidelity carelessly slipped from Ian's lips was because of the tunnel vision induced by his hormonally driven fixation to get to Cicely's house in order to rut.

In addition to these multiple reasons for Ian's sexual guilt, there is also the pull to remain within his mother's orbit. Perhaps, like Ezra Tull's mother (*Dinner at the Homesick Restaurant*), there is a part of Ian's mother that is content to let her son grow old with her, his bedroom still reflecting the outdated decor of boyhood. Is it merely coincidental that Ian doesn't seem free to marry until after Bee's death has occurred?

The type of woman whom Ian has been attracted to all his life has been an ultrafeminine type: Mrs. Arnett with her soft ivory skin in his boyhood dreams, Lucy in his adolescence with her extremely red lips and seamed stockings, and in adulthood Miss Pennington who wears the "sexy, constricting clothes" typical of the 1950s (251). In contrast, his mother was an unglamorous type, wearing dull slacks and a men's plaid shirt most of the time. The woman whom he finally chooses, Rita, seems to be a compromise between the alluring feminine type and the companionable, independent masculine type. Rita favors jeans and lumberjack shirts but is also willing to put on a dress and walk hand-in-hand with Ian to church. Although she is not the ideal pure and chaste Church Maiden of his earlier dreams, she does not belittle his beliefs as his parents always did. Whereas they could barely tolerate his saying a blessing before the meal, Rita asks Ian to pray for their child during her pregnancy.

It could be said that Rita represents a kind of wholeness or balanced integration of fundamental tendencies in Ian's life—masculine and feminine, sacred and secular, traditional and innovative—a balance that may be a prerequisite to realizing the vision of a "spinning green planet" whose inhabitants dwell in harmony and peace.

Ladder of Years
(1995)

"Just as she subverts the domestic with fantasy—her situations are earthbound until you notice that they are gliding along two inches above the earth—she subverts fantasy with the domestic."

Richard Eder on Anne Tyler

Ladder of Years marks a watershed for Anne Tyler because it is the last of her novels to be completed before the death of her husband Taghi Modarressi. In addition to exploring once again the complexities of family life and the impulse to run away, Tyler's central character faces aging and her fears about her husband's mortality. Delia imagines her husband lying alone in the cemetery and waiting for her, as on those nights when she stayed up to watch television and then slipped under the covers to join him where he was already sleeping.

Like many of Anne Tyler's novels, *Ladder of Years* is circular in structure. The central character Delia Grinstead abandons her family during their summer vacation at the beach and returns to them approximately a year later after another trip to the beach. The novel is written from Delia's point of view and follows her sequentially in time without significant flashbacks. In form, the novel is a comedy whose main plot and subplots involve complications between couples that are resolved at the end, much like the Shakespearean comedies. But on a deeper level, the novel is also a meditation on identity, autonomy, and death.

PLOT

Delia Grinstead is a middle-class mother in the throes of a midlife crisis. She lives with her husband, three maturing children, and unmarried sister in the same big old house that she grew up in, located in the fashionable Roland Park area of Baltimore. Her father was a physician, and one wing of the house contains the office where he saw patients. Shortly after high school, Delia married Sam, several years her senior, who took over her father's medical practice.

Sam moved into the house, and Delia's accustomed pattern of life went on without much interruption. Sam continued to see patients in the old office used by Delia's father. Delia continued to be the secretary-receptionist, taking care of the office for Sam as she had for her father. And her father too continued to live in the house after his retirement, up until his death a few months before the beginning of the novel.

The action begins when Adrian Bly-Brice, a handsome yuppie, suddenly thrusts himself into Delia's life at a supermarket, asking her to pretend to be his girlfriend until his estranged wife and her lover leave the store. This unexpected encounter produces a kind of psychological dislocation in Delia, akin to Charlotte Emory's suddenly being caught up in a bank robbery at the beginning of *Earthly Possessions*.

Delia begins fantasizing about Adrian and sneaks over to his house for secret romantic encounters that have the restrained quality of high-school flirtation. After some weeks of this, Adrian's elderly mother-in-law bursts into a family gathering at Delia's home, accusing her of wrecking Adrian's marriage. Delia's family laughs the old lady off as senile, sarcastically remarking that Delia is hardly a "siren." As much as she dreaded being caught in infidelity, Delia now feels equally humiliated by her husband and children's condescension.

While on an annual family vacation at the beach, Delia impulsively deserts her family, hitching a ride to a neighboring town from Vernon, a local repairman. Without any definite plan in mind, she gets off at the town of Bay Borough, which coincidentally was founded by another de-serter—a soldier who ran away from his regiment. The town is a throw-back to Delia's high-school days: the old fashioned dime store, the luncheonette with the formica counter, the austere library that doesn't carry paperback novels. The stores in the town have comical names: the Gobble-Up Grocery, Pinchpenny Thrift Shop, Tricia's House of Hair.

Delia rents a room from Belle Flint and gets a job in the office of Attorney Pomfret whose prior secretary ran off with one of Belle's boarders. Like a child who is playing hide-and-seek (133), Delia keeps expecting her husband Sam to drive to Bay Borough and beg her to return home, but instead she only gets a businesslike letter from him that strikes her as emotionless. In the letter, Sam states he has tried to be "a rock" for his family, but to Delia it is precisely this stony, seemingly bloodless quality that she now resents. Angrily, she concludes that Sam has simply written her off.

Tiring of her new boss and his dictatorial ways, Delia takes another job as a live-in nanny for Noah Miller, son of the school principal, Joel Miller. Noah's mother recently ran away from her husband in order to pursue a career as a television anchorwoman in a nearby town. Delia concludes that almost everyone in Bay Borough had either run away from someone or was being run away from.

Delia has an encounter with Joel's estranged wife Ellie, who confesses having regrets about leaving her family, feeling she should have "stuck it out," but is too proud now to return (254). Gradually, Delia starts to feel uneasy about her living situation, as it begins to resemble the one she ran away from. Joel starts to fall in love with her, and Noah begins turning from a loving, open little boy into a surly, guarded teenager like the sons whom Delia deserted.

When Delia receives an unexpected invitation to her daughter Suzie's wedding in Baltimore, she decides to attend. She is surprised to find that all three of her children have moved out of the house because of disagreements with their father. She had imagined that her family did not need her, but now it appears that things have fallen apart in her absence. Nor does her daughter's wedding take place as planned. At the last minute, Suzie calls off the wedding because of a disagreement with her boyfriend, Driscoll, which Delia has to help resolve.

In the end, as in a Shakespearean comedy, all the couples are paired off. Suzie is back with Driscoll. Carroll is being eyed by a new girl, Courtney. And Sam, in his emotionally clumsy way, affirms his need for Delia's presence. It is eerie to see Delia slide seamlessly back into her accustomed place in the family, the way Pearl Tull (in *Dinner at the Homesick Restaurant*) had hoped Beck might come back when she kept his desertion a secret for so many years. As in that novel, the restoration of the broken relationships in *Ladder of Years* is symbolized by the sacra-

mental family meal in the final chapter where the dining room table has
to be expanded with all its extra leaves in order to include everyone.

The subplots involve relationships that are variants on Delia and Sam's
marriage. The relationship of Joel and Ellie, Driscoll and Suzie, Nat and
Binky demonstrate the same fundamental ambivalence.

CHARACTERS

Delia Grinstead is the central figure of the novel. Forty-one years old,
she is the youngest of three sisters. Her mother died when she was too
young to remember; consequently she became much more closely attached to her father than did her older sisters Linda and Eliza. When
Anne Tyler's male protagonists are too close to their mothers, like Ezra
Tull of *Dinner at the Homesick Restaurant*, the Oedipal closeness seems to
preclude marriage. Delia, in contrast, marries a man who is very much
like her father, but she allows herself to remain in many ways a young
maiden. Just as Ian Bedloe of *Saint Maybe* does not fully grow up until
his mother's death, Delia's journey to full maturity is sparked by her
father's death.

In the aftermath of her father's death, Delia becomes naggingly over-
protective of her husband, Sam, in his fifties, who recently had his first
attack of angina. She worries about his having a heart attack while he is
jogging or driving and insists upon chaperoning him on his house calls.
Meanwhile, her children, now in their teens and early twenties, either
ignore her or cut her off in midsentence. Carroll, her fifteen-year-old son,
rolls his eyes disgustedly every time she speaks. Ramsay and Suzie, who
are both in college, are angry that they have to continue rooming at home
because of the limited family finances.

Delia feels her home life is in disarray and describes herself as a "sad,
tired, anxious" woman in her forties who hasn't been taken to a cham-
pagne brunch "in decades" (18). Reading romance novels provides a
temporary escape from her burdens, and she consumes them guiltily
during the breaks between patients.

Delia is an acute observer with a wry sense of humor. For example,
she wonders why celery is not called "corduroy plant," which would be
much more descriptive of its appearance (5). Despite her perceptiveness,
Delia does not know her own self very well. She repeatedly resolves not
to embark on a particular course of action and then finds herself doing
that which she had protested she would not do. Thus, she becomes

Noah's caretaker despite herself and also abandons Noah despite herself. She often slides into decisions by degrees without committing herself at any one point, deluding herself that the decision is reversible. She is a stranger to herself, and her own heart withholds its secrets from her.

She overhears a remark that causes her to wonder whether Sam ever really loved her, or if he just married her so that he could inherit her father's practice. It is in the context of this malaise over her father's death and a creeping sense of estrangement from her husband and children that Delia begins acting out some of her romance novel fantasies with the young Adrian Bly-Brice.

Sam Grinstead is an aging man who is sad and tired in his own way, full of recriminations and self-doubt, although Delia does not realize this until the end of the novel. She is fooled by his air of bravado and certainty. He protests that he is "strong as an ox" when she worries about his heart condition (35). To Delia, it appears as though Sam is always certain that he is right and he seems to be always lecturing her on the proper way to do things. When she was young and first in love, Sam's aura of unshakable certainty was part of his appeal, but as Delia gets older it begins to annoy her. Sam is a man who does not like to "plead, or bargain, or reverse himself" and gives Delia the impression that "he had never made a mistake in all his life" (144).

Like Ira Moran of *Breathing Lessons* or Macon Leary of *The Accidental Tourist*, Sam's ability to cope with the world on a feeling level is limited, as becomes apparent when Delia leaves the household. Upon her return, she finds that everyone has become alienated and has moved out and that Sam is living on canned soup. The way in which Sam handles Suzie's last minute refusal to get married is typical of his limited, wooden style of responding to people. Sam can think of no other strategy than to "proceed as planned," assuring the others that his daughter will somehow "come around" and change her mind (282). Not knowing how to try to talk to Suzie, and unable to cajole Delia into doing so, Sam simply starts up the music for the wedding procession and waits expectantly for Suzie to emerge. When she does not, he reluctantly announces that his daughter's wedding has been "postponed."

In his own way, Sam is more passive than Delia, never taking the initiative to talk face to face with his missing wife in Bay Borough. He has difficulty with the candid admission of his emotions. As he tells Delia, "I don't have a very . . . wide nature" (307). The letter he writes to Delia in Bay Borough has the constricted quality of Daniel Peck's letter to his missing brother in *Searching for Caleb*. Its phrases are stiff and formal: "It is my understanding that you have requested some time on your own" and "You may rest assured that I will not invade your privacy" (125). Only some heavily crossed-out lines suggest his struggle around including more personal feelings.

Even after Delia returns home and has taken the initiative of sliding into Sam's bed uninvited, he has difficulty mustering up a forthright confession of emotion. When she asks him what was in the crossed-out last line of the letter he sent her, he fumbles around evasively before finally managing to admit it was something like, "Was there anything that would, you know. Would persuade you to come back" (324).

Eliza Felson, one of Delia's older sisters, is a minor character whose function in the novel seems to be primarily a comic one. She never married, and like Delia she still lives in the old family home. After Delia disappears, Eliza makes a play for Sam. She is one of those eccentric characters of whom Anne Tyler seems so fond, wearing a safari-style pith helmet for gardening. She grows medicinal herbs and burns them in the house to clear the atmosphere of negative vibrations. She believes in reincarnation and is interested in homeopathic medicine and natural foods. Her feelings are hurt when the twins won't drink her homemade lemonade because it has "shreddy things" and seeds in it (45).

Sixty-seven-year-old Nat Moffat, Noah's maternal grandfather, is a significant minor character because he represents for Delia another version of her deceased father. Nat enjoys pickly relishes and other sour treats, as did Delia's father. Nat lives in an elderly housing complex and has a fiancée, twenty-nine years younger than himself, named Binky, who gets pregnant by him. Nat and Binky's relationship dramatizes by proxy Delia's attraction to a father figure.

Since Freud, we view the marriage between a younger woman and an older man as carrying some flavor of the Oedipus complex in which the young child longs for the totality of the parent's love. "When I grow up I'm going to marry you" represents a childish fantasy that is unrealizable because as the child reaches maturity the parent has already advanced into old age or even death. This is nature's trick, the trick of time. But time loops back upon itself in its usual circular fashion, as Delia realizes when, in relating to her son Carroll, she notices she is dealing with a new version of her husband, Sam, uttering the same pet phrases, *"If you say so, Dee,* and *Have it your way"* (206).

As usual, significant bits of Anne Tyler's personality are sprinkled among several of the major and minor characters. Delia expresses Tyler's rich inner world and her impulse to run away and live a simple, austere life. Eliza shares Tyler's interest in gardening and her background as a librarian. Attorney Pomfret represents Tyler's fascination with mail order catalogs. Adrian Bly-Brice shares her fascination with time.

Like a recurring dream, some of the minor characters are vaguely reminiscent of earlier Anne Tyler novels. For example, Ramsey's single mother, cosmetologist girlfriend, Velma, with her six-year-old daughter calls to mind Jesse Moran's ex-wife, Fiona, in *Breathing Lessons*. And the household of Vanessa and her three brothers who manufacture herbal remedies is reminiscent of the eccentric Leary "boys" who live with their sister Rose in *The Accidental Tourist*. And the elegant Rosemary Bly-Brice with her silk dresses and asymmetrical haircut is a younger version of Mrs. Scarlatti from *Dinner at the Homesick Restaurant*.

LITERARY DEVICES

In *Ladder of Years*, Anne Tyler demonstrates a love of literary playfulness for the pure joy of it, not connected to any linear, utilitarian need to advance the plot or expound on some profound theme. She keeps subtly weaving into the narrative the motif of the cat in a teasing manner. Delia is very fond of cats, and her sister Eliza, who believes in reincarnation, speculates that Delia, with her felinelike aversion to water, was a cat in a prior life. Cats, with their proverbial nine lives, symbolize Anne Tyler's idea of leading "more than one life." Anne Tyler playfully incorporates this notion of Delia as cat in various sections of the text. For example, Delia receives a letter from her mother-in-law that she considers insulting. Simultaneous with her reaction, a "furry paw reached out to bat the page" (144). In the context of the passage, there is a moment when it is not made immediately clear *who* has batted the page. Her pet kitten's paw acts as an extension of Delia and recollects an earlier passage when Delia herself, in annoyance at her niece's insulting remark, "had an urge to bat her voice away" (61).

Here are a few of the many other playful references to cats: Delia's washcloth feels "rough and warm as a mother cat's tongue" (128); when Delia hums, it sounds "not much different from purring" (158); she laughs uncontrollably when introduced to a couple whose last name is Mewmew. These teasing references embody in their whimsy the kind of play for the pure joy of it that we find so endearing in relating to kittens.

At one point, the author subtly connects the cat motif with the allusions to fairy tales that are scattered throughout the novel. The scene is

just before Delia abandons her family on their summer vacation. She
enters the beach cottage, calling her pet cat, Vernon, to her. She is startled
when a young man named Vernon appears instead, as if her pet had
been magically transformed. Like the magical coachman in Cinderella,
this Vernon fulfills Delia's wishes by driving her away to a fantasylike
adventure in Bay Borough.

This encoded fairy tale reference echoes back to the other parts of the
novel where Delia makes explicit references to fairy tales, such as the
story of the wood chopper's honest son or the three marriageable sisters.
And her return to her house at the end of the novel has some quality of
Rip Van Winkle as she marvels at the changes that have occurred in her
absence. Part of Delia's preoccupation with fantasy is the way she so
frequently relates her experiences either to fairy tales or to romantic novels like *Captive of Clarion Castle*, which structurally are quite similar to
fairy tales.

This kind of layering of allusions was noticed years ago by John Updike (1982) in an early review of Anne Tyler's fiction. He called attention
to the multiple "strands of continuity" that are "cross woven" into
threads of her novels (277). Another example of such interweaving is the
way the ending of *Ladder of Years* recapitulates a fantasy that Delia had
as a young bride. She worried that Sam would die before her. And she
had imagined him in the cemetery lying alone and waiting for Delia to
join him as she did on those nights when she stayed up late "watching
some silly movie" and afterward "slipped between the covers" to cuddle
with him while he was sleeping (213). These images are echoed in the
final chapter when Delia, having returned from a year on her own in
Bay Borough, slips into bed with Sam who has been lying there half
awake.

This parallelism with Delia's earlier fantasy makes the final scene ambiguous by layering conflicting connotations onto her action. Is returning
to her place in the household analogous to a living death as she joins
Sam in an entombed existence? Or was her year away from home just a
dreamlike diversion from her "real" life, analogous to getting caught up
in a late night television movie? As usual, Anne Tyler leaves this open
ended, perhaps herself undecided, illustrating Susan Gilbert's (1990)
point: "Tyler seems intrigued by the possibility of turning her ideas inside out and she achieves subtlety through alternation and juxtapostion"
(141).

THEMES

On one level, this novel is a light, semiromantic comedy. On another level, it deals with themes that strike a deep chord: the meaning of love, the nature of identity, the role of fantasy, the significance of time—topics that have been explored from different angles in previous Anne Tyler novels. Like *Breathing Lessons*, this novel is an exploration of the later stages of marriage, when many of the romantic illusions have been pared away or at least irreparably eroded. Like Charlotte Emory in *Earthly Possessions*, Delia runs away from home. Like Mary Tell in *Celestial Navigation*, she secretly hopes her husband will pursue her and beg her to come back. Like Macon Leary in *The Accidental Tourist*, she finds herself passively drawn back to her house and her spouse, resuming her place there almost as if she had never left. But unlike Charlotte Emory or Mary Tell or Macon Leary, Delia does not as clearly reach a point of conscious choice in her life. At the end of the novel, she is still largely drifting with the flow of events as in the beginning. Her real moment of choice is when she walks several feet across the hallway to Sam's bedroom and when she stifles an impulse to walk out as he begins evading her directness. But perhaps such tiny moments of choice are as significant as the more dramatic ones.

Delia's passivity brought negative reactions from many critics. In the beginning, there is also a certain self-centered petulance about Delia that is rather unattractive, although in all honesty most readers will recognize an aspect of themselves reflected there. This can be a disagreeable experience for the reader, seeing oneself in the mirror without makeup or flattering lighting, and there can be a tendency to reject it—"No, that's not me." Without an heroic character to aggrandize one's identity with, the narrative puts the reader in the same emotional situation that Delia describes as the late stage of marriage: "No hopes of admiring gazes anymore, no chance of unremitting adoration. Nothing left to show but their plain, true, homely selves, which were actually much richer anyhow" (324).

This realization—that our "true, homely selves" are actually much richer than any idealized image—is a theme that has been implicit in Anne Tyler's writing since the beginning, as I have tried to demonstrate in the previous chapters. And it represents the enduring kernel of a Quaker sensibility that has stayed with Tyler since childhood.

Many of Anne Tyler's fictions are about identity, where the heroine tries to sift out a sense of self from among the layers of fantasy and the definitions of oneself that have been imposed by others. Tyler's characters often alternate between an attempt to define a sense of self through possessions—house, furniture, children, husband—and a bulimic purging of all this from oneself as her women dream of abandoning their families and living unencumbered. Delia takes this radical paring down a step further. She spends the winter evenings in Bay Borough like an anchorite in her cell, sitting on the mattress in her bare cubicle and staring into space, trying to empty her mind: "She had always known that her body was just a shell she lived in, but it occurred to her now that her mind was yet another shell—in which case, who was 'she'? She was clearing out her mind to see what was left" (127).

Delia never reveals what—if anything—she discovered at the secret core of herself. Instead the novelist lets the reader explore the outer periphery of Delia's identity, defined by various strands of fantasy and daydream. In a Bay Borough clothing shop, she tries on an old-fashioned gray dress, and it becomes a costume. Suddenly, she is transformed into "The Secretary," and she finds herself walking differently, to the accompaniment of a mental voice-over: *"Here is the secretary, Miss X, speeding back to her office"* (89). Next, she looks for a "boardinghouse" that she imagines will be run by an "ancient landlady, dressed in black" (89). The effect is a bit like that in Jane Austen's *Northanger Abbey* where the heroine fancies herself living out a Gothic novel, imagining that the laundry list she finds is a secret document.

The interweaving of the inner life and the outer life, so central to Jeremy Pauling in *Celestial Navigation*, is represented in Delia's case by the way in which images from romance novels get intermingled with her experience of daily life. For example, while Delia is reading *Captive of Clarion Castle*, the character Eleanora's imagined facial features keep forming themselves into the image of her mother-in-law, Eleanor. The process also works in the other direction. Stock elements from the romances are projected into her current life. When the doorbell rings unexpectedly during a family barbecue, Delia momentarily supposes it is Adrian who has come to take her away with him like some wild-eyed hero, and she imagines allowing him to lead her passively to his carriage before the stunned gazes of her bewildered family.

Time, which is another central preoccupation of Anne Tyler, is alluded to in various sections of the novel, beginning with Adrian Bly-Brice, who edits a quarterly on time machines, to Nat at the end, who keeps saying, "It's a time trip" (322). As with her favorite author, Gabriel García Márquez, time for Anne Tyler is circular. Delia begins *Ladder of Years* by reexperiencing the emotions of teenage dating in her trysts with Adrian Bly-Brice, whom she later realizes is just a younger version of her husband, Sam. By leaving her family and becoming the caretaker for Joel's son, Delia manages, as Sam says, to "roll the clock back" to the "easy" days before her children turned into difficult adolescents (308). And at the very end, Delia again turns back the clock for a moment by installing the elderly Nat in her deceased father's bedroom, kissing his forehead just as she used to with her father "all those nights in the past" (323). In the final pages, as she walks barefoot through the house, she steps across "cool floorboards, then scratchy rug, then cool floorboards once again," the familiar terrain she has traveled "since the day she first learned to walk" (324).

As if it were not clear enough, the circularity of the novel's plot is further signaled by one of Delia's sons who gives her a detailed summary of the plot of *Groundhog Day*, the movie in which comic actor Bill Murray gets trapped in a time-warp and keeps reliving the same day over and over. This reverberates, like a missing jigsaw puzzle piece, with the curious coincidences that accompany Delia's departure and return. Delia leaves her family during a trip to the beach. A year later, just before she returns to her family, Delia is at the beach again listening to the same music ("Under the Boardwalk") and reading the same book (*Captive of Clarion Castle*).

It is almost as though everything that happened in between was just a dream. Or like the Buñuel film *The Exterminating Angel* (1962), in which, from the start of the movie, people become trapped in an alternate reality that they escape from only by rearranging the circumstances exactly as they were at the beginning. In a sense, Delia's extended sojourn in Bay Borough is analogous to Anne Tyler's book-length periods of immersion in her creative process, during which she becomes abstracted from her family and daily routine.

A FEMINIST READING OF *LADDER OF YEARS*

As discussed in Chapter 12, feminist analysis tends to focus on what is unique about women's experience, including the power differentials between men and women that are often so routinized that they go unnoticed. Anne Tyler exposes her male characters' failings, but without anger or bitterness. She does not consider herself a political feminist because, like Justine Peck of *Searching for Caleb*, she is cursed with the ability to see all sides of the question.

But like the best women authors of the nineteenth and early twentieth centuries, Anne Tyler does give a distinct voice to women's experience. As Maggie Moran says in *Breathing Lessons*, men are "shielded from everything truly important" (262), by which she means childbirth and mothering. Perhaps in retaliation, men have conspired to exclude women from what the masculine world has construed as important. Therefore, Delia can't get the plumber to discuss the pipes with her because he's the type who thinks only the man of the house is "worth talking to" (20). Yet these workmen—one of whom is outrageously name Lysander—expect her to fetch the ice from the fridge for them. Lysander must be the type of man who "didn't know" where his wife kept the spoons, Delia muses with only faint annoyance (32).

One of the primary feminist themes in this novel is the importance of female bonding. Delia is a "daddy's girl" whose mother died when she was very young. She was not particularly close to her sisters and seems to have never formed close friendships to other women her age. Like many of Anne Tyler's women, Delia was hoping to get a new, substitute mother when she married. But her mother-in-law, Eleanor Grinstead, proved instead to be a sharp-tongued and formidable paragon of self-reliance and plain living in whose presence Delia always feels incompetent and spendthrift.

When her father dies, Delia seems to go into mourning not only for him but also for her mother. It's as if, in her father's absence, the painful old wound of her mother's early death is reopened. Feeling that the other males in her life—her husband and her two sons—don't care about her, Delia embarks on an odyssey in which a great deal of self-healing occurs through the relationships she forms with other women.

The early signs of this self-healing occur in Delia's relationship with Adrian Bly-Brice. Just as Cody in *Breathing Lessons* is attracted to Ruth, as if hoping thereby to magically obtain some quality of Ezra's which he lacks, Delia seems to be less interested in Adrian than in his estranged wife Rosemary, with whose image she is fascinated. Being with Adrian allows Delia to fantasize herself as a different person, someone chic and elegant like Rosemary, who travels light, unencumbered, with a purse the size of a sandwich. Like Goldilocks at the Bears' house, Delia's main interest in visiting Adrian is to peek in at the bedrooms. Rosemary left everything behind when she moved out (an action that Delia imitates when she deserts), and like a child rummaging through an absent parents' belongings, Delia is mesmerized by the artifacts in Rosemary's closets and drawers.

In Bay Borough, Delia forms a friendship with Belle Flint, whose incongruous name suggests a combination of traditional femininity and a steely will. More significant is Delia's encounter with Ellie, the television anchorwoman and mother of Noah, the young boy whom Delia is hired to care for. Like Rosemary, Ellie is "the other woman," and Delia watches her on television with some of the same curious fascination that she had about Rosemary. But this time Delia actually makes contact, and the two women have a heart-to-heart conversation in which they share some of the burdens of womanhood in contemporary society: "Funny how men always worry ahead of time that marriage might confine them. Women don't give it a thought. It's afterwards it hits them" (228).

Delia uses this new capacity for woman-to-woman conversation when she returns to her home in Baltimore and discovers her daughter Suzie in crisis over her wedding. Suzie tells her mother what bothers her about her fiancé Driscoll, complaints strikingly similar to those that Ellie voiced about Joel and that Delia harbors about Sam. For example, when Suzie tells Driscoll she has decided to call off their marriage ceremony he closes his eyes for a moment and then—acting as if Suzie has said nothing important—leaves to go dress for the wedding. This type of inflexible, mechanical response is similar to the way Joel Miller overlooks the emotional content of what people are saying and focuses instead on their errors in grammar or word usage, or the way Attorney Pomfret wrongly assumes Delia could not help him diagnose what's wrong with his computer.

At the end, it becomes clear that Delia has a certain strength, as do Suzie, Eliza, Linda, and Eleanor. As in Anne Tyler's first novel, *If Morning Ever Comes*, it becomes clear that this household really depends on strong women and that paternalism is fundamentally a fantasy that they sometimes buy into.

A Patchwork Planet
(1998)

In May 1998, as this book headed to press, Knopf released *A Patchwork Planet*, Anne Tyler's fourteenth novel. *A Patchwork Planet* is dedicated, "In loving memory of my husband, Taghi Modarressi," and is the first book Anne Tyler has published since his death in April 1997. The novel covers familiar ground in the manner Tyler's public has come to expect, but does not represent a significant advance stylistically or thematically over her previous work.

In this novel, Anne Tyler indulges at length her abiding interest in older people, a fascination that can be glimpsed in many of her short stories and in such novels as *The Clock Winder*, *Breathing Lessons*, and *Ladder of Years*. In fact, this novel gets its title from the patchwork quilt made by an elderly woman, Mrs. Alford, who dies shortly after its completion. "Planet Earth, in Mrs. Alford's version, was makeshift and haphazard, clumsily cobbled together . . . and likely to fall into pieces at any moment" (261).

PLOT

Barnaby Gaitlin, who is about to turn thirty at the beginning of the novel, is drifting through life. His wife has divorced him and found another man, and Barnaby is gradually losing touch with his young daughter, Opal. He is the black sheep of the Gaitlin family, a stuffy clan that resembles the Pecks of *Searching for Caleb*. Barnaby's mother disapproves of him because he got into trouble with the law as a teenager and had to be sent to an elite residential school for wealthy delinquents. The family paid off the various people he had robbed, in order to avoid criminal charges. Barnaby's mother constantly reminds him about the $8,700 they had to spend to keep him from going to jail as a teenager, and she nags him about his lack of ambition. She criticizes his low-paying job at Rent-a-Back, Inc., an agency that provides handyman services in the homes of elderly people. Ironically, the service he provides for his elderly clients, and the lessons their lives teach him, are the only redeeming qualities in Barnaby's otherwise unfocused life.

There is a curious tradition in the Gaitlin family. Each of the males for four generations has had a turning point in his life as the result of a brief encounter with a female believed to be an angelic messenger in disguise. Barnaby's life begins to change after he meets his "angel," Sophia Maynard. She is a steady and solid kind of person who works in a bank and has a conventional social graciousness that Barnaby lacks. With her by his side Barnaby begins to receive some positive attention at family gatherings. He launches a campaign to regain his daughter's affections. Most dramatically, he sells his prized Corvette in order to pay off the $8,700 his mother is always complaining about, thus ransoming his autonomy.

Things begin to go sour when Sophia's elderly aunt, Mrs. Glynn, loses a substantial amount of cash that she keeps stashed in her flour bin, a relic of her distrust of banks from the Great Depression. Having learned about Barnaby's delinquent past, Mrs. Glynn accuses him of having stolen her money. At her own initiative Sophia sneaks into her aunt's house and replaces the missing money with cash from her own savings, but then becomes resentful about this sacrifice, mentioning it frequently to Barnaby—the same way that his mother used to make him feel guilty by always mentioning the $8,700. Barnaby realizes that Sophia secretly believes he really did steal the money from Mrs. Glynn, so he breaks into the old woman's kitchen and finds the wad of money she misplaced originally. He then retrieves the money that Sophia had put in its place and returns it to her. At the novel's end it is clear that the relationship with Sophia is over, and in its place Barnaby has found the love of a kindred spirit in his coworker Martine.

CHARACTERS

The central character in the novel, Barnaby Gaitlin, is an almost-thirty-year-old, left-handed, divorced underachiever who rents a basement room from a family in Baltimore. His social life is practically non-existent.

The tale is told entirely in the voice of Barnaby—the first time since *Earthly Possessions* that Anne Tyler has narrated an entire novel from the first person point of view. With his dislike of phoniness and his penchant for outdated slang expressions (like "Geez!"), Barnaby sounds almost like a middle-aged version of Holden Caulfield, the teenage protagonist of J. D. Salinger's famous *The Catcher in the Rye*.

Like Morgan Gower (*Morgan's Passing*), and like the author herself, Barnaby has an incurable curiosity about other people's lives. As a teenager he indulged this voyeurism—breaking and entering into people's homes, not to steal valuables, but to peer at their photograph albums, read their diaries, look through their personal letters. At times he would carry away some memento. Now, as an employee of Rent-A-Back, he gets to peer legitimately into his elderly clients' lives and sort through the forgotten possessions in their attics. Like Anne Tyler, he notes all the quirky little details of their homes, such as when he discovers Christmas wrapping so out-of-date that Santa Claus is portrayed smoking a cigarette.

Barnaby has an anarchistic streak. As a teenager he used to amuse himself at dinner by imagining turning the soup tureen upside down over his parents' heads. As an adult, he almost gives in to an "irresistible impulse" to grab his sister-in-law's firm buttocks at the family's Thanksgiving dinner (243). As a teenager this impulsivity once got quite out of hand. He got into what he ludicrously calls "a little trouble": he locked his parents out of the house and set the dining room curtains on fire (255).

Barnaby sabotages himself through a spiteful, self-destructive streak. If he thinks someone has a low opinion of him, he will often be tempted to fulfill their worst expectations out of stubborn spite. But underneath all this rebelliousness he is being suffocated by a lot of guilt, so he retreats to his privacy to lick his wounds and to indulge in feeling sorry for himself.

Barnaby's passivity is illustrated by his actions after his wife Natalie divorces him. He and Natalie had been living in her parents' garage.

After they divorce and she moves out, he continues to live in his former-in-laws' garage, until finally they ask him to leave when he begins dating other women.

Barnaby travels from Baltimore to Philadelphia irregularly to visit his daughter Opal. Natalie suggests that the inconsistency of these erratic visits might be doing Opal "more harm than good" (19). Opal herself seems ambivalent about spending time with Barnaby. Drifter that he is, Barnaby at first seems ready to follow his ex-wife's cue and fade out of the picture, rather than battle to establish a continuing place for himself in Opal's affections. This changes after Sophia enters his life and he decides to try to make something of himself.

Sophia is Greek for "Wisdom," which is often depicted iconographically as a celestial female or goddess. When Barnaby first glimpses Sophia, she is wearing a coat imprinted with a pattern that looks like angelic feathers and her blond hair seems golden, braided into almost the semblance of a halo. Thinking he has finally met his angel, Barnaby begins paying special attention to her every word. But there is another side to Sophia as well. His first impression of her is as "a schoolmarm sort" (5). Like Barnaby's family she is too predictable and lacking in adventurousness, which is undoubtedly why she makes such a good impression on them. As her relationship with Barnaby unfolds it becomes clear that she can be quite controlling in a subtle way. She has plans to make Barnaby over in her own image, by getting him to quit Rent-a-Back and take a job in the bank, like her.

In previous chapters we have seen how some of Anne Tyler's characters remain "stuck" in mutually dependent relationships with their mothers, which Sigmund Freud might have termed as having an Oedipal quality (see Chapter 5, pp. 61–62). This kind of Oedipal entanglement can be primarily positive, as was true for Ian Bedloe (*Saint Maybe*), or can be primarily negative. Barnaby's is the negative type. He has the kind of conflicted relationship with his mother that characterized Macon Leary (*The Accidental Tourist*) and Cody Tull (*Dinner at the Homesick Restaurant*). Whereas Cody Tull became an overachiever in response to his mother's disapproval, Barnaby stubbornly remains an underachiever. As a result, juvenile patterns of child-mother relationship are prolonged far into adulthood, giving Barnaby's relationship to his mother the kind of stunted quality.

Sophia's emotional support helps Barnaby to reverse the relationship to his mother, establishing it on a more mature plane by severing the ties of guilt and negative dependency. He announces this shift through the symbolic act of paying back the $8,700 that his mother has used as a reminder of all that he owes her. Paying her back is his way of "trying hard to grow up" (251). Ironically, however, Sophia then begins to take the place of his mother as she attempts to keep Barnaby emotionally indebted to her by constantly reminding him of the money she gave her aunt, Mrs. Glynn, in order to "clear" Barnaby of the accusations of theft. Like Barnaby's mother, Sophia enjoys having something to hang over his head. As Barnaby tells her, "You prefer it that I'm beholden to you for your sacrifice" (254).

Like Ian Bedloe in *Saint Maybe*, Barnaby eventually decides against a woman who is conventionally feminine, Sophia, and instead is drawn to an offbeat and somewhat androgynous partner, Martine Pasko. She is described, not very attractively, as a "tiny little cat-faced girl with sallow skin and boxy black hair squared of above her earlobes." Her appearance is a study in incongruities. Weighing ninety pounds at most, Martine is so petite she has to sit on a cushion to drive a car. Yet she wears motorcycle boots and baggy overalls whose figure-eight shaped brass clasps clink when she breathes. Her voice is "raspy" and she is "tough," descended from a clan of steelworkers. Before they become lovers Barnaby admits he "never really thought of Martine as a woman" but as "just this scrappy, sharp-edged little *person*" (185). Nevertheless, her body radiates a "concentrated, fierce heat" (236) and she considers Barnaby to be "good-looking" enough that she is willing to overlook his sarcastic moodiness (237). Martine is clearly jealous of Sophia's relationship with Barnaby, although he is too oblivious to notice.

Like Macon Leary with Muriel in *The Accidental Tourist*, Barnaby finds himself physically drawn to the spiky Martine almost against his will, in a scene which comes closer to depicting raw passion than Anne Tyler's understated prose usually allows. At first Barnaby tries to dismiss it as a mere accident of physical appetite, but in the end he comes to realize that Martine gladdens his heart, and he expresses his love to her by quoting from Shakespeare's Sonnet 29, a poem he was forced to memorize at boarding school. As in *The Accidental Tourist*, social class issues are a subtext in the couple's relationship. Barnaby's match with Martine is a reverse image of his parents' marriage. Unlike his father, Barnaby is "downwardly mobile" economically. Unlike his mother, Martine is one working-class ethnic who does not aspire to "society."

The backdrop characters for the novel are the Gaitlin family. Barnaby's father is a well-bred patrician who dislikes displays of emotion. His brother Jeff is a stockbroker turned philanthropist who is married to a preppy type of woman named Wicky and has a young son named Jeffrey Parnel the Third ("J. P." for short). His mother, Margot, is a social climber from Polish working-class stock (maiden name Kazmerow). Chairperson of the local arts club, she fancies herself a patron of culture, installing a hideous modern sculpture on the front lawn of the family's Tudor home.

Like the Peck dynasty in *Searching for Caleb* the Gaitlins trace their traditions back to an eccentric patriarch—Barnaby's great-grandfather—whose Gaitlin Woodworks manufactured shoe trees and artificial limbs. He made his fortune by inventing the "Gaitlin Faithful Feminine Twinform" at the suggestion of his "angel," and used the resulting profits to establish the Gaitlin Foundation for the Indigent, whose letterhead incorporates a drawing of an angel (35). The archives of the foundation include elaborately bound reminiscences by four generations of Gaitlins with titles like *The Light of Heaven* and *A Possible Paranormal Experience*.

The other set of minor characters are Barnaby's elderly clients, whose differing personalities represent the variety of strategies for dealing with the infirmities of old age. For example, Mrs. Alford is the "ultra civilized" type of person who maintains her good humor even though her "joints are aching nonstop" (263). In contrast, Maud May is a spunky "let-it-all-hang-out" type (263). Tyler lovingly chronicles the challenges faced by the elderly: memory problems, hearing problems, abandonment by family. An elderly client is asked in the supermarket if she wants plastic or paper. "I can pay for it," she says (99), mistaking "paper" for "pay for." Another client tapes reminder notes all over the house: *"Take afternoon pill with FULL GLASS OF WATER"* (230).

THEMES

Anne Tyler has long been fascinated with the interrelated themes of time, old age, and death. In *Ladder of Years* she explored Delia's reaction to the death of her father and the resultant fears about her husband dying. In *A Patchwork Planet* Barnaby lives with the constant knowledge that the elderly clients he has become fond of are likely to die at any moment. In fact, his favorite client, Mrs. Alford, dies unexpectedly at the end of the novel.

Like Rita, the Clutter Counselor in *Saint Maybe*, or Charlotte Emory in *Earthly Possessions*, tending elderly people gives Barnaby a different perspective on money and possessions: "Every now and then, in this job, I suddenly understood that you really, truly can't take it with you" (284). All the decades spent acquiring, arranging, and tending objects are for naught.

He sees that true value lies in relationships, not objects. Working for Rent-a-Back he meets couples who have been married for fifty or sixty years, caring for each other in illness, dealing with the challenges of money and failing memories, and the crises of their children and grandchildren. Seeing this teaches him the value of "staying power," a quality which Martine, in a pique, tells Barnaby he does not have.

Like Maggie Moran in *Breathing Lessons*, Barnaby comes to the conclusion that love is a decision: "I was beginning to suspect that it made no difference whether they'd married the right person. Finally you're just with who you're with. You've signed on with her, put in half a century . . . and she's *become* the right person. Or the only person" (219).

The true meaning of charity is another theme explored in the novel. The Gaitlin family runs a charitable foundation, yet they look down upon the concrete work of charity that Barnaby is doing. Theirs is a bureaucratic, institutional approach that requires no sacrifice in lifestyle, while his is a hands-on approach that is more physical and emotional. The Gaitlin family's lack of generosity is also revealed in the way Barnaby is never allowed to forget how indebted he is to them for the money they paid to keep him out of jail as a youth. In contrast, Pop-Pop, Barnaby's working-class maternal grandfather, gave Barnaby his prize possession, his vintage Corvette. He did so because at that moment everyone else in the family was angry with Barnaby, and Pop-Pop wanted to make a gesture that would communicate to Barnaby that he was loved.

This contrast between the Gaitlin's superficial charity and Pop-Pop's heartfelt giving is one that Anne Tyler has explored in other writings. For instance, in *The Clock Winder*, Elizabeth Abbott says that the sympathy routinely shown by her mother—a minister's wife—was as contrived as the casseroles she kept in the freezer to be defrosted and sent to the mourning family whenever some parishioner died. Similarly Tyler's short story "The Saints in Caesar's Household" demonstrates how a mentally ill young woman resents the kind of pity that her neighbors demonstrate, because they feel sorry for her out of a forced, self-conscious sense of "Christian charity," which only reinforces the perceived barrier between her and them.

A final theme of *A Patchwork Planet* is the magical dimension of life. Anne Tyler has explored this theme in many of her previous novels, often somewhat teasingly, hinting at a deeper dimension to life, and then seeming to sweep it away dismissively. This reflects her own ambivalence about spirituality and her awareness of the excesses to which it is sometimes carried in popular culture. At the time that this novel was written, American culture was saturated with books, movies, and television programs catering to a renewed popular fascination with all things angelic.

In *A Patchwork Planet* Anne Tyler satirizes the current vogue for angels, but also demonstrates how elusive a sense of the transcendent can be. In her satirical mode Tyler lampoons the Gaitlins' posturing about their angels. For the Gaitlins, angels have been "one of those . . . insider things that helps them imagine they're special" (37). But now that angels have become the latest rage Barnaby's mother fears the family will appear to be merely "faddish," their angels lumped in with those "tacky newcomer angels" (74).

In contrast to Margot Gaitlin's comical social anxieties, Anne Tyler also explores the serious side of this phenomenon. As in *Saint Maybe*, Tyler looks at how a vision of the supernatural may temporarily become real, at least in terms of its concrete effects upon a human life. Because Barnaby at first views Sophia as being an angel, he pays special attention to her words, and as a result they begin to have a transformative effect upon his life. Even though he ultimately realizes she is not "really" an angel, it may nevertheless be said that he has had a true angelic encounter, because grace somehow entered his life at that point.

Bibliography

NOVELS BY ANNE TYLER

Note: All citations in the text are to paperbound editions as listed below in alphabetical order.

The Accidental Tourist. New York: Berkley Books, 1986.
Breathing Lessons. New York: Berkley Books, 1989.
Celestial Navigation. New York: Ivy Books, 1993.
The Clock Winder. New York: Berkley Books, 1983.
Dinner at the Homesick Restaurant. New York: Berkley Books, 1983.
Earthly Possessions. New York: Ivy Books, 1993.
If Morning Ever Comes. New York: Ivy Books, 1992.
Ladder of Years. New York: Knopf, 1995.
A Patchwork Planet. New York: Alfred A. Knopf, 1998. (Hardcover.)
Saint Maybe. New York: Ivy Books, 1992.
Searching for Caleb. New York: Ivy Books, 1993.
A Slipping-Down Life. New York: Ivy Books, 1992.
The Tin Can Tree. New York: Berkley Books, 1983.

SELECTED ESSAYS AND REVIEWS BY ANNE TYLER

Arranged in alphabetical order:

"Because I Want More Than One Life." *Washington Post*, 15 August 1976: sec. G, 1, 7. Reprinted in Alice Hall Petry, ed., *Critical Essays on Anne Tyler*, 45–49. New York: G. K. Hall, 1992.

"Fairy Tales: More Than Meets the Ear." *National Observer*, 8 May 1976: 21.

"The Fine Full World of Welty." *Washington Star*, 26 October 1980: D1+. Reprinted in Rosemary M. Magee, ed., *Friendship and Sympathy: Communities of Southern Women Writers*, 142–148. Jackson: University Press of Mississippi, 1992.

"Introduction." In Anne Tyler and Shannon Ravenel, eds., *The Best American Short Stories, 1983*, xi–xx. Boston: Houghton Mifflin, 1983.

"Introduction." In Anne Tyler and Shannon Ravenel, eds., *Best of the South: From Ten Years of New Stories from the South*, vii–xii. Chapel Hill, N.C.: Algonquin Books, 1996.

"Introduction." In *The Available Press/P.E.N. Short Story Collection*, ix–x. New York: Ballantine, 1985.

"The Ladies and the Tiger." Review of *Right-Wing Women*, by Andrea Dworkin. *New Republic* 188 (20 February 1983): 30–32.

"*The Lonely Hunter*: The Ballad of a Sad Lady." Review of *The Lonely Hunter*, by Virginia Spencer Carr. *National Observer*, 16 August 1967: 17.

Review of *The Basement*, by Kate Millet. *New Republic* 181 (7 and 14 July 1979): 35–36.

"Still Just Writing." In Janet Sternburg, ed., *The Writer on Her Work*, 3–16. New York: Norton, 1980.

"Trouble in the Boys Club: The Trials of Marvin Mandel." *New Republic* 177 (30 July 1977): 16–19.

"A Visit with Eudora Welty." *New York Times Book Review*, 2 November 1980: 33–34. Reprinted in Rosemary M. Magee, ed., *Friendship and Sympathy: Communities of Southern Women Writers*, 148–153. Jackson: University Press of Mississippi, 1992.

"Why I Still Treasure *The Little House*." *New York Times Book Review*, 9 November 1986: 56.

"Writers' Writer: Gabriel García Márquez." *New York Times Book Review*, 4 December 1977: 70.

SELECTED SHORT STORIES OF ANNE TYLER

Arranged in alphabetical order:

"The Feather Behind the Rock." *New Yorker* 43 (August 1967): 26–30. Reprinted in William Blackburn, ed., *A Duke Miscellany: Narrative and Verse of the Sixties*, 154–162. Durham: Duke University Press, 1970.

"The Geologist's Maid" *New Yorker*, 28 July 1975: 29–33. Reprinted in Benjamin Forkner and Patrick Samway, eds., *Stories of the Modern South*, 343–354. New York: Bantam, 1978.

"Half-Truths and Semi-Miracles." *Cosmopolitan* (December 1974): 264–265.

"A Knack for Languages." *New Yorker*, 13 January 1975: 32–37.
"Uncle Ahmad." *Quest 77* (November–December 1977): 76–82.

INTERVIEWS WITH ANNE TYLER

Arranged in chronological order:

"Authoress Explains Why Women Dominate in South." Interview by Jorie Lue-loff. *Morning Advocate* (Baton Rouge), 8 February 1965: sec. a, 11. Reprinted in Alice Hall Petry, ed., *Critical Essays on Anne Tyler*, 21–23. New York: G. K. Hall, 1992.

"Anne Tyler: A Sense of Reticence Balanced by 'Oh, Well, Why Not?' " Interview by Clifford Ridley. *National Observer*, 11 (July 1972): 23. Reprinted in Alice Hall Petry, ed., *Critical Essays on Anne Tyler*, 24–27. New York: G. K. Hall, 1992.

"Olives Out of a Bottle." Transcript of panel discussion with Anne Tyler. Duke University *Archive* 87 (Spring 1975): 70–79. Reprinted in Alice Hall Petry, ed., *Critical Essays on Anne Tyler*, 28–39. New York: G. K. Hall, 1992.

"Anne Tyler, Writer 8:05 to 3:30." Interview by Marguerite Michaels. *New York Times Book Review*, 8 May 1977: 13, 42–43. Reprinted in Alice Hall Petry, ed., *Critical Essays on Anne Tyler*, 40–44. New York: G. K. Hall, 1992.

"An Interview with Anne Tyler." Interview by Wendy Lamb. *Iowa Journal of Literary Studies* 3 (1981): 59–64. Reprinted in Alice Hall Petry, ed., *Critical Essays on Anne Tyler*, 53–62. New York: G. K. Hall, 1992.

"A Writer—During School Hours." Interview by Bruce Cook. *Detroit News*, 6 April 1980: sec. E, 1, 3. Reprinted in Alice Hall Petry, ed., *Critical Essays on Anne Tyler*, 50–52. New York: G. K. Hall, 1992.

"An Interview with Anne Tyler." Interview by Sarah English. *The Dictionary of Literary Biography Yearbook: 1982*, 193–194. Detroit: Gale Research, 1983.

"Interviews with Seven Contemporary Writers." Interview by Laurie L. Brown. *Southern Quarterly* 21 (Summer 1983): 3–22.

"Searching for Anne Tyler." Interview by Natalie Harper. *Simon's Rock of Bard College Bulletin* 4 (Fall 1984): 6–7.

Interview by Paul Bail through unpublished personal correspondence, March–December 1997.

REVIEWS AND CRITICISM

If Morning Ever Comes

Booklist 61 (15 October 1964): 193.
Harper's 230 (November 1964): 152.
Kirkus Reviews 32 (15 August 1964): 837.

Library Journal 89 (15 November 1964): 4563.
New York Times Book Review 69 (25 September 1964): 52.

The Tin Can Tree

America 113 (30 October 1965): 507.
Booklist 60 (15 October 1965): 196.
Harper's 231 (December 1965): 133.
Kirkus Reviews 33 (15 August 1965): 849.
New York Times Book Review 70 (21 November 1965): 77.
Saturday Review 48 (20 November 1965): 50.

A Slipping-Down Life

Booklist 65 (15 June 1970): 1261.
Kirkus Reviews 38 (1 January 1970): 24–25.
Library Journal 95 (15 March 1970): 1050.
New York Times Book Review 75 (15 March 1970): 44.

The Clock Winder

Booklist 68 (1 July 1972): 930.
Choice 9 (November 1972): 1134.
Kirkus Reviews 40 (1 February 1972): 158–159.
Library Journal 97 (15 September 1972): 2971.
New Republic 166 (13 May 1972): 29.
New Statesman 85 (16 February 1973): 240.
New York Times Book Review 77 (21 May 1972): 31.
New Yorker 48 (29 April 1972): 140.
Saturday Review 55 (17 June 1972): 77.
Virginia Quarterly Review 48 (Fall 1972): 120.

Celestial Navigation

Booklist 70 (1 July 1974): 1182.
Kirkus Reviews 41 (15 December 1973): 1380.
Library Journal 99 (1 March 1974): 679.
New Republic 170 (25 May 1974): 32–33.
New York Times Book Review 78 (28 April 1974): 34–35.
Southern Journal 14 (December 1973): 1298.
Washington Post Book World 24 (March 1974): 2.

Searching for Caleb

America 134 (10 April 1976): 319.
Atlantic Monthly 237 (March 1976): 107.
Choice 13 (July 1976): 668.
Library Journal 100 (15 December 1975): 2345.
New York Times Book Review 80 (18 January 1976): 22
New Yorker 52 (29 March 1976): 110–112.
Saturday Review 3 (6 March 1976): 28.

Earthly Possessions

Booklist 73 (1 May 1977): 1327.
Choice 14 (September 1977): 867.
Hudson Review 30 (Winter 1977–78): 611.
Library Journal 102 (15 May 1977): 1213.
Ms. 6 (August 1977): 35.
New Republic 176 (28 May 1977): 35.
New York Review of Books 24 (26 May 1977): 39.
New York Times Book Review 81 (8 May 1977): 12.
New Yorker 53 (6 June 1977): 130.
Sewanee Review 14 (January 1978): 170.

Morgan's Passing

Atlantic Monthly 245 (May 1980): 102.
Commonweal 107 (5 December 1980): 696.
Booklist 76 (1 March 1980): 102.
Hudson Review 33 (Autumn 1980): 440.
Library Journal 107 (15 March 1980): 746.
New Republic 182 (22 March 1980): 28.
New York Review of Books 27 (3 April 1980): 34.
New York Times Book Review 85 (30 March 1980): 8.
New Yorker 56 (23 June 1980): 94.
Saturday Review 7 (15 March 1980): 38–39.
Southern Review 17 (Summer 1981): 619.
Virginia Quarterly Review 56 (Autumn 1980): 138.

Dinner at the Homesick Restaurant

Booklist 78 (15 December 1981): 522.
Esquire 97 (April 1982): 123–124.

Library Journal 107 (15 February 1982): 476.
London Review of Books 4 (21 October 1982): 23.
Ms. 10 (June 1982): 75.
New York Times Book Review 87 (14 March 1982): 1.
New Yorker 58 (5 April 1982): 189.
Saturday Review 9 (March 1982): 62.
School Library Journal 28 (August 1982): 132.

The Accidental Tourist

Antioch Review 44 (Spring 1986): 249.
Atlantic 256 (October 1985): 106.
Commonweal 112 (29 November 1985): 679.
Library Journal 111 (January 1986): 50.
Ms. 14 (November 1985): 28.
New York Review of Books 32 (7 November 1985): 15.
New York Times Book Review 91 (8 September 1985): 1.
New Yorker 61 (28 October 1985): 106.
Newsweek 106 (9 September 1985): 92.

Breathing Lessons

Commonweal 116 (24 February 1989): 120.
Kirkus Reviews 56 (1 July 1988): 931.
Library Journal 114 (1 May 1989): 44.
Ms. 17 (September 1988): 86.
Nation 247 (7 November 1988): 464.
National Review 40 (30 December 1988): 48.
New York 21 (12 September 1988): 110.
New York Review of Books 35 (10 November 1988): 40.
New York Times Book Review 94 (11 September 1988): 1.
Time 133 (2 January 1989): 95.

Saint Maybe

America 166 (4 January 1992): 18.
Belles Lettres 7 (Fall 1991): 27.
Christianity Today 36 (22 June 1992): 42.
Commonweal 118 (8 November 1991): 656.
London Review of Books 14 (12 March 1992): 23.
New York Review of Books 39 (16 January 1992): 53.
New York Times Book Review 98 (4 October 1992): 32.

Southern Literary Journal 37 (December 1991): 149.
Southern Review 28 (Winter 1992): 168–173.

Ladder of Years

America 173 (30 September 1995): 26.
Christian Century 112 (13 September 1995): 859.
Commonweal 122 (15 June 1995): 859.
English Journal 95 (April 1996): 88.
Library Journal 120 (1 April 1995): 127.
National Review 67 (26 June 1995): 59.
New York 71 (8 May 1995): 89.
New York Times Book Review 101 (21 April 1996): 44.
New Yorker 71 (8 May 1995): 89.
People 43 (15 May 1995): 31.
Time 145 (15 May 1995): 74.
World & I 10 (July 1995) 252.

A Patchwork Planet

Booklist 94 (1 March 1998): 1045.
New York Times Book Review 103 (19 April 1998): 13.
Publisher's Weekly 245 (16 March 1998): 51.
Time 151 (27 April 1998): 80.

ARTICLES AND BOOKS ABOUT ANNE TYLER

Betts, Doris. "The Fiction of Anne Tyler." *Southern Quarterly* 21 (Summer 1983):
    23–28. Reprinted in Peggy Whitman Prenshaw, ed., *Women Writers of the
    Contemporary South*, 23–37. Jackson: University Press of Mississippi, 1984.
———. "Tyler's Marriage of Opposites." In C. Ralph Stephens, ed., *The Fiction
    of Anne Tyler*, 1–15. Jackson: University Press of Mississippi, 1990.
Binding, Paul. *Separate Country: A Literary Journey Through the American South.*
    New York: Paddington Press, 1979.
Croft, Robert W. *Anne Tyler: A Bio-Bibliography.* Westport, Conn.: Greenwood
    Press, 1995.
Eder, Richard. [Review of *Ladder of Years*, by Anne Tyler.] *Los Angeles Times Book
    Review.* 7 May 1995: 3+.
Evans, Elizabeth. *Anne Tyler.* New York: Twayne, 1993.
———. "Early Years and Influences." In Dale Salwak, ed., *Anne Tyler as Novelist*,
    1–14. Iowa City: University of Iowa Press, 1994.
Gerstenberger, Donna. "Everybody Speaks." In Dale Salwak, ed., *Anne Tyler as
    Novelist*, 138–146. Iowa City: University of Iowa Press, 1994.

Gilbert, Susan. "Anne Tyler." In Tonette Bond Inge, ed., *Southern Women Writers: The New Generation*, 251–78. Tuscaloosa: University of Alabama Press, 1990.

————. "Private Lives and Public Issues: Anne Tyler's Prize-Winning Novels." In C. Ralph Stephens, ed., *The Fiction of Anne Tyler*, 136–145. Jackson: University Press of Mississippi, 1990.

Gullette, Margaret Morganroth. *Safe at Last in the Middle Years: The Invention of the Midlife Progress Novel: Saul Bellow, Margaret Drabble, Anne Tyler, and John Updike*. Berkeley: University of California Press, 1988.

————. "The Tears (and Joys) Are In the Things: Adulthood in Anne Tyler's Novels." *New England Review and Bread Loaf Quarterly* 7 (Spring 1985): 323–334 Reprinted in C. Ralph Stephens, ed., *The Fiction of Anne Tyler*, 97–109. Jackson: University Press of Mississippi, 1990.

Jones, Anne. "Home at Last and Homesick Again: The Ten Novels of Anne Tyler." *Hollins Critic* 23 (April 1986): 1–13.

Kissel, Susan. *Moving On: The Heroines of Shirley Anne Grau, Anne Tyler, and Gail Godwin*. Bowling Green, Ohio: Bowling Green State University Popular Press, 1969.

Magee, Rosemary M., ed. *Friendship and Sympathy: Communities of Southern Women Writers*. Jackson: University Press of Mississippi, 1992.

Nesanovich, Stella. "The Individual in the Family: Anne Tyler's *Searching for Caleb* and *Earthly Possessions*." *Southern Review* 14 (Winter 1978): 170–176.

————. "The Early Novels: A Reconsideration." In Dale Salwak, ed., *Anne Tyler as Novelist*, 15–32. Iowa City: University of Iowa Press, 1994.

Petry, Alice Hall. *Understanding Anne Tyler*. Columbia: University of South Carolina Press, 1990.

————. "Bright Books of Life: The Black Norm in Anne Tyler's Novels." *Southern Quarterly* 31 (Fall 1992): 7–13.

————, ed. *Critical Essays on Anne Tyler*. New York: G. K. Hall, 1992.

————. "Tyler and Feminism." In Dale Salwak, ed., *Anne Tyler as Novelist*, 33–42. Iowa City: University of Iowa Press, 1994.

Robertson, Mary F. "Anne Tyler: Medusa Points and Contact Ponts." In Catherine Rainwater and William J. Scheik, eds., *Contemporary American Women Writers: Narrative Strategies*, 119–142. Lexington: University of Kentucky Press, 1985.

Ross-Bryant, Lynn. "Anne Tyler's *Searching for Caleb*: The Sacrality of the Everyday." *Soundings* 73 (Spring 1990): 191–207.

Salwak, Dale, ed. *Anne Tyler as Novelist*. Iowa City: University of Iowa Press, 1994.

Saxton, Ruth O. "Crepe Soles, Boots, and Fringed Shawls: Female Dress as Signals of Femininity." In Dale Salwak, ed., *Anne Tyler as Novelist*, 65–76. Iowa City: University of Iowa Press, 1994.

Smith, Lucinda Irwin. *Women Who Write: From the Past and the Present to the Future*. Englewood Cliffs, N.J.: Prentice Hall, 1989.

Stephens, C. Ralph, ed. *The Fiction of Anne Tyler*. Jackson: University Press of Mississippi, 1990.

Templin, Charlotte. "Tyler's Literary Reputation." In Dale Salwak, ed., *Anne Tyler as Novelist*, 175–196. Iowa City: University of Iowa Press, 1994.

Updike, John. "Family Ways." *New Yorker*, 29 March 1976: 110–112. Reprinted in John Updike, *Hugging the Shore*, 273–278. New York: Random House, 1983.

———. "Imagining Things." *New Yorker*, 23 June 1980: 97–101. Reprinted in John Updike, *Hugging the Shore*, 293–292. New York: Random House, 1983.

———. "On Such a Beautiful Green Little Planet." *New Yorker* 5 April 1982: 193–197. Reprinted in John Updike, *Hugging the Shore*, 292–299. New York: Random House, 1983.

Voelker, Joseph C. *Art and the Accidental in Anne Tyler*. Columbia: University of Missouri Press, 1989.

Wagner-Martin, Linda. "*Breathing Lessons*: A Domestic Success Story." In Dale Salwak, ed., *Anne Tyler as Novelist*, 162–174. Iowa City: University of Iowa Press, 1994.

Willrich, Patricia Rowe. "Watching Through Windows: A Perspective on Anne Tyler." *Virginia Quarterly Review* 68 (Summer 1992): 497–516.

Zahlan, Anne R. "Anne Tyler." In Joseph M. Flora and Robert Bain. eds., *Fifty Southern Writers After 1900: A Bio-Bibliographical Sourcebook*, 491–504. Westport, Conn.: Greenwood Press, 1987.

ADDITIONAL WORKS CITED

Bacon, Margaret Hope. *The Quiet Rebels: The Story of the Quakers in America*. Philadelphia: New Society Publishers, 1985.

———. *Mothers of Feminism: The Story of Quaker Women in America*. San Francisco: Harper Row, 1986.

Bail, Paul. *John Saul: A Critical Companion*. Westport, Conn.: Greenwood Press, 1996.

Baker, John F. "*PW* Interviews: Reynolds Price." *Publishers Weekly*, 4 August 1975: 12–13. Reprinted in Jefferson Humphries, ed., *Conversations with Reynolds Price*, 50–53. Jackson: University Press of Mississippi, 1991.

Baym, Nina. "The Rise of the Woman Author." In Emory Elliott, gen. ed., *Columbia Literary History of the United States*. 298–305. New York: Columbia University Press, 1988.

Beja, Morris. *Epiphany in the Modern Novel*. Seattle: University of Washington Press, 1971.

Betts, Doris. "Introduction." In Tonette Bond Inge, ed., *Southern Women Writers: The New Generation*, 1–8. Tuscaloosa: University of Alabama Press, 1990.

Brown, E. K. *Willa Cather: A Critical Biography*. New York: Knopf, 1953.

Burton, Virginia Lee. *The Little House*. Boston: Houghton Mifflin, 1942.

Campbell, Joseph. *The Hero with a Thousand Faces*. New York: Pantheon, 1949.

Carr, Virginia Spencer. *The Lonely Hunter: A Biography of Carson McCullers*. Garden City, N.Y.: Doubleday and Company, 1975.

Cockshutt, Rod. "A Glimpse into the Very Private World of a Novelist." *The Raleigh News and Observer*, 24 January 1971: sec. 4, 3. Reprinted in Jefferson Humphries, ed., *Conversations with Reynolds Price*, 30–35. Jackson: University Press of Mississippi, 1991.

Dillard, Annie. *Pilgrim at Tinker Creek*. New York: Bantam, 1975.

———. *Holy the Firm*. New York: Harper and Row, 1997.

Elgin, Kathleen. *The Quakers: The Religious Society of Friends*. New York: McKay, 1968.

Ezell, Margaret J. M. "The Myth of Judith Shakespeare: Creating the Canon of Women's Literature." *New Literary History* 21 (1990): 579–592.

García Márquez, Gabriel. *One Hundred Years of Solitude*. Translated by Gregory Rabassa. New York: Harper and Row, 1970.

Humphries, Jefferson. "Feast Thy Heart: An Interview" In Jefferson Humphries, ed. *Conversations with Reynolds Price*, 220–266. Jackson: University Press of Mississippi, 1991.

Isherwood, Christopher. *Exhumations*. New York: Simon and Schuster, 1966.

Kauffman, Wallace. "Notice I'm Still Smiling: Reynolds Price." *Shenandoah* 17, no. 4 (Summer 1966): 70–95. Reprinted in Jefferson Humphries, ed., *Conversations with Reynolds Price*, 5–29. Jackson: University Press of Mississippi, 1991.

McCullers, Carson. "A Tree, A Rock, A Cloud." In *Collected Short Stories and the Novel: The Ballad of the Sad Café*, 98–105. Boston: Houghton Mifflin, 1955.

Mason, Bobbie Ann. "Graveyard Day." In Anne Tyler and Shannon Ravenel, eds., *The Best American Short Stories, 1983*, 178–190. Boston: Houghton Mifflin, 1983.

Miller, William D. *All Is Grace: The Spirituality of Dorothy Day*. Garden City, N.Y.: Doubleday, 1987.

Mitchell, Stephen. *Parables and Portraits*. New York: Harper, 1990.

Modarressi, Taghi. *The Book of Absent People*. Garden City, N.Y.: Doubleday, 1986.

———. *The Pilgrim's Rules of Etiquette*. Garden City, N.Y.: Doubleday, 1989.

O'Connor, Flannery. *The Habit of Being*. Edited by Sally Fitzgerald. New York: Farrar, Straus, Giroux, 1979.

Price, Reynolds. "An Interview with Reynolds Price." *Ariel* 10, no. 2 (Winter 1972): 3–17. Reprinted in Jefferson Humphries, ed., *Conversations with Reynolds Price*, 162–170. Jackson: University Press of Mississippi, 1991.

Renfer, Linda H. *Daily Readings from Quaker Writings Ancient and Modern*. Vol. 2. Grants Pass, Ore.: Serenity Press, 1995.

Salinger, J. D. *Frannie and Zooey*. New York: Bantam, 1964.

Scheick, William J. "Annie Dillard: Narrative Fringe." In Catherine Rainwater and William J. Scheik, eds., *Contemporary American Women Writers: Narrative Strategies*, 51–67. Lexington: University of Kentucky Press, 1985.

Suzuki, D. T., *Manual of Zen Buddhism*. New York: Grove Weidenfeld, 1960.

Voll, Daniel. "The Spy That Stayed: A Conversation with Reynolds Price." *Tobacco Road* (April 1983): 4–6. Reprinted in Jefferson Humphries, ed., *Conversations with Reynolds Price*, 162–170. Jackson: University Press of Mississippi, 1991.

Welty, Eudora. *One Time, One Place: Mississippi in the Depression: A Snapshot Album*. New York: Random House, 1971.

———. *The Eye of the Story: Selected Essays and Reviews*. New York: Random House, 1978.

———. *The Collected Stories of Eudora Welty*. New York: Harcourt, Brace, and Jovanovich, 1980.

Woolf, Virginia. *A Room of One's Own*. 1929. Reprint. New York: Harcourt, Brace, Jovanovich, 1957.

Index

About the Author

PAUL BAIL is the author of *John Saul: A Critical Companion* (Greenwood, 1996). He teaches graduate courses on cross-cultural psychology at Fitchburg State College in Massachusetts. He holds a doctorate in clinical psychology from the University of Michigan. He has reviewed fiction for *The Drood Review* and was a contributor to *Great Women Mystery Writers: Classic to Contemporary*, edited by Kathleen Gregory Klein (Greenwood, 1994).

Critical Companions to Popular Contemporary Writers
Kathleen Gregory Klein, Series Editor